LITTLE
GIRL
LOST

Judy in a publicity photo for *The Wizard of Oz.*

Little Girl Lost

Al DiOrio, Jr.

ARLINGTON HOUSE·PUBLISHERS
NEW ROCHELLE, N. Y.

Manufactured in the United States of America

Library of Congress Cataloging in Publication Data

DiOrio, Al, 1950-
     Little girl lost: the life and hard times of Judy
Garland.

     Includes bibliographical references.
     1. Garland, Judy. I. Title.
ML420.G253D56   784'.092'4 [B]   74-3466
ISBN 0-87000-255-4

For my grandfather, Ettore Breve,
and my uncle, Michael Santoianni.
Also, for my parents,
Albert and Martha DiOrio.

Publisher's Note
To help round out the author's
research, he would be most
grateful for any information
concerning sources not credited
or cited in this book. He may be
reached through his publisher.

CONTENTS

Thoughts from Judy

Youth isn't all it's cracked up to be. There are so many terrible things to find out about.

DATE UNCERTAIN

Wouldn't it be wonderful if we could all be a little more gentle with each other, and a little more loving, have a little more empathy and maybe we'd like each other a little bit more.

JANUARY, 1964

I've been told that I represent people's dreams. I'm grateful, but if I represent people's dreams, then I represent more than I really am . . . What it amounts to, really, is that I've been a little girl who hasn't quite known where she was going. But now, at last, I know. Finished? Why, I'm right at the beginning of something.

MAY, 1967

Acknowledgments

A sincere and heartfelt thank you to all who helped me with this book. Some may not have done anything tangible, but in many cases, just their encouragement did far more good than they could possibly realize. I doubt if I could ever list all their names, but I'll try.

First, a very special thank you to Suzanne and Robert Berkowsky, Bianca and Robert DiOrio, John Fricke, Ken Young and Karen and Terry Regan. Also to those people who submitted comments for use in the book and those who granted special permissions. I must not forget to take this chance to tell Mr. Douglas McVay how grateful I am for his foreword and to thank Miss Pat Hetherington without whom, I would have been lost.

Also, ABC Television Network, Jamie Aronson, Donna Arthur, Ray Avery's Rare Records, Nancy Barr, Charles Blair, Barbara Bruno (of M-G-M Records), Pam Campbell, Capitol Records, Cheryl Childs, Anthony Catalano, CBS Television Network, Lexie Chasman, Barb Collins, Cynthia and John Contino, Creative Management Associates, Decca Records, Dana Dial, Dianna Daugherty, Shirley Dorman, Agarn Dumler, Kathy Egan, Cathy Enslin, Neva Foley, Maralee Hastings, Rich Henderson, Frank Louzon, Jack Lynch, Fred McFadden, Memory Shop, Metro-Goldwyn-Mayer, NBC Television Network, Charles Petzold, Gwen Potter, Tod Roberts (of NBC–TV), Kay Salzstein, John Santoianni, Screen Actor's Guild, Screen Director's Guild, Ken Sephton, Lorna Smith, Charlotte Stevenson, Sue Strimel, Ed Sullivan Productions, Twentieth Century Fox, United Artists, Ethel Van Den Berg, Mary Ann Venditto, Warner Brothers and my sister, Barbara DiOrio.

FOREWORD

What you feel about Garland depends on what you value most about popular performing art and artists. If you like a hearty laugh better than anything else—well, you probably find her quite agreeable, but would still tend to think that there have been a good many movie comediennes equaling or surpassing her. If, on the other hand, a nice cry is your specialty, then you'll doubtless be ready to admit that—in the dressing-room sobbing-breakdown sequence of *A Star Is Born*, the witness-stand sobbing-breakdown sequence of *Judgment at Nuremberg*, or the offstage sobbing-breakdown sequence of *I could Go on Singing*—she gives you your money's worth in that department. Whether these sequences add up to "great dramatic acting" in your book will, however, depend on whether the ability to jerk tears consititutes for you the supreme sign of histrionic genius. If it does not, then you may prefer that loftier, more regal kind of poignancy achieved by Garbo; or even the stoical irony of Dietrich; or perhaps the defiant, tough, self-reliant pose with which Jane Fonda masks her vulnerability. Should you, alternatively, be a sucker for an "all-around entertainer," then once again you might decide that Garland lacks the virtuoso versatility of, say, Sammy Davis. And if you simply flip over feminine glamour and sexual oomph, then the variable face and figure of Garland the screen heroine will in all likelihood give you less of a charge than the allure of dozens of other celluloid queens.

Even on the question of her singing, controversy seems endless, and a matter of the most personal taste. Everybody agrees that she was a great belter: but not everyone likes belting. Nor has she achieved a lasting reputation as a "singer's singer," in the sense in which this term is applied to a Mel Torme, an Ella Fitzgerald, a Sarah Vaughn, a Billie Holiday, or a Peggy Lee. But here we begin to approach the heart of the problem. Garland's attitude to ballads is no longer fashionable, in period when the concept of emotional "cool"—a defense mechanism against a world in which atrocities of all types appear more frequent, varied, and appalling than ever before—has become dominant in art. Although the lyrics, and often the music, by the classic "standards" of the twenties through the

13

fifties, remain anything but reticent, anything but restrained in their am-
orous joy or sorrow, nowadays it is considered artistically old-fashioned,
tasteless, and slightly vulgar for the vocalist to be similarly uninhibited in
his or her interpretation. Instead, a "cool" reading is favored, in which
impeccable musicianship, immaculate phrasing, and a minimal amount of
vibrato combine to suggest emotional sophistication and worldly-wise
poise. A style such as Garland's, in which the degree of musical, technical
accomplishments was inconsistent, but the intensity of emotional response
unflagging, now becomes suspect to most critics and many members of the
discriminating public. Billie Holiday, though herself far from deficient in
emotional sensitivity, is praised today mainly for her jazz expertise; and
her most famous venture into outright emotionalism, "Strange Fruit," has
come increasingly under attack.

I know, for example, of no version of "I Can't Give You Anything But
Love" that begins remotely to match hers. Her equally unflawed, disci-
plined, yet deeply sensuous treatment of "Do It Again" surely destroyed
for ever the archly shallow view of this song patented by Alice Delysia.
Garland's "Stormy Weather," "The Man That Got Away," and "Have
Yourself a Merry Little Christmas" strike me as superior to Sinatra's; while
her rendering of "Last Night When We Were Young" possesses more
bittersweet force (if a shade less subtle polish) than his. Her "But Not for
Me," again, is infinitely more moving than Ella Fitzgerald's: her two ver-
sions—one youthfully lyrical, the other maturely elegiac—of "Danny Boy"
outstrip even Harry Belafonte's fine interpretation in beauty and affecting
tenderness. Her "While We're Young" at least equals Peggy Lee's, and her
handling of "Happiness Is Just a Thing Called Joe" leaves Lee's treatment
standing (it can, indeed, only be compared with Ethel Waters' celebrated
performance). Her "If I Love Again" dwarfs Lee Wiley's; her "Yes" oblit-
erates Doris Day's; while "By Myself" is, by its more deeply felt nature,

At this point I ought belatedly to declare my own aesthetic bias. I
reject the concept of "cool." For me, "Strange Fruit" ranks among Holiday's most imperishable renditions, just as "Les Blouses Blanches" ranks
among Piaf's, or "Pirate Jenny" among Lenya's. And my regret is that
Garland, whose supreme gift has always seemed to me to be that of a
ballad singer of potentially tragic proportions, was never fortunate enough
to find a song of genuine tragic quality like the three mentioned above.
All the same, she contrived to leave her unique imprint on perhaps twenty
numbers expressing, if not stark tragedy, then at any rate true heartache
—coupled, in several instances, to courage and hope. And she supple-
mented these ballads with another twenty or more which voiced compen-
sating emotions of fulfilled love or gratified aspiration. An artist's stature
can only ultimately be gauged by his or her success with the most demanding, memorable material; and by a comparison between this success and
the successes of professional rivals with the identical material. From such
a test, Garland, to my way of thinking, emerges with high distinction.

greater in impact (though no more perfect) than Fred Astaire's. Then, in addition, there is a whole string of other numbers that she has seemingly made her personal property, and which it is hard to imagine any other singer ever claiming from her: "Alone Together," "It Never Was You," "How About Me?," "Happy New Year," "Just Imagine," "Better Luck Next Time," "You Can Do No Wrong," "Melancholy Baby," "It's a New World," "Look for the Silver Lining"—and, of course, "Born in a Trunk." A standard such as "More than You Know" is so infallibly touching and exquisite a composition as to be virtually singer-proof, and indeed I have heard half-a-dozen admirable readings of it. Nevertheless, Garland's remains the most potent of them all. In fact, offhand I can think of only two ballads—"My Man" and "Never Will I Marry"—in which she has been unmistakably outshone: in both cases, significantly, by Streisand, who alone among popular vocalists of either sex has managed on occasion to challenge her as a vibrant, visual-vocal, singing-acting, stage-and-screen personality.

So this is my particular Judy Garland: not the clown, the game little trouper, the riotous concert entertainer, the lovable human being, the tear-jerking straight actress, the neurotic, or even (some say) the bitch—but the dramatic, romantic, heroic, graceful, often surprisingly quiet and gentle interpreter of some of the best ballads in popular music. My particular Judy is also to be found, at moments, in Al DiOrio's book. But Mr. DiOrio's biography has room for almost all those other Garlands too. It is, in every sense, a labor of love, which means that it is a book that can be safely recommended to anyone with more than a token interest in its subject.

DOUGLAS MCVAY
(Author of *The Musical Film*, New York: A. S. Barnes, 1967)

INTRODUCTION

In the two years that I was putting this book down on paper, one question was constantly asked of me: "What made you decide to write a book about Judy Garland?" Other questions often asked were: "Why did you like her?" and "When did you start liking her?"

I'll answer these questions in backward order, starting from the last.

During the summer of 1963, the Philadelphia newspapers were giving a big buildup to the Judy Garland television series. At this time I was only thirteen years old and knew Judy only as Dorothy in *The Wizard of Oz*. Nevertheless, the publicity releases made her sound fascinating. My parents and relatives mentioned her and her forthcoming series and whenever they did, they spoke of her as if she were someone special.

I remember one of the Sunday papers (probably the *Inquirer*) running a large photo of Judy on the first page of its entertainment section. It was a typical Garland shot: Legs apart, one hand up, dressed in a dark, beaded suit. As I remember the photo I conclude that it was a shot of Judy onstage at the Sahara Hotel in Las Vegas. I remember that my aunt and uncle were visiting our house that Sunday and I recall my aunt saying, as she glanced at that page of the paper, "They say that when she's onstage —just like that—there's no one like her." I always remembered that comment. It was my first clue as to just how powerful a performer Garland was.

Well, the publicity for the series grew and I began reading all of it. Other than a vague recollection of her television special with Frank Sinatra and Dean Martin, I had never seen Garland the woman—only Garland the teenager of *Oz* and *Andy Hardy*. Nevertheless, I began looking forward to the series.

Then, on Sunday, September 29, 1963, *it happened*. I watched the opening segment of "The Judy Garland Show" (on a small fifteen-year-old Philco). It was as if I had been hypnotized. From the moment she walked out and sang "Call Me Irresponsible" as her opening number, I was a permanent, concrete member of her fanclub.

I never missed any of the Garland shows. I decided immediately, on that September eve, that there really was no one like her.

That Christmas I was given my first Garland album, a Decca re-release of some of her old hits. Three days later my uncle bought me another, and in six months I had ten of Judy's albums.

In February of 1964 I began collecting photos and stories on Garland and writing to television stations to show her old films.

Then, in March, when her show ended, I felt as if I'd lost an old friend. I couldn't understand why it had been taken off the air. It had seemed to me that everyone loved Judy!

When Judy almost died in May, I stayed by my radio for hours listening to the news reports.

Then, in September, I received a letter from Judy's secretary, Renee Keiser, and a beautiful autographed photo of Judy in acknowledgment of a letter I had written. Then, in December, I found out about the *Garland News*, a magazine published semimonthly about Judy, and about her two fan clubs. I joined all three groups and soon my collection was growing by leaps and bounds. Through the *News* and the fan clubs I had a chance to learn how Judy had affected the lives of so many others besides myself.

Not only did I feel that Judy was a good friend, but through these clubs I was introduced to a number of wonderful people who are now among my closest friends. Pam, John, Charlotte, Neva, Dana, Max, Mike, Nancy, Charles, Linda, and Ken have all helped with this book in their own way, some merely by encouraging me when things got rough and some in more substantial ways. All of them agreed that a fitting tribute was needed for Judy.

In May of 1967, I saw Judy in person for the first time at the taping of "The Jack Paar Show." Then, the following July, she did a week of concerts at a music fair near my home and I attended every performance.

One month later, I was in the audience at the Palace Theatre on her closing night and in December I saw one of her shows at Madison Square Garden. She was part of my life now, and would always remain so.

Finally, in July of 1968, I was at the Kennedy Memorial Stadium in Philadelphia to see the last concert she was to give in the United States. It would be impossible to convey the impact of that beautiful evening. Judy's voice was in fine shape and she was in a terrific mood. The most descriptive statement I've heard concerning the show was not from any of the local papers. It came out of the mouth of my eight-year-old cousin, John. I'd brought him to see Judy several times when she appeared near my home and so he was, indeed, a veteran of Garland concerts. As we left the stadium, well shaken by the brilliance of Judy's performance, he muttered, almost to himself, "That wasn't Judy . . . that was double Judy!"

I guess it was the next day when the seed was first planted in my mind to write this book. The reviews of the show were all good but the writers just couldn't let well enough alone. They twisted Judy's comments during the show around so that it appeared as if she had been terribly insecure onstage that night. As usual, they tried to make her the poor helpless waif instead of letting her be the mature performer in full command of herself and her audience that she actually had been.

I went all out now, gathering everything I could on Judy, and in January, 1969, I began writing. I was not yet nineteen years old. By that May, I was finishing my freshman year in college and had completed the first draft of my book.

In June, Judy died.

I'll never forget that week. I guess I went through it half in a daze. The only thing that helped me was my constant telephone calls to a good friend in New York—a friend who understood because she was going through the same thing. The next month our phone bills were enormous but I like to think that we helped each other. It would have been much harder without her.

After not being able to look at my manuscript for weeks, I decided that now there really was a need for it—it was a necessity.

Since then, it has been rewritten and retyped over and over until it has reached the state you see here.

I hope it at least suffices until a more deserving tribute to our Judy comes along to takes its place.

Sincerely,
ALBERT J. DIORIO, JR.

January 1, 1974

I

In the last few months it has become increasingly evident to me that one of the hardest things a writer can attempt is to get the story of Judy Garland on paper. The reasons for this are equally hard to explain.

Judy Garland began in show business when she was two and a half years old. She was well known to the public by the age of thirteen. From 1935, until her death in 1969, she was a part of that illusive dreamland, Hollywood. In her last years she confessed to hating Hollywood, and she very rarely visited it, but nonetheless she was a part of it.

Millions loved her and millions didn't, but even those that didn't— those who somehow remained untouched by her—will admit that there was something different about Judy. She had something that no other performer could claim.

Just what it was no one has been able to pinpoint. Some have called it magic. Some have called it charisma. And some have simply attributed it to love. Whatever it was, it was there and its presence is still felt.

When Judy Garland walked onto a stage, whether at the Palace, the Palladium, or Carnegie Hall, she built her audience into an unequaled frenzy of excitement. Keep in mind that no small number of her fans were professionals. In 1961, at New York's Carnegie Hall, an audience of 3,165 people, including such show business luminaries as Phil Silvers, Rock Hudson, Harold Arlen, Polly Bergen, Jule Styne, Betty Comden, Adolph Green, Myrna Loy, Richard Burton, Dore Schary, Carol Channing, Henry Fonda, Julie Andrews, Merv Griffin, Anthony Perkins, and Maurice Chevalier, were so entranced by her wizardry that they wouldn't let her leave the stage, giving her standing ovation following standing ovation. The same thing happened in California, where 28,000 people (among them Carol Lynley, Jill St. John, Rock Hudson, and Marilyn Maxwell) sat in the rain while Mort Lindsey and his orchestra played the Garland overture, and again at the Palladium in London shortly after Judy was

21

released from the hospital where she had been treated for a seriously infected liver.

The list of successes could go on. In the last few years the successes came less often. There were concerts all right, and good ones, but an unfair press and a quick-to-criticize public managed to put a damper on things.

Compare: In September of 1967, 108,000 people showed up for a Garland concert on the Boston Common. One month later, Bushnell Auditorium in Hartford, Connecticut could fill only half of its 5,000 seats when Judy played there.

No performer could claim as many misquotes by the press as Garland could, no one could claim as many out-and-out lies. Why did they get away with it? As Judy once said, "Just how many people can you sue for libel?"

Most people believed Garland to be a sick woman, but very few knew just how sick she was—not only emotionally but physically. Years of diets, poorly prescribed medications, and nervous breakdowns were gnawing at her body.

By January of 1969, her once beautiful legs were as thin as rails and in her face one could see the illness in her sunken eyes and hollow cheeks. When she died, six months later, she was even thinner.

Her voice, once an instrument obeying her every command, was getting weak and stubborn. There were times when she could hit every note with the old Garland wallop, and then there were times when she couldn't sustain a note she'd been holding for years.

All her life she searched for some peace, some happiness, and some understanding. Sometimes she would insist that she had found it, but these times usually lasted for only a brief duration. Many people, however, think of her only as a very unhappy, depressed woman—always "looking for a rainbow"—these people are as mistaken as those who say that all of Garland's faults were products of the country's newspapers. There were times when she could be the happiest woman in the world and her happiness, the sound of her wonderful laughter, was by far more infectious than any Asian virus.

Perhaps her problems stemmed from the fact that her life was seldom her own. Beginning in her infancy there was always someone around to tell her what to do. If someone wasn't telling her what to do they were doing it for her. In an article she wrote for the *Ladies' Home Journal* in 1967 she suggested that the title of her life story be "They Didn't Ask Me." It's true, they seldom did.

Judy Garland represented, as no entertainer before or since, the glamour, the glitter, and the heartbreak that was Hollywood.

The Story

Judy's father was Frank Gumm, a graduate of Sewanee University in Tennessee. Frank's family wanted him to become a doctor, a lawyer, or a member of some other equally respectable profession. Frank, however, had gotten a whiff of greasepaint somewhere and decided to go into show business as a song and dance man. He put together a short act and toured the vaudeville circuits of the Midwest.

In 1914 he found himself appearing at a small theatre in Superior, Wisconsin. The pianist in the theatre was a young woman named Ethel Marion Milne. The two of them organized community singing sessions at the theatre between the features and struck up quite a friendship. A short while later, they were married. The Gumms put together an act and called themselves "Frank and Virginia Lee—The Sweet Southern Singers." They toured the vaudeville houses in the northern states and were fairly popular. Soon, however, the tour had to be called off—Ethel was pregnant.

Frank Gumm was adamant in his feelings that his family was to have a secure home to help stabilize the children's early years, and since he no longer enjoyed performing as a solo he decided to go into another business. He couldn't get show business completely out of his system, though, and so, as a compromise between his heart and his conscience, he bought the New Grand Theatre in Grand Rapids, Minnesota (not to be confused with Grand Rapids, Michigan). Then, he and Ethel did their best to settle down and establish their business.

Well, the first child was born in 1915 and it was a girl. They named her Mary Jane Gumm. After the child's birth, Ethel went to work in her husband's theatre as the house pianist. Once in a while, when an act didn't show up in time, "Jack and Virginia Lee" would take their costumes out of the closet and sub for them—this was as close as Ethel would ever come to the glories she dreamed of achieving on the stage.

In 1920, Ethel gave birth to their second child, also a daughter. Although named Virginia, she was later to change her name to Jimmy, just as Mary Jane was to change hers to Suzanne. Around the time of Virginia's birth, Mary Jane was added to her parents' on-again, off-again act.

Fate must have worked overtime to prepare for the birth of the Gumms' third daughter. I can just imagine how the stars must have glittered on June 10, 1922, when Ethel Gumm gave birth to Frances Ethel. From the beginning there was something special about Frances. It's hard to say what it was, but if one looked closely, he probably would have seen an extra sparkle in the eyes and a kind of magnetism.

By the time Frances was two and a half years old, both of her sisters were performing with Frank and Ethel. The first time Frances (or "Babe," as her family called her) appeared on the stage has become famous in the annals of show business. Her grandmother, Mrs. Milne, was irritated because Frances wasn't onstage with her two older sisters. Finally, Mrs. Milne picked up Frances, carried her up front, and set her on the stage in front of Mary Jane and Virginia. Judy described the moment in "There'll Always Be Another Encore," an autobiographical article that appeared in *McCalls Magazine* in January-February, 1964:

> The roar of the crowd—that wonderful, wonderful sound—is something I've been breathing in since I was two years old. I'll never forget the first time I heard it. My sisters were singing on the stage in my father's theatre and I was sitting on my grandmother's lap. Grandmother got annoyed that I wasn't up there, too. So she walked down the aisle and put me on the stage. The only song I knew was "Jingle Bells," and I sang it over and over again. I liked the applause so much I wouldn't stop. My mother was playing the piano in the pit and kept saying, "Get off. Get off." My two big sisters had enough class to head for the wings, but my father finally embarrassed himself by coming onto the stage, picking me up, and carrying me off. The audience loved it. So did I."

Well, little Frances became a regular part of her family's act after that. The winters in Minnesota were getting too hard for Frank's health—remember, he had been used to the milder weather common to the Tennessee area. Soon, the family decided to move west, to California—it must have been like deciding to move to the "new world."

Mrs. Gumm became obsessed with the idea of fame and fortune—if not for herself, then for her daughters. She'd seen the Jackie Coogan films and the *Our Gang* comedies and assured herself that there was no reason her children couldn't become just as famous.

Until her death Judy was never quite sure that she had fulfilled her mother's ambitions for her or that her life wouldn't have been much happier if her family had never left Grand Rapids.

The Gumms worked their way across the country by playing one-night stands in theatres and vaudeville houses. It took them three months, during which Frank drove and the kids sang . . . and sang . . . and sang. No one could describe the Gumm's act—onstage or backstage—as well as Judy did in "There'll Always Be Another Encore":

> Daddy had a wonderful voice; but my mother didn't sing well, and she played the piano very badly. It was a lousy act. And we kids were terrible, too. We appeared separately as "Jack and Virginia Lee" and "The Gumm Sisters." First, we'd sit out front and applaud for Mother and Daddy, and then they'd do the same when we were on stage. Mother's song, "I've Been Saving for a Rainy Day," always made me cry. She was terribly untalented but very touching. I cried and applauded all the way to California. She was a very lonely and determined woman, and I guess I'm the same way.

After Mother's and Father's act, she'd dash into the pit to play the piano, and he would dress us in our costumes backstage. I did those horrible Egyptian belly rolls, in an Egyptian outfit with those big balloon pants and a lot of ankle bracelets and spangles. My sisters wore Spanish costumes, with those funny hats with little balls hanging all around the brims and toreador pants, and sang "In a Little Spanish Town." While they were singing, Father was backstage trying to get me dressed. It was dark and all he had was a flashlight. Can you imagine trying to dress a two-year-old belly roller in the dark? Well, he usually managed to get both of my legs in one pant leg so there would be a big, ballooning pant leg left over. Then, he'd run to the wings to tell my sisters to do another chorus. No wonder they hated show business. They had to sing fifteen choruses of "In a Little Spanish Town" while I was getting dressed.*

Unfortunately, the audiences didn't consider the Gumm Sisters very good either. Virginia, Mary Jane, and Frances were bombarded with all sorts of things, including tomatoes and rotten eggs. Once, Suzanne was hit in the stomach with a piece of cheese. But even after all they were hit with, the three girls would still join hands and bow gracefully at the end of their act.

The family moved into a green stucco bungalow in Los Angeles for about six months while Mr. Gumm looked for a theatre to take over. He finally found one in Lancaster, a small town about eighty miles north of Los Angeles. There wasn't another theatre for about fifty miles around so the Gumms made out fairly well. The girls grew up watching Rudolph Valentino, Vilma Banky, Theda Bara, Richard Barthelmess, and Mary Pickford and appearing onstage in the breaks between the features.

While still in Los Angeles, Mrs. Gumm had signed the children up with the Meglin Kiddies, a booking agency run by Ethel Meglin, a former ballroom dancer. The Kiddies toured as a group and gave shows around the Los Angeles area. Frances's portion of the show usually consisted of singing "I Can't Give You Anything But Love, Baby" and joining her sisters in "In a Little Spanish Town." Years later, while showing a film clip of the three girls at work, a television narrator was to say, "But as the littlest Gumm Sister comes on, be prepared to be dazzled by sheer artistry."

In 1929, Warner Brothers decided to do a series of short fairy-tale-type movies aimed at the younger set and the Meglin Kiddies were signed to appear in them. "Babe" was tested for the title role in *Cinderella* but she was thought to be too plain. She did, however, appear as one of the many children in *The Old Lady in the Shoe*. The features weren't very successful, though, and the series was soon canceled.

Around this time the Gumm Sisters (and the Meglin Kiddies) also

*Judy Garland, "There'll Always Be Another Encore," *McCalls Magazine*, January-February, 1964.

25

appeared in a series of films produced by Mayfair Films. There were also two color films entitled *The Vitaphone Kiddies* in 1930. They featured Hollywood kid acts and were produced by Warner Brothers.

Mrs. Gumm started bringing the three girls to Los Angeles from Lancaster every weekend (fifty miles was quite a drive in 1929) to find jobs for them. After Mary Jane and Virginia were enrolled in school, Mrs. Gumm began bringing Frances alone, booking her as a single. Sometimes she would earn as much as fifty cents for one performance!

At times Frances and her mother would stay in Los Angeles overnight, other times they would drive all the way back to Lancaster. Once, during the Christmas season, they had to make the round trip every night because Mr. Gumm decided that he wanted them home every night—if only Frank had been around ten years later when Judy would really need him.

By the time Frances was in school there were problems at home. There were times when Mrs. Gumm would pack up and leave, sometimes taking only Frances with her and leaving the other two girls home with their father. One of these times Ethel and Frances stayed at the Hotel Gates in Los Angeles. Other times the hotels weren't as nice. Judy always remembered those days painfully. In "There'll Always Be Another Encore" she said:

> It was during these times that mother would take me out on trips, sometimes driving as far away as Seattle, to find jobs for me. I guess I wasn't any better than any other little girl of five or six, and mother always took pride in the fact that she never spanked me. But when I was naughty or bad, we were inevitably in a strange hotel room in a strange town—like Vancouver or something. And instead of giving me a wallop on the behind, which I would have welcomed, she wouldn't tell me what I'd done wrong. She'd just slowly pack her own suitcases —in silence—to add to the agony.
>
> Then, I'd sit there all alone, terrified. Just sitting there waiting, hoping she'd come back. It has a lot to do with my loneliness today. I'm afraid at night. I didn't know how to use the phone when I was a scared little girl. But now, I do know how to use the phone and make all those nocturnal calls to all my friends—at about three in the morning. I resent the fact that they're sleeping and they're not around here. If they'd just sleep around my pool or something, it might be different. It's almost like everybody were Mama and everybody went away and I'm alone again.*

It is evident by Judy's words that she was never really happy as a child performer. She longed for a home life. She always wanted a mother and father she could be close to and boyfriends and girlfriends she could play

Ibid.

26

with. As it was, she was waking up late, doing the shows she had been booked for on that particular weekend, and then going to bed in the middle of the morning. She only saw her father in the middle of the week when she and her mother were home, and he was always busy in the evenings anyway. Being a vaudevillian, she was shunned by other children in the towns she would travel through. This bothered her. The people in her own town, Lancaster, wouldn't allow their children to play with her or her sisters. She had to confine her friendships to children in the same business or the offspring of acts on the same tour. When she was five, she met Donald O'Connor on the circuit. She said that he was her first "boy-friend." They were both lonely children and no one really paid any attention to either of them. They would play hide-and-seek backstage and Donald taught Judy how to play jacks. Together they would watch the shows from the wings.

Finally, the Gumms left Lancaster. Mrs. Gumm and Frances moved to Los Angeles first, and then Frank and the older girls followed. They rented a house, which they later bought, in the Silver Lake district.

By this time it was 1929 and Frances, Mary Jane, and Virginia were enrolled in Mrs. Lawler's School for Professional Students. There was another student there destined for great stardom—one who was later to become something of a legend in his own right. His name was Joseph Yule —he later became Mickey Rooney. In her 1964 *McCalls* article Judy reminisced about the first day they met:

> I was ten years old. The first day we met we played Post Office. A boy would choose a girl, and they'd go behind a curtain and get kissed. Mickey choose me, and he was the first person, I think—excluding my mother, father and sisters—who ever kissed me.*

After moving to Los Angeles, Virginia and Mary Jane began to lose interest in show business. Mrs. Gumm didn't, though. She was determined that at least one of her girls was going to make it. Meanwhile, she and Frank were having their problems. Judy described the situation in "There'll Always Be Another Encore":

> My parents were separating and getting back together all the time. It was very hard for me to understand these things, and of course, I remember clearly the fear I had of these separations. When my father and sisters joined my mother and I in Los Angeles, he bought a theatre in Lomita, one of the suburbs. The trouble really began in our family in Lancaster. From the moment we moved there, we weren't able to communicate with one another. The surroundings were so terrible— the scorching heat, the snakes and desolation sort of made us all with-

Ibid.

27

draw into ourselves just to stay alive. It was a great contrast to the green friendliness of Minnesota, and we just couldn't make the adjustment.*

In 1934, Mrs. Gumm and the three girls got into the family touring car and drove until they reached Denver, Colorado, without even stopping for a rest. There they played a theatre and a nightclub and then traveled on to Chicago to play at the World's Fair. They appeared there for three months but were never paid. Finally they left the Fair and found jobs at the Oriental Theatre in Chicago.

When they arrived at the theatre, their names were up in lights— below that of George Jessel, the headliner. There had been a mistake, though, and they were billed as the "Glum" Sisters. Needless to say, Ethel Gumm raised quite a commotion.

Jessel came out to see what all the excitement was about. He saw little Frances (by now she was almost twelve years old) and asked her what the matter was. She tearfully explained it to him and he suggested that the family's name be changed. That night, New York theatre critic Robert Garland was backstage. Garland was a friend of Jessel's. When George was about to introduce the three girls to the audience, an inspiration hit him —he introduced them as the "Garland" Sisters. At the time there was a very popular tune being played on the radio. It was one of Hoagy Carmichael's greatest hits and it was a favorite of Frances's. The title of it was "Judy." Thus, Judy Garland was born!

Judy's performance at the Oriental Theatre included her sitting on a piano singing "My Bill." Jessel has described the 1934 Garland style as that "of a woman with a heart that had been hurt." She was very successful and *Variety* reported: "The youngest, Frances, handles ballads like a veteran and gets every word over with a personality that hits audiences. Her sisters merely form a background."

Judy's star began its ascent.

*Ibid.

2

Well, the girls made enough money at the Oriental Theatre to pay for their return to California. Judy had these recollections of their homecoming:

> All the time we were away from home my sisters and I were lonesome for my father, but we didn't dare mention it to mother. We hit Los Angeles at three o'clock in the morning and my father was outside the house. It was the first and the only time I can remember that I ran into his arms. I cried out of happiness—and that was a first, too. It's hard to explain, but all the times I had to leave him, I pretended he wasn't there; because if I'd thought about him being there I'd have been full of longing.*

The Gumms were back together again—but not for long. For two summers, the Garland Sisters appeared at the Cal-Neva Lodge at Lake Tahoe. This was the scene of Judy's first "discovery."

It was the summer of 1934 and Judy, her sisters, and her mother were piling into the car for their return to Los Angeles. Suddenly, Jimmy realized that she had left her hatbox in her room and Judy was sent to fetch it. As she left the cottage, Bones Remer, one of the owners of the lodge, spotted her and asked her to come over to the casino to sing for some friends of his. His friends were Lou Brown—the casting director for Columbia Pictures, Harry Akst—the songwriter, and Al Rosen—a Hollywood talent agent. They all told her to go ahead and sing. Judy asked, "Does anyone know how to play 'Dinah'?" To which Akst replied, "I should, I wrote it." So they listened to her sing.

Judy wasn't impressed by the audition. All she could think of was her "poor family" sitting out in the car waiting for her and the hats and she

*Ibid.

29

was afraid that "they'd all be mad at me—or leave." Rosen gave her a slip of paper with his name and phone number on it and told her to have her mother call him when they got back to Los Angeles. He became her first agent.

Back in Los Angeles, Rosen sent Judy on a tour of all the studios and although everyone was nice to her, they didn't know what to do with a twelve-year-old girl. You had to be either five or eighteen—there was no in-between.

Finally, one day while Judy was outside doing some gardening, a call came from Al Rosen saying that MGM wanted to hear her. Mrs. Gumm wasn't at home, so Frank took Judy just as she was—in old clothes and covered with mud!

At the studio Mr. Gumm played the piano and Judy sang "Zing! Went the Strings of My Heart" for Jack Robbins, then the Metro talent chief. Robbins called in Louis Mayer's secretary, Ida Koverman. Then they called in Roger Edens. Edens was the rehearsal piano player for the lot at the time and he had just returned from New York where he had played for Ethel Merman. As Judy recalled in "There'll Always Be Another Encore":

> Daddy was beaming because it was the only time he had the chance to be that kind of father. My face was still dirty but he was proud of me.*

Finally, Ida Koverman decided to call Louis B. Mayer. When she hung up the phone she said, "He's coming." Neither Judy nor Frank Gumm knew exactly who "he" was, all they knew was that suddenly everyone was acting "as if it were the resurrection." Soon Mayer came in, with papers and secretaries flying all over the place. He was furious with Ida Koverman for interrupting him but nevertheless he took a seat and listened to Judy sing. The expression on his face didn't change at all. When it was over he and his secretaries left the room without saying a word. Mr. Gumm was a little angry at Mayer's obvious indifference to his daughter's singing so he grabbed little Frances and they headed home. "Daddy and I both thought it was a big nothing," she later remarked.

Just two short months later Judy was signed to a contract with Metro-Goldwyn-Mayer. Mr. Mayer was obviously not as indifferent as Judy and Frank thought. Judy Garland was the first person ever to be signed to a movie contract without a screen or sound test. If they had asked her to read some music they would have found that she couldn't—and never could—read a note!

She reported to Metro every day but they didn't really have anything

Ibid.

for her to do. Rumor has it that she was always Louis B. Mayer's favorite of the child performers and that those around the studio were hesitant about putting her in a film for fear that it would flop and Mayer would take his anger out on them. For two years Judy simply attended classes. Her schoolmates included Mickey Rooney, Lana Turner, Jackie Cooper, Deanna Durbin, and Freddie Bartholomew. Judy spoke often of her class. She used to like to recall how "Mickey and Lana used to raise their hands all the time to go out and smoke!" and how their teacher was "a real Simon Legree." Indeed, the school system was very strict. The children had to attend a certain number of class hours every day. While Judy was filming *The Wizard of Oz* a few years later, Ray Bolger (the Scarecrow) would have to help her with her homework between scenes.

The first real tragedy of Judy's life occurred three months after she signed her contract with Metro. Her father had been very ill and bedridden for a while. Everyone was worried about him. Then, one night, Judy was to perform on the Al Jolson radio show. Before the show her father's doctor called to tell her to sing extra special that night because her father would be listening. It was then that Judy knew her father was dying because until then he hadn't even been allowed a radio. The next day he died. Judy described her reaction in the 1964 *McCalls* article:

> It was on my mother's birthday, I remember. And it was a sudden death—spinal meningitis. I think my father's death was the most horrible thing that ever happened to my life. I can say that now, because I'm more secure than I was then. But the terrible thing about it was that I wasn't able to cry at my father's funeral. I'd never been to a funeral. I was ashamed because I couldn't cry; so I feigned it. But I just couldn't cry for eight days, and then I locked myself in a bathroom and cried for fourteen hours.
>
> I wasn't close to my father, but I wanted to be all my life. He had a funny sense of humor, and he laughed all the time—good and loud, like I do. He was a gay Irish gentleman and was very good looking. And he wanted to be close to me, too, but we never had much time together.*

The tragedy of her father's death was one that Judy carried with her until her own. Many psychiatrists have tried to explain her numerous marriages by claiming that she was in search of a father. It is possible that her first two marriages uphold this theory (although I doubt that there is any connection) since both men were much older than she. However, her last two marriages were both to much younger men. Her third marriage, to Sidney Luft, found her with a man of her own age. There seems to have been a lack of love between Judy, her mother, and her sisters. Actually,

Ibid.

the love must have been there, but they were all too involved in their own lives to show it. Judy saw this much, wanted love from her father, and when he died her need for love simply grew. Often, she thought that she had found this love but was betrayed or disappointed. She continued her search for love until she died and it's possible that finally, just four months before her death—she found love enough to fulfill her desire.

For over a year Judy was just another girl on the lot. Any time a star or a Metro executive gave a birthday party they would ask her to entertain for them. It's funny, but with all the parties she was invited to attend, Judy was seldom asked to join the celebrities during their meal until she was one of the biggest of them all! It seems that in the old Hollywood there really was a class-consciousness. Meanwhile, she continued to grow up around the stars she loved so much—Spencer Tracy, Jean Harlow, Clark Gable, and the only other real legend Hollywood has created—Garbo.

Finally, Metro got around to giving Judy a screen test. They put Deanna Durbin in it, too. Both Judy and Deanna were unknowns at the time and shortly thereafter they made a two-reel short together. It was entitled *Every Sunday Afternoon* (often referred to simply as *Every Sunday*). In it they dueted with a little number called "Opera vs. Jazz." The film wasn't seen around much.

Soon after Metro signed Judy, she was also signed by Decca Records as a singer. Through her inactive year as a film hopeful she had been recording for Decca and her first discs were mild successes. Her very first record was entitled "Swing Mr. Charlie" and it was backed by "Stompin' at the Savoy." Also, in 1935, shortly after the signing of her contract, she was introduced on Wallace Beery's radio show as a new discovery. She sang a swinging version of "Broadway Rhythm" and knocked the audience for a loop. She was asked back again the next month. (It should be noted here that at the time Wallace Beery was one of MGM's biggest stars.)

Now it was 1936 and MGM let Deanna Durbin go. Universal Pictures picked her contract up (Joseph Pasternak later confessed that he really wanted Judy for a role in *Three Smart Girls* but Mayer wouldn't release her) and she became one of the top stars of the day. Metro was determined not to let another studio have the upper hand so they decided that they would make Judy into just as big a star. Ironically, their first step was to loan her out to Twentieth Century–Fox Studios for a role in the film *Pigskin Parade.*

The stars of the film were Tony Martin, Betty Grable, and Stuart Erwin. Although her part really wasn't much at all, Judy did get to sing some songs and show her first real movie audience what she had to give them. A friend of mine still remembers his mother saying, as they left the movie theatre after seeing *Pigskin Parade,* "that little girl is going to be a very big star someday." How true—how very, very true.

The *New York Times* had this to say in its review of the film:

32

Also in the newcomer category is Judy Garland, about twelve or thirteen now, about whom the West Coast has been enthusing as a vocal find . . . she's cute, not too pretty, but a pleasingly fetching personality who certainly knows how to sell a pop.*

Both MGM and Judy decided that she came across on the screen looking like "a fat little pig with pigtails." And so, with Judy's very first feature film she was started on her never-ending diet routine.

At this time Judy was earning $150 a week. By 1940 she was earning $2,000 a week! And by 1945 her salary had jumped again to $2,500 a week. No one knows just where all that money went. While Judy was a child under her mother's supervision the money was spent—with no regard for saving towards the future. It seems Mrs. Gumm had a penchant for bad investments. When Judy grew into adulthood she never had the good sense to have someone wise about such matters invest for her. Had she done so she would have never had the financial problems that plagued her throughout her life and that inadvertently helped give her the insomnia which, in its own turn, caused her to rely on sleeping pills and caused her death.

Clark Gable's birthday in 1936 inspired Roger Edens to write a special treatment of the song "You Made Me Love You," which he called "Dear Mr. Gable." The studio assigned Judy to sing it at the party on the lot. In her autobiographical article for *McCalls* Judy wrote:

> One of the big events in my life was Clark Gable's birthday party. Roger Edens wrote a song entitled "Dear Mr. Gable," a cute little thing about a teenager with a big crush on Clark, and I was supposed to sing it for his birthday party. He was making "Parnell" on the lot at the time. And I sang the song for him. He was one of the finest men I ever knew, a truly gentle man. He gave me a bracelet that I still cherish. But the funny thing is that whenever I sang that song that big, wonderful man wept. And he always stood up while I sang. Years later, just before his death, he told me, "Judy, I had a birthday the other day, and I hid. I was afraid you'd jump out at me and sing that song again."**

Judy sang the song so well that it was written into *Broadway Melody of 1938*, which, of course, was made in 1937. This was her third film (if you count *Every Sunday Afternoon*). The movie had an all-star cast including such screen luminaries of the day as Sophie Tucker, George Murphy, Eleanor Powell, and Buddy Ebsen. Judy's part was small but the public fell in love with "the little girl with the crush on Gable." In addition to singing "Dear Mr. Gable," Judy also sang "Everybody Sing" (which was one of her

*© 1936 by the New York Times Company. Reprinted by permission.
**Judy Garland, "There'll Always Be Another Encore," *McCalls Magazine*, January-February, 1964.

Decca hits) and participated in the finale. (See "Judy on Film" at the back of this book for a complete listing of credits and songs for all of Judy's movies.)

Regarding *Broadway Melody of 1938*, the *Herald Tribune* remarked:

> A girl named Judy Garland does a heart-rending song about her unrequited love for Clark Gable which the audience seemed to like.*

The studio still felt that Judy looked too plump for pictures, so Louis B. Mayer sent orders to the studio commissary. No matter what she ordered for lunch Judy was to be given nothing but chicken soup. In *McCalls* she remembered the studio as a cruel and domineering parent:

> Metro thought they were raising me. They were just dreadful. They had a theory that they were all powerful, and they ruled by fear. What better way to make a young person behave than to scare the hell out of her every day.**

Judy always liked to eat, though, and she started sneaking out between scenes to have malts, or she would smuggle chocolate bars into the rehearsals. Following is a sampling of Metro's interoffice correspondence of the time:

> Judy sneaked out between takes seven and eight this afternoon and had a malted milk.
> Garland gained ten pounds. Costumes refitted.
> J. G. brought three chocolate bars to rehearsal this A.M. Reported this to Mayer.†

Around this time, or a short while later, one of Metro's executives summoned Judy to his office and frankly told her that she was so fat she looked like a monster. Technicians who worked on the set at the time consider this just about the cruelest thing ever said to a child in the movie business.

One time, some while later, a director being held accountable to a very strict production schedule yelled: "Get on with it. Sing out and you won't feel so hungry!" And so she would "go on with it," and she would "sing out," but she would still feel hungry—nevertheless she continued to produce film after film as the studio tried to keep up with the public's seemingly insatiable desire for more and more Garland musicals.

With *Broadway Melody of 1938* Judy's star really began to rise. Her

*The *New York Herald Tribune*, 1937.
**Judy Garland, "There'll Always Be Another Encore," *McCalls Magazine*, January-February, 1964.
†© 1937 by the New York Times Company. Reprinted by permission.

next film was her first with Mickey Rooney. It was called *Thoroughbreds Don't Cry* and it also starred Sophie Tucker. Although it was a box-office success there wasn't much plot to it and Judy later referred to it as "inexcusable." During the filming of the picture, Sophie Tucker predicted that Judy would be America's next "red-hot mama." Judy recorded two songs for use in *Thoroughbreds* but only one of them ("Gotta Pair of New Shoes") was used. The other one, entitled "Sun Showers," was deleted from the final cut and hasn't been heard yet although it is still in Metro's vaults and hopefully will be released soon. (As this book goes to press there are very believable rumors that David Wolper has acquired all the cuts from MGM's musicals and that they *will* be used.

In his review of *Thoroughbreds Don't Cry*, Bosley Crowther, movie critic for the *New York Times*, wrote:

> Judy Garland is the puppy love interest who tosses off some scorchy rhythm singing.

She followed this with a good little film called *Everybody Sing*. She was really in good company in this one, with Alan Jones, Reginald Gardiner, Reginald Owen, and the immortal Fannie Brice to accompany her through her escapades as the teenage daughter of show business people who is kicked out of school for "swinging" Mendelssohn. Judy had slimmed down for this film and she looked good. In the *New York Times*, Bosley Crowther commented:

> It is only fair, of course, to admit that Judy Garland of the rhythm, writin' and 'rithmetic age is a superb vocal technician despite her not exactly underemphasized immaturity.*

By this time Judy was fifteen years old but the studio was still portraying her as the typical twelve- or thirteen-year-old. This was a constant frustration to her and although she did begin to play older characters, she very rarely played a girl or woman of her own age. In 1944, when she was twenty-two years old, she was playing a seventeen- or eighteen-year-old high school junior in *Meet Me in St. Louis*. Judy often claimed that this was one factor that led to her arguments with the studio and her eventual nervous breakdowns.

In quick succession, following *Everybody Sing*, Judy appeared in *Listen, Darling* with Mary Astor, Freddie Bartholomew, and Walter Pidgeon, and *Love Finds Andy Hardy* with Mickey Rooney, Lana Turner, and Lewis Stone. The first was just another "cute little film" that really didn't have much to offer, but it did have a good cast, good songs, and some general fun.

*© 1938 by the New York Times Company. Reprinted by permission.

35

Listen, Darling was the story of a teenager (Judy) who kidnaps her mother in the family house-trailer to match her up with a beau (Walter Pidgeon). Freddie Bartholomew played her "partner in crime." Her songs included "Ten Pins in the Sky" and "Zing! Went the Strings of My Heart."

Again quoting from the *New York Times,* but this time from Frank Nugent's review of *Listen Darling:*

> An extremely pleasant—winsome would be a better word—picture about two youngsters who kidnap a matrimonially eligible widow, lock her in a trailer, and start touring the countryside in search of a suitable husband. Freddie Bartholomew and Judy Garland—with little Scotty Beckett's unconscious assistance—conduct their matrimonial tour with charming unworldliness, despite the surface sophistication of their enterprise.*

Love Finds Andy Hardy was another in the long series of *Andy Hardy* flicks. This was Judy's first, though, and while she only appeared in two more pictures of the series, it is interesting that until her death Judy was identified with her character, Betsy Booth, and with the *Hardy* films in general. In this one Judy and Lana Turner were rivals for Andy's affections. Needless to say, Judy, playing the girl from Carvel, won. Meanwhile, she found an excuse to sing "Meet the Beat of My Heart" and "In-Between." She had also recorded "All I Do Is Dream of You," but it was cut out.

Howard Barnes wrote in the *New York Herald Tribune:*

> Judy Garland sings them and they are catchy enough pieces but they have no proper place in this sort of show. Miss Garland is the least effective of the young players who have a hand in this photoplay.**

Although up to this point all of Judy's films and parts had been fairly small, they had been noticed. In her fifteen years at Metro-Goldwyn-Mayer Judy appeared in twenty-eight feature films and none of them were anything but box-office successes. How many of today's stars can claim a record like that? I can't think of any. Even the inimitable and fascinating Julie Andrews (the closest thing to Judy Garland) has had bad luck with *Star* and *Darling Lili,* which is regrettable because both were fine films.

During this period Judy's radio career was fairly active also, and this helped to keep her in the public eye and ear. She appeared on "The Bob Hope Show," "The Screen Guild Radio Show," and other variety-type

Ibid.
**Howard Barnes, the *New York Herald Tribune,* 1938.

radio shows of the day. In addition, she continued to record for Decca, turning out such popular numbers as "Cry, Baby, Cry," "Sleep, My Baby, Sleep," and "It Never Rains But What It Pours." Her Decca recording of "Dear Mr. Gable—You Made Me Love You" was a tremendous success.

3

Sometime in 1936 or early 1937, MGM began planning a children's film based on the book *The Wizard of Oz* by L. Frank Baum. A deal was made with Shirley Temple's studio. MGM was going to loan them Jean Harlow and Clark Gable for their production of *In Old Chicago* and they were going to loan Metro Shirley Temple to play Dorothy in the *Oz* film. But then tragedy struck Jean Harlow and she died at the age of twenty-six. With that, the deal to borrow Shirley Temple fell through. Not long before her death Judy recalled the following to national beauty columnist Arlene Dahl:

> Though I was a contract player at Metro-Goldwyn-Mayer, I had never made a major movie. I went to school on the lot and one afternoon, after classes, I was playing softball with some other girls when a man walking by stopped dead in his tracks, pointed to me, and said "You're Dorothy!"
>
> "No, I'm Judy," I said.
>
> He turned out to be the producer who was planning a film called "The Wizard of Oz" and he thought I'd be perfect as the lead character, Dorothy, a girl whose experiences in The Land Of Oz have become one of the most famous stories in the world.
>
> I was called in to make a screen test of my features—brown hair and eyes, small pert nose and mouth that have always been uniquely mine; the features that, supposedly, were "perfect" for the part.
>
> But first, I had to pass through the make-up, hairdressing, and wardrobing departments.
>
> I emerged five hours later with blond hair, straight putty nose, rosebud mouth, sunken cheeks and a slim corsetted figure. The make-up, hairdressing, and wardrobing departments thought I looked great. So did I.

"Who are you?" the producer asked.

"I'm Dorothy," I replied.

He roared with anger and told them to get me out of there and return me to my original appearance—the "perfect" Dorothy.*

Needless to say, Judy did make that historic motion picture and she did have some fun while doing it although the production was far from simple. She once reminisced about director Victor Fleming:

I was with three very professional men, Ray Bolger, Jack Haley, and Bert Lahr. Remember that little dance we used to do down the yellow-brick road? Well, they used to crowd me out and I'd be BACK there. And Mr. Fleming, a darling man, he was always on a boom, would yell, "You three dirty hams, let that little girl in there!"

Evidently, working with the hundreds of midgets who played the Munchkins was also something of an experience:

They got all those little people and put them in one hotel. And at night they would all get drunk. Then the police would come around and pick them up in butterfly nets! Once, one asked me for a date and what could I say?, "I don't want to go out with you because you're short," so I said, "No, I don't think my mother would let me." So he said, "Aww, bring your mom along, too!"**

The cost of producing and filming *Oz* was extremely high. When Judy had a cold and couldn't work for three days, it added on an additional $150,000.

The movie was a great success and it established Judy as one of the top stars on the lot. All America fell in love with little Dorothy, the girl with the wistful, wide-eyed look of a young innocent, and they came to love Judy as well. In years to come, their children would fall in love with her, and, in turn, their children's children. The reviews of the film were all sensational:

A delightful piece of wonder-working which had the youngsters' eyes shining and brought a quietly amused gleam to the wiser ones of the oldsters. Judy Garland's Dorothy is a pert and freshfaced miss with the wonderlit eyes of a believer in fairy-tales.

—Frank S. Nugent, *New York Times*†

*Arlene Dahl, the *Philadelphia Daily News*, 1965.
**© 1939, The New York Times Company. Reprinted by permission.
†*Ibid.*

Judy Garland is perfectly cast as Dorothy. She is as clever a little actress as she is a singer and her special style of vocalizing is ideally adapted to the music of the picture.
—Kate Cameron, *New York Daily News**

Excellent. Brilliantly Technicolored . . . a beautiful and humorous fantasy the appeal of which is not limited to juvenile trade. The performances are beyond cavil. Miss Garland makes a delightful Dorothy. It's a picture to put on your things to do today list.
—Archer Winsten, *New York Post***

Not only did 1939 bring Judy's first encounter with real fame but it also brought her first encounter with the Motion Picture Academy of Arts and Sciences and its annual Academy Awards. On the night of the awards Judy was presented with a special miniature Oscar as the outstanding screen juvenile of the year. Mickey Rooney presented it to her and it was, indeed, one of the highlights of her career. But why did she have to stoop to accepting an award as a juvenile instead of a full-fledged Oscar? Age has, of course, been given as an excuse, but I honestly doubt that it was the real reason. The very same year, Mickey Rooney, who was only one year older than Judy, was nominated for his performance in *Babes in Arms* (a Garland-Rooney picture, no less) as Best Actor. But alas, that was the year that *Gone With the Wind* whooshed over Hollywood. No doubt Vivien Leigh would have won anyway for her astonishingly good performance as Scarlett O'Hara; nevertheless, Judy should have received a nomination. We will probably never know if age was the real reason or not, but on the surface it seems unfair and the first of many injustices Judy was to suffer at the hands of the Academy.

The song "Over the Rainbow" did, however, receive an award. This is most interesting when one realizes that the song was almost omitted from the final cut of the movie. Harold Arlen, who wrote the music for *Oz*, and E. Y. Harburg, who wrote the lyrics, had finished most of the needed music for the film ("Ding Dong the Witch Is Dead," "We're Off to See the Wizard," and "If I Only Had a Brain"), but Arlen felt that a ballad was needed to break up the monotony of the music they had written so far. The deadline was fast moving closer and Arlen was still without a melody. Finally, one night on the way to Grauman's Chinese Theatre it came to him. At first Harburg wasn't as positive about the song, he felt it was written in too grand a manner for a little girl to sing. Nevertheless he wrote the lyrics and called it "Over the Rainbow." It was deleted from the final print of the film three times. Arthur Freed, *Oz*'s producer, and Arlen fought for it, though, and the song was finally left in

*Reprinted by permission of the *New York Daily News.*
**Reprinted by permission of the *New York Post.*

the film. Incidentally, "Over the Rainbow" is the only sequence in *Oz* that was not directed by Victor Fleming. Fleming was assigned by Metro to direct *Gone With the Wind,* which was also being made on the lot at that time, so King Vidor directed the filming of the song.

As quoted by Edward Jablonski in *Harold Arlen: Happy With the Blues* (Doubleday, 1961), Judy had the following to say about her work in *Oz* and about "Over the Rainbow":

> I enjoyed it (working in "The Wizard of Oz") tremendously although it was a long schedule and very hard work; it was in the comparatively early days of technicolor and the lights were terribly hot. We were shooting for six months but I loved the music and I loved the director, Victor Fleming, and of course, I loved the story. I wasn't aware until the first preview of "The Wizard of Oz" that they were thinking of cutting "Over the Rainbow" out of the picture. I couldn't understand it because it was such a beautiful song. However, in those days I had very little to say about anything. As for my feelings towards "Over the Rainbow" now, it has become a part of my life. It is so symbolic of everybody's dream and wish that I am sure that's why people sometimes get tears in their eyes when they hear it. I have sung it dozens of times and it's still the song that is closest to my heart. It is very gratifying to have a song that is more or less known as my song, or my theme song, and to have had it written by the fantastic Harold Arlen.*

Unknown to many, a sequence of about fifteen minutes in length was deleted from *Oz* before the final release (at about the same time that the film was being tested without "Over the Rainbow"). After melting the Wicked Witch, Dorothy and her friends are led over a "rainbow bridge," which dissolves immediately after they cross it, and through a triumphant return to the Emerald City. In addition to this, a song entitled "The Jitterbug" was removed from the segment prior to Dorothy's capture by the Witch. The song can be heard though on Judy's Decca recording of the songs from *The Wizard Of Oz.*

The Wizard of Oz is one of *the* events of every television season. In 1955 CBS bought the rights to it and aired it. It wasn't rerun until 1959 and since then it has been shown annually and has never been lower than tenth in the year-long movie ratings. In 1965 an interesting rating system was noticed in Toronto. It seems that the home-viewers watching the movie were so enthralled by it that they wouldn't leave their seats for anything. As soon as the movie was over, however, the water department reported a simultaneous flushing of millions of toilets in the area!

CBS paid $250,000 for each of the first two showings of *Oz;* the price tapered down to $200,000 for each of the following seven showings, but

*© 1961 Edward Jablonski, *Harold Arlen: Happy With the Blues,* Doubleday and Company, Inc.

in 1968 MGM (getting desperate for money) raised the price and NBC picked up the option for $300,000 per showing. In 1971, the film was shown for the thirteenth time. The album from the film is still one of MGM's best-sellers.

And so, in 1939, a tornado in Kansas blew Judy into the turmoil of super-stardom.

Following *The Wizard of Oz* Judy and Mickey Rooney immediately began work on *Babes in Arms*, a delightful Busby Berkeley musical. The movie was a tour de force for Mickey since it gave him a chance to impersonate Clark Gable, Charles Laughton, and others. Judy, in turn, imitated Eleanor Roosevelt, sang some good Rodgers and Hart songs, and gave additional proof that she really could act.

There were a number of poignant scenes in the film as Judy and Mickey fought and then made amends with each other for the good of the show. Who can ever forget Judy singing, "I Cried for You"? In the film, there was a spoken verse in the middle of the song that showed just how easily Judy could wring tears out of her audience. The theatre's atmosphere was damp as she cried:

> I know I'm no glamour girl like Baby . . . like her. But maybe someday you'll realize that glamour isn't the only thing in this world. If your show's a flop you'll find you can't eat glamour for breakfast. Anyway, I might be pretty good looking myself when I grow out of this ugly duckling stage. And you're no Clark Gable yourself. But that's all right. You go your way and I'll go mine. Don't worry about me. I'll recover. Time is a great . . . healer. But in the future if we should meet again at the opera or at a ball and I'm dazzling in my diamonds and furs and ermine wraps and surrounded by Lords and Dukes and Princes, you'll probably be sorry . . . and you'll probably realize that life is just an idiot's delight. And as I speed through the dark night into the abyss of oblivion I can only say thanks . . . thanks for the memories.

Babes in Arms was one of the biggest hits of 1939 (the year of *Gone With the Wind* and *The Wizard of Oz*, both also from MGM). Thus, Judy had two great films in one year. Mickey, as I mentioned earlier, was nominated for an Academy Award as Best Actor but did not win.

Irene Thirer reviewed the film as follows for the *New York Post:*

> . . . a brightly entertaining screen version of Rodgers' and Hart's legit musical. Perked up by . . . Mickey's mugging and undeniable song and dance talents, and by Judy Garland's simply swell sense of swing . . . "Babes in Arms" is quite a show. It moves fast, with guaranteed laughs and lots of sure fire tunes.*

*Reprinted by permission of the *New York Post.* © 1939, the New York Post Corporation.

On August 19, 1939, *The Wizard of Oz* made its premiere at the Capitol Theatre in New York. Judy and Mickey appeared at the Capitol all week in a vaudeville show in between screenings of *Oz*. They did five shows a day and worked terribly hard. Judy collapsed backstage after one show from exhaustion but nevertheless she was revived and "pepped up" in time for the next show. The first day found 15,000 people waiting to get into the theatre, which seated only 5,400. Forty policemen were needed to handle the crowds.

In the autumn of 1939, Judy was asked to place her footprints in the forecourt of Grauman's Chinese Theatre. Luckily Judy always had a sense of humor, because it was going to come in handy that night. Because of her nervousness she had bitten her nails almost completely off, so she went to Metro's makeup department and had them put on false fingernails. That night, she arrived in a gown and fur with Mickey by her side and proceeded to stick her hands in the wet cement. As she did so she felt the wet cement seep between her own nails and the false ones. Of course she couldn't do anything about it then and it took weeks of filing to get the artificial nails off.

In her *McCalls* article Judy did not remember those days at Metro as being very happy ones:

> When we were in production, they had us working days and nights on end. They'd give us pep-up pills to keep us on our feet long after we were exhausted. Then they'd take us to the studio hospital and knock us cold with sleeping pills—Mickey sprawled out on one bed and me on another. Then, after four hours, they'd wake us up and give us the pep-up pills again, so we could work another seventy-two hours in a row. Half of the time, we were hanging from the ceiling but it became a way of life for us. This sort of thing went on all the time at Metro and it started when I was fourteen and executives were worried about my weight.
>
> Even after "The Wizard of Oz" they treated me like a poor relation at the studio. They convinced me I wasn't any good. They kept telling me I wasn't any good as a performer. Neither Mickey or I was ever exposed to the fact that we were important properties.
>
> My inability to sleep, however, was not MGM's fault. All my life I've never adjusted to sleeping at night, and it began when I was a child working in theatres. Vaudeville is night work. We'd finish at 10:30 or 11:00 at night, and then we'd all get to bed about three in the morning. We'd sleep very late, getting up at noon, and do the first show at two o'clock in the afternoon. When I got into the movies I had to get up at five in the morning and was supposed to go to bed at nine at night, but it never worked that way.
>
> I was still on my old timetable, only I was getting to bed at four in the morning and being awakened at five. I'd rush to the make-up department, where they painted eye balls on my lids, I think, to make me look awake.

In addition to my lack of sleep my head was always buzzing with too many numbers. Too many lyrics, too many dances, too many warnings. But I had to sleep because at 6:00 A.M. I had to start all over again.*

Babes in Arms was followed by another of the *Andy Hardy* films. This one was called *Andy Hardy Meets Debutante*. It had the usual *Andy Hardy* cast (Rooney, Lewis Stone, Fay Holden, Cecilia Parker, and Ann Rutherford) and a couple of songs. The movie was nothing spectacular but it was well liked and full of the expected Garland-Rooney fun. *Time* reported:

> "Andy Hardy Meets Debutante" marks Mickey Rooney's ninth appearance as bratty Andy Hardy . . . As such oldsters as Wallace Beery, Lionel Barrymore and Lewis Stone have discovered, Mickey Rooney thrives on his ability and determination to steal anything up to a death scene from a colleague. Some of Cinemactor Stone's heartiest chuckles may be explained by the fact that seventeen year old Judy Garland, growing prettier by the picture and armed for this one with two good songs, "Alone" and "I'm Nobody's Baby," treats Mickey with a dose of his own medicine.**

The second film Judy made in 1940 was *Strike up the Band*, again with Mickey Rooney. This was their third film in a row together. They were a national institution now—America's sweethearts—and the public just couldn't get enough of them. In *Strike up the Band* they sang "Our Love Affair," "Nell of New Rochelle," and "Do the La Conga." Busby Berkeley directed the film and his touch was seen throughout. The review in the *New York Herald Tribune* read:

> Following the general pattern of "Babes in Arms," Mickey Rooney and Judy Garland romp through another boisterous screen musical in "Strike up the Band." The title and the title song have been lifted from the Gershwin-Kaufman show but otherwise . . . the offering bears no resemblance to its stage namesake. Instead of a satirical war continuity it offers a series of jam sessions. Instead of Clark and McCollough it presents Rooney and Garland getting well into the groove for MGM. The important point is that the juvenile stars give the show all the punch of a sure fire hit.†

Next came the film that is generally considered Judy's first adult role. The movie was *Little Nellie Kelly*—based on a story by George M. Cohan. It was a huge success, with Judy's millions of fans watching her get her first "screen kiss" (from George Murphy). The old Garland verve and bounce

*Judy Garland, "There'll Always Be Another Encore," *McCall's*, January-February, 1964.
**© 1939, *Time*. Time-Life, Inc.
†The *New York Herald Tribune*, 1940.

45

were there and she got her most dramatic scene yet when she died after giving birth to a baby girl. (Louis B. Mayer, incidentally, objected to this part of the film. He went around the studio yelling, "You can't let that baby have a baby!") Watching these old films on television, it's moments like this one that make you wonder whether the stars of today really have much talent. Few of them show any signs of ability to give comparable performance.

In *Little Nellie Kelly* Judy played a dual role—Nellie Kelly and Nellie's mother. For the first half of the film Judy mastered an Irish brogue for use as Mrs. Kelly.

Besides George Murphy, the cast included Charles Winninger and Douglas McPhail. Judy's songs included "Nellie Kelly, I Love You," "A Pretty Girl Milking Her Cow," and "Singing in the Rain." Metro's one mistake was in deleting Judy's version of "Danny Boy" from the final print of the film. Kate Cameron of the *New York Daily News* wasn't too fond of the picture, though, and her review went as follows:

> Long drawn out battle of the sexes and an over sentimental story of an Irishman's love for his daughter and the latter's efforts to escape the parental influence.
>
> Judy Garland in the double role . . . does her best, but even her beguiling exuberance and her sweet way with a ballad cannot entirely overcome the deficiencies of the story.*

It was around this time that Judy decided to get away from her mother's domination for once and all. She decided to move into her own apartment. She found a girl to share the apartment with and they became close friends. Judy was heartbroken when she found out that her "friend" was being paid by Metro to report her every move to them. MGM used the same technique when Judy was home—they paid Mrs. Gumm a salary, and she reported Judy's comings and goings in detail—what she ate, who she went out with, when she got to sleep, and so on.

Careerwise Judy started off 1941 in a big way. She was chosen as one of the three leads in *Ziegfeld Girl* with Lana Turner and Hedy Lamarr. The cast also included Jimmy Stewart, Edward Everett Horton, Charles Winninger, Tony Martin, and Jackie Cooper. Judy and Jimmy Stewart received top billing. Although Judy's role didn't require much of an actress there were a lot of good songs, some beautiful costumes, and a few good scenes. She danced and joked her way through a delightful routine with Charles Winninger called "Laugh? I thought I'd Split My Sides," and she gave a beautiful rendition of "I'm Always Chasing Rainbows," which was to become one of her big hits for Decca records. She was also the lead singer in the finale. The musical highlight of the film, however, was the Calypso number, "Minnie from Trinidad." Up to that point in her career

*Reprinted by permission of the *New York Daily News*.

it was "the production number to end all production numbers" and it was all hers!

Howard Barnes of the *New York Herald Tribune* said:

> Judy Garland is especially good as a youngster who becomes a star under a strict code of showmanship.*

But Judy's personal life was far from peaceful during this period. Her mother's domination over her was second only to that of the studio and Louis B. Mayer. They told her who to date, how to dress, what to say, and practically when to breathe. She was still having trouble sleeping and her nerves were always on edge from the different studio-induced pills.

Around this time she had been dating Artie Shaw (only briefly) but then he eloped with Lana Turner (after canceling a date with Judy for the same night) and that was the end of that. She was also seen around a great deal with Robert Stack, Guy Madison and Van Johnson.

Tyrone Power and Judy had planned on being married when he returned from the service. But while he was away, the studio (in Judy's words now) "convinced me I was in love with the cover of Photoplay."

When Judy was in love, her love was very deep and very loyal. But when she was unloved or without love she felt incomplete. A friend of Judy's has admitted: "She had more love than anyone I've ever known. She needed more love than anyone. She had to feel love . . . to know that she was loved in order to be happy. When she was in love with someone she could be the most wonderful woman in the world. She never gave anyone reason to doubt her love. You always knew it was there."

And so, when Judy met David Rose, she was a very confused and lonesome girl. Rose cheered her up and made her eat all sorts of things that she warned him Metro wouldn't allow. He made her laugh and feel like a human being for the first time in years. She felt so good when she was around him that she began calling him "Mr. Sunshine." She needed him, she really did, and so on her nineteenth birthday (June 10, 1941), against the wishes of both her mother and the studio, and possibly in rebellion against both, she and Rose announced their engagement.

They were married on July 28, 1941 in Las Vegas. Mrs. Gumm accompanied them on their honeymoon! It was, indeed, an unpromising beginning. Not long after their honeymoon, Judy and David Rose moved into the lavish mansion that had belonged to Jean Harlow. Judy's wedding gift to her husband was a beautiful new depot for his miniature railroad collection (which included over 1,000 feet of track).

Soon after their marriage, Judy went to work in what was to be her last *Andy Hardy* film. The name of it was *Life Begins for Andy Hardy*, and although it was big at the box office her public wondered why she was

*Howard Barnes, the *New York Herald Tribune,* 1941.

47

songless. This hasn't been explained yet and I doubt if it ever will. She had recorded four songs for use in the film: "Abide With Me," "The Rosary," "Easy to Love," and "America," but none of them was used—although she did get to sing a Happy Birthday telegram!

The following review by Robert Dana appeared in the *New York Herald Tribune:*

> "Life Begins for Andy Hardy" is just another exposition of the lad who braves the big city for a while, has his hungry days, learns some sense by his experiences and returns home ready to follow his father's suggestion of a college education.
>
> Mickey Rooney, Judy Garland, Lewis Stone and two newcomers, Patricia Dane and Ray McDonald, work hard to sustain the film . . .
>
> . . . Judy Garland as the faithful hopeful admirer of the Hardy heir is helpful in both the Carvel and New York settings.*

Her last film of 1941 was *Babes on Broadway* starring Judy and . . . that's right, Mickey again. The film gave them a chance for their usual spats and duets. The cast included Virginia Weidler (in a role originally planned for Shirley Temple) and Donna Reed. Busby Berkeley directed. Here is Howard Barnes's review from the *New York Herald Tribune:*

> Judging from the line outside the Music Hall yesterday, "Babes on Broadway" was the perfect choice for a New Years celebration at the Radio City playhouse. It is a brash and engaging entertainment for any holiday season. Mickey Rooney and Judy Garland are getting a bit on in years to be designated as babes, but they have lost none of their shrewd showmanship in their passage through adolescence.**

Judy's marriage to David Rose didn't really last very long. Let's face it, it did have its problems. Judy, in "There'll Always Be Another Encore," said:

> When I was just nineteen, I was married to David Rose, the composer. David and I were very much in love. Our marriage gave me a chance to get away from my mother and the domination of the studio. But the studio just muscled in and tried to humiliate him, and even kept him out of work. He couldn't fight a big, powerful studio. We had a wonderful marriage until my professional life tore me one way and David another. Our happiness lasted less than a year and a half and ended in despair. I was tired, and the regimen at Metro wouldn't let me stop working long enough to be really married.†

*Robert Dana, the *New York Herald Tribune,* 1941.
**Howard Barnes, the *New York Herald Tribune,* 1941.
†Judy Garland, "There'll Always Be Another Encore," *McCalls Magazine,* January-February, 1964.

Judy and Deanna Durbin (top) on the set of their first film, *Every Sunday*. (Courtesy of Metro-Goldwyn-Mayer) Tony Martin, Judy, and Jack Haley (bottom) in a publicity shot for *Pigskin Parade*. (Courtesy of 20th Century–Fox)

Stuart Erwin (top left) whispers in Judy's ear in a scene from *Pigskin Parade*. (Courtesy of 20th Century–Fox) Ronald Sinclair, Judy, and Mickey Rooney (top right) in a publicity shot for *Thoroughbreds Don't Cry*. (Courtesy of Metro-Goldwyn-Mayer) Judy and Sophie Tucker (bottom) in a scene from *Broadway Melody of 1938*. (Courtesy of Metro-Goldwyn-Mayer)

Allan Jones, Judy, and Henry Armetta (top) in a scene from *Everybody Sing*. (Courtesy of Metro-Goldwyn-Mayer) Fannie Brice, Henry Armetta, Judy, and Allan Jones (bottom) in a scene from *Everybody Sing*. (Courtesy of Metro-Gold-wyn-Mayer)

Judy, Mary Astor, Walter Pidgeon, Freddie Bartholomew, and Scotty Beckett (top) in a publicity shot for *Listen, Darling*. (Courtesy of Metro-Goldwyn-Mayer) Freddie Bartholomew and Judy (bottom) in a scene from *Listen, Darling*. (Courtesy of Metro-Goldwyn-Mayer)

Judy in a publicity photo for *Love Finds Andy Hardy*. (Courtesy of Metro-Goldwyn-Mayer)

Jack Haley, Judy, and Ray Bolger in a scene from *The Wizard of Oz*. (Courtesy of Metro-Goldwyn-Mayer)

Judy and Mickey Rooney (top) impersonating Franklin and Eleanor Roosevelt in *Babes in Arms*. (Courtesy of Metro-Goldwyn-Mayer) Judy and Mickey Rooney (bottom) in *Babes in Arms*. (Courtesy of Metro-Goldwyn-Mayer)

Judy and Mickey Rooney (top) in a scene from *Andy Hardy Meets Debutante*. (Courtesy of Metro-Goldwyn-Mayer) Lewis Stone, Cecilia Parker, Fay Holden, Sara Haden, Mickey Rooney, and Judy (bottom) in a publicity photo for *Andy Hardy Meets Debutante*. (Courtesy of Metro-Goldwyn-Mayer)

Larry Nunn, Judy, and Mickey Rooney (top) in a scene from *Strike Up the Band*. (Courtesy of Metro-Goldwyn-Mayer) Judy and Mickey Rooney (bottom) singing "Our Love Affair" in *Strike Up the Band*. (Courtesy of Metro-Goldwyn-Mayer)

Judy and George Murphy (top) in a scene from *Little Nelly Kelly*. (Courtesy of Metro-Goldwyn-Mayer)Edward Everett Horton, Judy, and Charles Winninger (bottom) in a scene from *Ziegfeld Girl*. (Courtesy of Metro-Goldwyn-Mayer)

Hedy Lamarr, Judy, and Lana Turner (top) in a publicity photo for *Ziegfeld Girl*. (Courtesy of Metro-Goldwyn-Mayer) Judy and Mickey Rooney (middle left) in a scene from *Life Begins for Andy Hardy*. (Courtesy Metro-Goldwyn-Mayer)

Judy (middle right) in a scene from *Life Begins for Andy Hardy*. (Courtesy of Metro-Goldwyn-Mayer) Ray McDonald, Mickey Rooney, Judy, Virginia Weidler, and Richard Quine (bottom) in a publicity photo for *Babes on Broadway*. (Courtesy Metro-Goldwyn-Mayer)

Judy and Mickey Rooney (top) in a scene from *Babes on Broadway.* (Courtesy of Metro-Goldwyn-Mayer) Judy and Gene Kelly (middle left) in a scene from *For Me and My Gal.* (Courtesy Metro-Goldwyn-Mayer)

Judy and Gene Kelly (middle right) in a publicity photo for *For Me and My Gal.* (Courtesy Metro-Goldwyn-Mayer) George Murphy, Judy, and Gene Kelly (bottom) in a publicity photo from *For Me and My Gal.* (Courtesy of Metro-Goldwyn-Mayer)

Judy and Van Heflin (top) in a scene from *Presenting Lily Mars.* (Courtesy of Metro-Goldwyn-Mayer) Judy (middle left), singing "The Joint Is Really Jumpin' Down at Carnegie Hall" in *Thousands Cheer.* (Courtesy of Metro-Goldwyn-Mayer)

Judy and Van Heflin (middle right) in a scene from *Presenting Lily Mars.* (Courtesy of Metro-Goldwyn-Mayer) Judy and Mickey Rooney (bottom) in a scene from *Girl Crazy.* (Courtesy of Metro-Goldwyn-Mayer)

Judy, Lucille Bremer, and Tom Drake (top) in a scene from *Meet Me in St. Louis.* (Courtesy of Metro-Goldwyn-Mayer) Judy and Henry Daniels, Jr. (middle left) in a scene from *Meet Me in St. Louis.* (Courtesy of Metro-Goldwyn-Mayer)

Judy (middle right), singing "The Boy Next Door" in *Meet Me in St. Louis.* (Courtesy of Metro-Goldwyn-Mayer) Judy and Tom Drake (bottom) in a publicity photo from *Meet Me in St. Louis.* (Courtesy of Metro-Goldwyn-Mayer)

Judy and Robert Walker
(top) in a publicity photo
for *The Clock.* (Courtesy
of Metro-Goldwyn Mayer)
Judy (middle left), singing
"In the Valley" in *The
Harvey Girls.* (Courtesy
Metro-Goldwyn-Mayer)

Preston Foster, Angela
Lansbury, Judy, and
John Hodiak (middle
right) in a publicity
photo for *The Harvey
Girls.* Judy and Robert
Walker (bottom) in a
scene from *The Clock.*
(Courtesy of Metro-Gold-
wyn-Mayer)

Judy and Gene Kelly (top) singing "Be a Clown" in the finale of *The Pirate*. (Courtesy of Metro-Goldwyn-Mayer) Judy and Gene Kelly (middle left) in a publicity photo for *The Pirate*. (Courtesy of Metro-Goldwyn-Mayer)

Judy (middle right), as Marilyn Miller in *Till the Clouds Roll By*. (Courtesy of Metro-Goldwyn-Mayer) Judy (bottom), singing "Who?" in *Till the Clouds Roll By*. (Courtesy of Metro-Goldwyn-Mayer)

4

In 1942 Judy made one of her most popular movies, *For Me and My Gal*. In it she appeared with a young dancer who was making his film debut, Gene Kelly. Judy sang many great songs in this one but nothing compared with her brokenhearted rendition of "After You've Gone." She's alone, onstage, and the camera comes in for a beautiful close-up. Judy stumbles over the timing of the song and tears come into her eyes, she's afraid Gene Kelly is leaving her. And who could stop himself from crying with her as she let out her final "... till we meet again," in the song of the same name, as her brother left for a war from which he was destined not to return? Decca released a recording of Judy and Gene singing "For Me and My Gal" and "When You Wore a Tulip," and it went on to be a big seller.

Her acting was good, too. The familiar catch in her voice was there and she had some good scenes. Her best, undoubtedly, was the scene in which Gene Kelly finally realizes that he's in love with her. Then, there's the one where she tells Gene, whom she had earlier told never to see her again, that she doesn't really hate him. And let's not forget the big closing where she just happens to see Harry (Kelly) in the middle of an audience of hundreds of identically dressed soldiers; and what should she be singing at that precise moment? "When Johnny Comes Marching Home Again," of course. As Judy rushes through the soldiers to Gene, the entire audience, for some unexplained reason, begins singing "For Me and My Gal"! Then, the famous MGM lion roars *The End*.

In the *New York Herald Tribune*, Howard Barnes wrote:

> Miss Garland is someone to reckon with. Of all the youngsters who have graduated into mature roles in recent years, she has the surest command of her form of make-believe.
> Barring the corny aspects of the continuity (film), she turns in a

65

warm, persuasive, and moving portrayal of the diffident hoofer and singer who loves a heel.*

Joseph Pasternak produced Judy's first film of 1943, *Presenting Lily Mars*. Originally the story (by Booth Tarkington) had been bought as a property for Lana Turner but then someone got the inspiration that with a little music it would be perfect for Judy. Pasternak's special touch and Judy's special acting, along with that of the rest of the cast, carried this film into the "something special" category. There were some tender scenes between Judy and her co-star Van Heflin (who had recently won an Academy Award). Who can forget the quiver in Judy's voice when she said, "I'm not a star, I'm not even an actress, I want to go home." Then she cried into the arms of her lovable but somewhat daffy mother, played by Spring Byington.

She swung "Tom, Tom, the Piper's Son" like it's never been swung since, and participated in a particularly poignant duet with Connie Gilchrist, called "Every Little Movement." The movie ended with a big and beautiful, (although obviously out of place) finale. Judy came out in yards and yards of black tulle and sang "Broadway Rhythm" and "Three O'Clock in the Morning."

The *New York Times* reported:

> MGM . . . is again having her [Judy Garland] show off her best points in "Presenting Lily Mars." Miss Garland is fresh and pretty—she has a perky friendliness that is completely disarming. She is a gifted young lady. [But] for all its sweetness "Presenting Lily Mars" is uninviting film fare . . . Perhaps MGM should let Miss Garland grow up and stay that way.**

Above all, throughout the film, Judy looked better than she had ever looked before. This, in itself, is remarkable, for during the production of this film her problems with her marriage were reaching their peak, and she was soon to start divorce proceedings against Rose.

On July 10, 1943, Judy appeared in her first concert. It took place at the Robin Hood Dell in Philadelphia, Pennsylvania, and it was her only concert during her fifteen-year contract with Metro. The Dell is an enormous outdoor theatre and that night they had to turn away 15,000 people. There just wasn't enough room for them. The show was, to say the least, a success.

Time magazine reported:

> Judy Garland was never so petrified in her whole life. With hands clasped demurely before her, she had just walked on the stage of

*Howard Barnes, the *New York Herald Tribune*, 1942.
**© 1943, the New York Times Company. Reprinted by permission.

Philadelphia's Robin Hood Dell to make her concert debut. Behind her sat ninety of the finest orchestral musicians in the world—the men of the Philadelphia Orchestra. At her side stood a man who had conducted for nearly every famous prima donna in the business—Andre Kostelanetz. In front of her, covering benches, aisles, roof tops, trees, steps and hillsides was all of her public who could possibly crowd themselves into the Dell amphitheatre—a sea of nearly 36,000 faces and a Dell record anyway it was counted.

There was little of the typical Garland exuberance in Judy's first group which consisted of four Gershwin love songs: "Someone to Watch Over Me," "Do, Do, Do," "Embraceable You," and "The Man I Love." Except for her startling red-blonde hair, she looked like a girl who had just arrived at her first formal party and was scared stiff nobody would dance with her.

With "Strike up the Band" which followed, she began to feel the beat which Kostelanetz was coaxing from the orchestra. And after intermission, when she got into the songs from her own movies— "Over the Rainbow," "For Me and My Gal," and "You Made Me Love You"—Miss Garland relaxed and slid right into the groove. At her finale, "The Joint Is Really Jumpin' Down at Carnegie Hall," neither she nor her audience were feeling any pain.

"I thought to myself," she said afterward, "that they were probably thinking what was I doing there anyway, so I just sang louder." Needless to say, the crowd roared, stamped, clapped, and whistled. To get the proper beat for this one, incidentally, Kostelanetz imported six hot saxophonists, one jazz trumpet, and one boogie-woogie pianist into the staid confines of Philadelphia.

Although David Hocker, the Dell's astute young manager, had to maneuver for two years to make this non-symphonic debut possible, it was definitely a success and Miss Garland said it was more fun than anything she'd ever done. A concert tour next winter might result, "but it would never be any more serious than this!"*

Of course, this hadn't been Judy's first adult contact with a live audience. Since the beginning of World War II she had been very active in entertaining the troops. She was entertaining at Fort Ord the day Pearl Harbor was attacked. Throughout the war, she was an active participant in shows for the guys in the service, especially through the dozens and dozens of radio performances she did on the Armed Forces Radio Network. After her shows at the bases she would tell the boys: "I love everyone of you. If it will help you, write to me. I'll try to answer your letters. And I beg you to come back. You're all too wonderful to have anything happen to you. I couldn't bear it." Then she'd sing "Over the Rainbow" and cry. And the men would cry. She did try to answer many of those letters and before long she was the most popular entertainer at the camps.

*© 1943, *Time*, Time-Life, Inc.

67

She was the girl next door, the girl they had waiting for them at home, the girl they wanted to marry.

Later, Judy was to learn that her recording of "For Me And My Gal" had been aired on one of the Normandy invasion barges and that there had been two bombers named for her. "Just imagine," she thought rather solemnly, "me bombing Hitler twice a day."

Thousands Cheer was one of MGM's big, all-star, wartime extravaganzas. No one star was in the film for very long, but almost everyone on the Metro lot made an appearance. Judy's spot consisted of singing one song, "The Joint Is Really Jumpin' Down at Carnegie Hall" with Jose Iturbi at the piano. "Judy Garland," remarked the *New York Herald Tribune*, "is attractive as she gets Iturbi to bang out some swing rhythms on the piano." In its first week at the Astor Theatre in New York City, it grossed $534,000 (and at 1943 prices!).

But alas, the year 1943 also brought the last of the great Garland-Rooney flicks. Together, they starred in George Gershwin's *Girl Crazy*. The songs were good and the movie was generally flawless. It got very good reviews and the critics reacted favorably to the excitement Judy and Mickey injected into the film merely by the force of their personalities. *Time* magazine printed the following review:

> He [Rooney] is a natural dancer and comedian, and his little parlor tricks—especially one burlesque broadcast—are a pleasure to watch. Even better is Judy Garland. As sung by Cinemactress Garland, "Embraceable You," and "Bidin' My Time" become hits all over again and the new "But Not for Me" sounds like another. Her presence is open, cheerful and warming. If she were not so profitably good at her own game she could obviously be a dramatic cinema actress with profit to all.*

Throughout the late thirties and forties there were dozens of properties bought by MGM specifically with Judy in mind. Some of them, such as "Girl Crazy," "The Clock" and "The Pirate" were made but many more just never made it to the screen for one reason or another (most usually because of the impossibility of fitting them into Judy's already overcrowded schedule). Some of these were *Very Warm For May, Babes In Hollywood, The American Symphony, Good News* (later filmed with June Allyson and Peter Lawford) and a screenplay entitled *The Captured Shadow* written by F. Scott Fitzgerald for Judy, Mickey and Freddie Bartholomew. For a while her schedule called for her to star in a remake of *Show Boat* immediately following *Presenting Lily Mars* but then *Meet Me In St. Louis* came along and she had to rush into that. Later she was scheduled to star in a remake of *Roberta* with Gene Kelly but that couldn't be fit in either. Also, in 1937, while casting *Gone With The Wind*, Judy

Ibid.

68

was one of the first actresses tested by David O. Selznick for the part of Scarlett O'Hara's younger sister. This role, however, went to Ann Rutherford.

Throughout this whole time, Judy continued to record for Decca. Her recordings were among the most popular of the day. Although all of them were well received, there are a few standouts, such as the disc with Kelly and the supremely beautiful "You'll Never Walk Alone." Some of her other cuts of this period were "The End of the Rainbow," "Blues in the Night," "The Last Call for Love," and "A Journey to a Star." She also had a tremendous success with her recordings of "On the Sunny Side of the Street" and "That Old Black Magic." There was always something about a Judy Garland recording that was special (try and find them now—antique dealers buy them up and sell them at preposterous prices). She never made a recording that wasn't "perfect" in the strictest sense of the word. Where such performers as Sinatra and Streisand might change the words to a song or ad-lib during a recording session, Garland always had the strictest regard for a songwriter's lyrics. It's true that she would sometimes ad-lib in front of a live audience but this was no more than an immediate reaction to the mood of her audience. Joseph Pasternak recalled:

> The musicians always looked forward to making a recording with her because they knew she would make a great foreground to their background. Musicians are the biggest critics in the world. If they don't think a singer is doing justice to an orchestration they feel sad. But not with her. When she did a song for me, she would go over it once or twice with Roger Edens at the piano and then, take one—finished. Perfect.

5

In 1944 Judy Garland made the second most popular film of her career at Metro. (The first, of course, was *The Wizard of Oz*). The name of it was *Meet Me in St. Louis* and it was based on Sally Benson's *New Yorker* series about the Smith family and most particularly about Esther Smith. Judy's co-stars were Mary Astor, Lucille Bremer, Leon Ames, and Margaret O'Brien. The director was Vincente Minnelli.

Oddly enough, Judy didn't want to make this picture. As a matter of fact she was dead set against it. She even had her mother speak to Arthur Freed. Nevertheless, they talked her into it. (Later, she was to find out that they could talk her into almost anything.) It became one of her favorite films. Of the fourteen Garland pictures produced by Arthur Freed for MGM this one was Freed's particular favorite. It was also the most success-ful. Until that time Metro's biggest grosser was *Gone With the Wind. St. Louis* came closer to overtaking *Gone With the Wind* than any other Metro picture in four years. It even surpassed *Oz*, although *Oz* later caught up through re-releases. Needless to say, *St. Louis* has been listed by *Variety* as one of the All Time Box Office Champions.

The film was produced so beautifully that it prompted James Agee, film critic for *Time* magazine, to proclaim: " 'Meet Me in St. Louis' is a musical that even the deaf should enjoy."

Agee most certainly wasn't alone in his opinion of the film. I don't think there was a critic with a criticism of the film other than the fact that it couldn't last longer. Its 112 minutes went by much too quickly. Movie critic Douglas McVay wrote the following many years later in *Films and Filming* when summarizing Judy's film career:

> The performances of Judy Garland in Vincente Minnelli's "Meet Me in St. Louis," and "The Pirate," Charles Walter's "Easter Parade," and "Summer Stock" and George Cukor's "A Star Is Born" are some

of the finest the American cinema has to afford; so much so, that it is impossible to convey their magic in print.

As Esther Smith in "St. Louis" she was a picture of flowering adolescence, with a will-o-the-wisp, lump in the throat fragrance; "high cheekboned face innocently on the edge of beauty, adorable bow of mouth, great dark gazing pools of eyes, long soft silks of auburn hair" (the infatuated quotation of the author)—and all with that voice! "The Trolley Song"; the wistful "Boy Next Door"; her little song over the banisters to this same boy next door when she's lured him into helping her turn down the house lights after a party. The scene where Esther's young sister, Tootie, comes home with false accusations against the boyfriend and Esther rushing round and piles into him out of family loyalty. Their kiss at reconciliation, and Esther bemusedly eating ice cream at the memory of it. And finally, his proposal to her after the Christmas ball, when it seems they are to be parted because her parents are leaving the city. Going upstairs, she discovers Tootie, also distressed at the thought of migration; slowly throwing aside the hood of her cape, she begins to sing to her in an effort of solace "Have Yourself a Merry Little Christmas." Judy's version of this exquisite Hugh Martin–Ralph Blane number makes even Sinatra's pedestrian; and Minnelli shoots her in shadow Technicolor close-ups, with love. If I could only save one sequence of film for a desert island, it wouldn't be Odessa, not the end of "The Great Adventure," mighty and inspiring as they are, it would be this . . .

McVay covers just about everything there is to cover concerning the highlights of *Meet Me in St. Louis* and I couldn't agree with him more about the scene between Tootie and Esther; but there is one thing I would like to add. In my opinion, Garland made only two films during her career that were totally perfect. They were *Meet Me in St. Louis* and *A Star Is Born.* (I will admit that both *Easter Parade* and *In the Good Old Summertime* came close to perfection.)

In my opinion it is impossible to find anything wrong with *St. Louis.* The casting of each role was perfect, the directing was done with love— sheer love—and the acting of all roles was superb. Indeed, the only word for *Meet Me in St. Louis* is *perfect.* Every camera angle, every close-up, every scene, every costume, every nuance of each performer was beyond criticism. There really isn't any more I can say without overdoing it, and I may have done so already.

If *Meet Me in St. Louis* had been made in the sixties Judy would undoubtedly have been nominated for an Academy Award. But in the forties, the Academy still felt that musical actresses just weren't the same as strictly dramatic actresses and didn't deserve awards. At best, this was a foolish attitude.

"The Trolley Song," which was written especially for this picture and for Judy to sing, went on to be nominated for an Academy Award but it was beaten by "Swinging on a Star" from the Bing Crosby hit, *Going My Way*.

Vincente Minnelli, the director, was relatively new to Hollywood. It is possible that he is the reason for the perfection of *St. Louis*. Actually, most Minnelli films are at least near-perfect. During the shooting of *St. Louis* he saw to it that each take was done over and over until it met with his satisfaction. Judy and Minnelli fought constantly during the filming of *Meet Me in St. Louis* over his constant ordering of retakes. Judy was a perfectionist in her work and she resented his disagreeing with the way a scene had been done if she thought it had gone well. But Judy, along with everyone else, admitted at the end that it had all been worth it.

Before release, one of Judy's songs was deleted from the final version of *Meet Me in St. Louis*. In the first half of the film, Rose, Esther, and their friends visit the site of the St. Louis Exposition. While there, Esther (Judy) and John (Tom Drake) compare the building of the fair to the building of their relationship and Esther sings a song entitled "Boys and Girls Like You and Me." This song had been written by Rodgers and Hammerstein for use in *Oklahoma!* but was never used. Minnelli found it and thought it appropriate for *St. Louis*, but in trying to shorten the final film he felt that either this song or "The Boy Next Door" would have to go. Since "The Boy Next Door" held more of a "story point" the other song went. It can still be heard on the Decca album of music from *Meet Me in St. Louis*.

Here is a sampling of the generally excellent reviews that followed the premiere of *Meet Me in St. Louis*:

> A charming movie. Miss Garland is full of exuberance as the second sister of the lot, and sings . . . with a rich voice that grows riper and more expressive in each new film. Her chortling of "The Trolley Song" puts fresh zip into that inescapable tune . . .
> A ginger peachy show.
>
> Bosley Crowther, *New York Times**

> A period family portrait . . . enchanting in its characterizations, incident and color.
> Fortunately MGM has never been at a loss to have the right performer for the right role . . . Judy Garland is on hand to sing several songs expertly and to give dramatic effects to the small crises of family life . . . little Margaret O'Brien is wonderful.
>
> Howard Barnes, *New York Herald Tribune***

> If you're looking for a picture that represents sheer, unadulterated enjoyment . . . the story of the Smiths is told to the accompaniment

*© 1944, The New York Times Company. Reprinted by permission.
**Howard Barnes, the *New York Herald Tribune*, 1944.

of a number of hearty laughs, one quick tear and a couple of good
tunes . . .

Judy Garland and Tom Drake . . . carry on romantically together
and Judy of course, gives out in song whenever the spirit moves her,
which is often enough to please her loyal following but not too often
to interfere seriously with the thread of the story.

Kate Cameron, *New York Daily News**

Judy made one other film in 1944 but it wasn't released until 1946.
Kay Thompson and Roger Edens, both very good friends of Judy's, wrote
a sketch for her to perform in Metro's "extravaganza of extravaganzas,"
Ziegfeld Follies. Thompson, a well-known entertainer in her own right,
had been very helpful in shaping Judy's film personality and in bringing
out her keen sense of humor and satire. She seemed to know exactly what
was best for Judy. The sketch was called "The Interview" or "A Great
Lady Has an Interview." It was a take-off of a "big star" being interviewed
and throughout the segment Judy gave a great impersonation of a Tallulah
Bankhead–type character. It was comedy at its most sophisticated and like
nothing Judy had ever done before. Minnelli had been asked to direct the
film and he and Judy got along much better than during *St. Louis.* In the
New York Times, Bosley Crowther described Judy as "giving promise of
a talent approaching that of Beatrice Lillie and Gertrude Lawrence."

Although the government had imposed wartime economics on the
film industry, *Follies* was very expensive. To avoid being panned by the
government, the public, and the critics for going overboard during such
a difficult time, Metro put the finished film away for two years.

Before the gossip columnists had even finished writing about the
arguments between Judy and Vincente on the set of *Meet Me in St. Louis,*
she shocked all of them by requesting that he direct her in her next film,
The Clock. Fred Zinnemann had originally been signed as director but he
and Judy weren't getting along. It was during the filming of *The Clock* that
Judy and Vincente fell in love and announced their engagement.

Except for *Life Begins for Andy Hardy,* when all four of Judy's songs
were deleted, *The Clock* was Judy's first straight dramatic and songless
film and she did it well. The critics all agreed that Judy had once and for
all shown them that she could be a sensitive actress. Again, the film liter-
ally reeked of perfection. Otis L. Guernsey remarked in the *New York
Herald Tribune:*

A sincere and touching examination of the war-time marriage
problem. Miss Garland, who doesn't sing a note in "The Clock," works
considerable sympathy into her role. She maintains the impression of
variety in the continual boy-girl relationship.

She reacts to the ugliness and red tape of a municipal wedding and

*Reprinted by permission of the *New York Daily News.*

74

then keeps the relationship from becoming too sugary when the disappointment is amended.*

The Clock was released in June, 1945. On the basis of *St. Louis,* which had been released in December, 1944, and *The Clock,* Judy was one of the top-ten money-makers at the box office in 1945. This was Judy's third year on the list. In 1940 she and Bette Davis were the only women on the list and in 1941 she ranked within the ten also.

On July 15, 1945, Judy and Vincente were married in the garden of her Hollywood home. Ira Gershwin served as best man and Betty Asher was Judy's attendant. Louis B. Mayer gave the bride away. (Unfortunately for Judy, that's only a figure of speech.)

Judy's first film following her marriage to Vincente was *The Harvey Girls.* George Sidney was the director and the cast included John Hodiak, Angela Lansbury, Ray Bolger, and Marjorie Main. The film had a loosely drawn plot based on the founding of the chain of "Harvey" restaurants. Johnny Mercer and Harry Warren wrote the original music, and one song from the film went on to win an Academy Award. This was "On the Atchison, Topeka and the Sante Fe," which became one of many songs identified with Judy through the years.

The Harvey Girls was another of the bubbly-bouncy Garland vehicles with the bubbly-bouncy Garland songs. It was set in the Old West and even had short, thin, little Judy holding up a restaurant at gun-point. The film was released in January, 1946, and received many reviews like the following one by Howard Barnes, which appeared in the *New York Herald Tribune:*

> A great big animated picture post card. Judy Garland is the film's bright . . . star. Miss Garland is effectively glamorized in getups of the '90's and sings her songs pleasantly. Hodiak gives her valuable dramatic support. "The Harvey Girls" is a perfect demonstration of what Hollywood can do with its vast resources when it wants to be really showy . . . pretty girls . . . period sets and costumes . . . lilting tunes . . . super speedy dance shuffles.**

Following the filming of *The Harvey Girls* Judy went into production with *Till the Clouds Roll By.* The film was based on the life of Jerome Kern and Judy had been signed to play the Broadway singing sensation, Marilyn Miller. Publicity built the part up so that one would have thought Judy was the star; however, when the film finally came out, Judy wasn't seen on the screen for more than fifteen minutes. It was during the production of this film that Judy found out that she was pregnant with her first child. Her pink feathery gown started out with a normal waist but as her figure

*Otis L. Guernsey, the *New York Herald Tribune,* 1945.
**Howard Barnes, the *New York Herald Tribune,* 1946.

expanded the waistline was raised until, when the scene was finally shot, the gown had become an empire style. That took care of her singing "Who" (she found it quite funny, running along a row of young dancers singing, "Who stole my heart away, who makes me dream all day . . ." while in her condition), but they still had to film her singing "Look for the Silver Lining." By this time her pregnancy was very noticeable, but someone got the idea of putting her behind a kitchen sink, piling dishes all around her and having her wash them while she sang the song. The audience only saw her from the waist up. Immediately after completing the picture Judy went into confinement for the rest of her pregnancy.

Despite the size of her part, Judy was given second billing in the film, just under that of Robert Walker, who played Jerome Kern. Interestingly enough, several people have confessed to having sat through the film four or five times just to see Judy's small portion of the show. In his *New York Times* review of the film, Bosley Crowther said:

> Why did Metro cook up such a phony yarn? Why couldn't it simply have given us more such enjoyable things as Judy Garland playing Marilyn Miller and singing the melodious "Look for the Silver Lining" and "Who."*

While Judy was resting (for the first time in years), Metro released *Ziegfeld Follies*. The reviewers had more raves for Judy than for anyone else in the cast.

After Liza was born Judy began going into depressions and no one really knew why. She began to cry on the set and retire to her dressing room until she could compose herself and build up enough courage to face the camera again. Word began to leak out through "gossip" magazines that "Judy Garland is being difficult." She wasn't being difficult, she was sick. It should have been obvious that she just didn't belong in the life she was in. God knows she had the talent for it, but emotionally she wasn't able to cope with the problems. Basically she was a strong woman and she endured a hell that few others in the public eye have known, but there is a limit to just how much one woman can take.

Judy's marriage had started off happily and she and Vincente had a few happy years together. Judy was constantly unsure of herself, though, and Vincente had to convince her that she could act, that she could sing, and that she was a desirable woman. Years earlier the executives at Metro had convinced her that she didn't have any talent and it seems that more than a trace of this brainwashing had remained with her.

And as if all that wasn't bad enough, since her divorce from David Rose, she had been getting thinner and thinner. She couldn't gain any weight—even when she tried! She was working on nervous energy and approaching a breakdown.

*© 1947, The New York Times Company. Reprinted by permission.

Metro chose Judy for the starring role in a new project they were planning. This was to be a screen-musical version of the Alfred Lunt and Lynn Fontanne play, *The Pirate*. Cole Porter was signed to write the songs for S. N. Behrman's story and Vincente Minnelli was set to direct.

Judy was ill during the filming of *The Pirate*. She tried her best to cooperate, but there was a very serious problem. During the day Judy would argue and disagree with her director, and then at night she would go home to her husband. They were one and the same person. Judy and Vincente were both perfectionists, but their ideas on the subject differed. When Hedda Hopper visited Judy on the set of *The Pirate* she was locked in her dressing room, crying that "no one loves me . . . no one gives a damn about me."

Judy's costumes in *The Pirate* were lavish, the performances were good, and Porter's songs were gems, but the film was greeted with mixed reviews. Some thought it too dull, others considered it the best of Judy's career. Arthur Freed, the producer of *The Pirate*, has expressed the opinion that the film was ahead of its time and that had it been released now it would have been an even bigger hit. In the same article quoted on page 35, Douglas McVay said:

> The scene provoked visual echos in "The Pirate," with a long close-up of her during the slow, quiet "evening star" section of "Mack the Black" (where to quote the writer again, "she shakes down her red, red hair and sings her heart out") and in her tender "You Can Do No Wrong." And her period portrayal here, if not possessing the peculiar charm of "St. Louis," has an equally individual panache. Ravishing whenever she has her hair loose (as in "Mack" and the earlier bedroom sequence with Gladys Cooper), she exhibits a notable development in the zest for parody which had been briefly apparent in Minnelli's "Ziegfeld." "He wants me," she murmurs grittily between clenched teeth, as another eager lady offers to step into the breach when she's summoned to the dread Macoco; and her come hither pretence prior to bombarding the unwary buccaneer with the contents of her boudoir wouldn't have disgraced Mata Hari.
>
> In the closing reprise of "Be a Clown" with Gene Kelly, she beats tempo with her foot, waits cheerfully for Kelly to finish singing his share, then joins him in a fade-out of mirth. They are, one feels, no longer Serafin and Manuela but Gene and Judy (as in their "When You Wore a Tulip" disc when they actually address each other by their real names); and they are celebrating not simply clowning and pierrots, but all types of song and dance, including the American musical. A rich connoisseur's pleasure.

One of the most favorable of the reviews was this one by Howard Barnes in the *New York Herald Tribune*:

A gala screen musical has been made out of S. N. Behrman's romantic costume play, "The Pirate." MGM has played considerable hob with the original Alfred Lunt–Lynn Fontanne starring vehicle. Most of it is to the good. At the Music Hall there is more dancing than script; more production pomp than practical staging. But with Gene Kelly hoofing like a dervish, Judy Garland changing character at the drop of a hat, and resplendent trappings, the show is bounding and beautiful. The important thing is that his [Behrman's] original notion has inspired a fetching film.

Miss Garland dances in a trance, sings pleasantly, and does a superb job of crockery smashing in a scene in which she discovers that her beloved pirate is only an itinerant mummer. Although the stars are backed up by hundreds of extras and panoply galore, they are in charge of "The Pirate" on the screen as surely as were Lunt and Fontanne behind the footlights.*

Soon after completion of *The Pirate*, Judy was taken to a psychiatric home to ward off a complete nervous breakdown. By now, it was late 1947. The home was charging Judy $300 a day and for this she got nurses sneaking into her bureau drawers and doctors disturbing her. Once, Judy woke up to find three men standing at the foot of her bed. The conversation went something like this (as told by Judy in her 1964 *McCalls* article):

"Now, Miss Garland," one of the doctors said, "We're sorry to disturb you, but we just wanted to come in and talk to you."

I was disgruntled to say the least but I wasn't going to show them. "Certainly," I said. "What can I do for you?"

"Well," one of them said, "we've been making a survey of your case, and we'd like to ask you a few questions."

"All right. Go ahead."

"First, do you see things?"

"See things—what do you mean, did I ever see? What kind of things?"

"Well, little things that crawl or fly."

"How dare you come in here and ask me things like that? And stop treating me like a nut. I'm here for a rest. I'm exhausted. Between that idiot nurse who comes around looking for things and you asking me do I see things, I'll really be eligible for this place. Now get out of here, so I can get some sleep."**

Judy missed Liza while she was away and finally talked the doctors into letting her see the baby. When Liza was brought to the home, Judy just sat and held her. She was so happy to see the child that when they took

*Howard Barnes, the New York Herald Tribune, 1948.
**Judy Garland, "There'll Always Be Another Encore," *McCalls Magazine*, January-February, 1964.

Liza home Judy cried terribly. Soon, Metro called Judy back from the home so that she could appear in *Easter Parade.*

Metro decided that the Garland-Kelly team deserved better than they'd been given. They came up with *Easter Parade,* which had seventeen songs in it—all of them by Irving Berlin. During the dance rehearsals, though, Gene Kelly sprained an ankle and MGM managed to get Fred Astaire, who was then in semi-retirement, as Kelly's replacement. At first it was hoped that Vincente would direct the film but Judy's doctors advised against it so Charles Walter's was called in." Judy had gained some weight while she was away and now the studio put her back on a strict diet to take it off. Soon her health was failing again because of the diet. The production of *Easter Parade* was strenuous to begin with because of the dancing rehearsals and all the songs, but her lack of energy made it even worse. Later, she recalled: "I didn't know how I was going to get through it."

At first Judy was afraid of working with Astaire. She had heard a lot of rumors about how demanding he was. Finally, she built up the courage to ask him, "Where's that whip you're supposed to crack?" Answered Fred, "I never cracked it on anyone but myself." Throughout the filming they got along fine.

Easter Parade was one of the biggest film successes of Garland's career. Along with *The Harvey Girls* it was added to *Variety*'s "All Time Box Office Champions" list.

Again turning to the article by Douglas McVay:

> Charles Walters wasn't able to lavish on Judy in his two films the decorative flair of Minnelli. In "Easter Parade" especially, she is only well coiffured during the "It Only Happens When I Dance With You" reprise and in the "Ziegfeld Follies" and "Better Luck Next Time" sequences, and only well costumed in the last of these. Moreover, in directing her and Fred Astaire, Walters permitted both in acting and dancing a shade too much forced grinning.*

This film also received generally excellent reviews. For example, Howard Barnes wrote in the *New York Herald Tribune:*

> Irving Berlin, Fred Astaire, and Judy Garland have pooled their musical and dancing talents in a smart and fetching screen carnival . . . Astaire is hoofing more superbly than ever and Miss Garland has matured to a remarkable degree in "Easter Parade" . . . a handsome and knowing actress. Her latest film performance is all together her best.**

*Douglas McVay, *Films and Filming.*
**Howard Barnes, the *New York Herald Tribune,* 1948.

With the success of the Astaire-Garland film, Metro decided to make a follow-up. It certainly was true that another good picture with the two of them would have been a good idea but Judy was exhausted and needed a rest. Nevertheless, she plunged right into rehearsals with Astaire for *The Barkleys of Broadway.* The dance rehearsals were strenuous and after three weeks Judy had to withdraw because of nervous exhaustion. Ginger Rogers was signed as her replacement and *The Barkleys of Broadway* is the last film Astaire and Rogers appeared in together.

It was only natural that Judy should be so exhausted. She had been making three films at once. In the middle of the filming of *Easter Parade,* Metro decided that some scenes in *The Pirate* had to be redone (it hadn't been released yet). Soon after this decision they began work on the production of *Words and Music,* the film biography of Richard Rodgers and Lorenz Hart. Judy had two songs in the film, one solo and a duet with Mickey Rooney. Thus, for a while Judy was actually working on three films. Later, she half-comically remembered finding herself on the wrong set with the wrong costume on.

Newsweek's review of *Words and Music* included the following:

> Lena Horne brings the film to its toes with her vocalization of "Where or When" and "The Lady Is a Tramp" . . . Judy Garland keeps it there with "I Wish I Were in Love Again" and "Johnny One Note."*

Judy rested for a while and then, when she felt she was ready to go back to work, she notified the studio. Around the same time, June Allyson announced that she was pregnant and would have to drop out of *In the Good Old Summertime.* Metro immediately replaced her with Judy. The film was a Joseph Pasternak production and Van Johnson was Judy's co-star. *In the Good Old Summertime* was a period remake of *The Shop Around the Corner* (which had starred Jimmy Stewart). In it, Judy sang one of the most beautiful songs of her entire career in films, "Merry Christmas."

In 1963 a play appeared on Broadway that was also based on *The Shop Around the Corner.* It was called *She Loves Me* and starred Daniel Massey and Barbara Cook with words and music by Sheldon Harnick and Jerry Bock.

Judy's performance in *In the Good Old Summertime* had many highlights. Unfortunately, it is one of the most overlooked of her career (and yet, one of the most often seen on television). Her most memorable line in the film was, coincidentally, her last one. After finding out that Van Johnson (the manager of the store where she works) was her secret pen pal and her one great love, she responds dreamily, "Psychologically I'm very confused, but personally I feel wonderful!"

*Newsweek, 1949.

For the closing scene of the film the studio needed a small girl to play the part of Judy and Van Johnson's daughter. Van suggested little Liza, now two and a half years old, and Liza got the part. She had no lines, all she had to do was to walk between her mother and Johnson and then let him pick her up. Liza insisted on dressing herself for the scene and when she came out of Judy's dressing room (which, at Liza's birth, had been turned into an elaborate dressing room and nursery) her mother discovered that Liza had forgotten her underwear! Needless to say, this problem was soon taken care of. *Newsweek*'s review of the film read:

> Films based on musical nostalgia have so often been saddled with silly plots that even Technicolor and important casts couldn't help keep them afloat. Hence, the unflagging sparkle of "Summertime" comes as a pleasant surprise . . . Miss Garland's voice, as appealing as ever, this time plays second fiddle to one of her best straight comedy performances.*

Judy's health during *In the Good Old Summertime* hadn't been as good as she'd hoped it would be, so she requested a vacation. The problem here should be obvious. Even though she'd had brief breaks after *The Pirate* and *Easter Parade*, she had never had enough time to get through the full cycle of a safe, supervised diet and then a regaining of her strength. Both times she had to put herself on another speedy diet to get thin for the cameras. And both times it had been done without any regard for her health. MGM decided to give her a long vacation. She made plans to visit Mexico and to stay in Carmel (just outside of Los Angeles) for a while and do a little golfing (her favorite sport).

Soon, Louis B. Mayer called her to his office. He handed her a script for the film *Annie Get Your Gun* and told her to look it over during her vacation. Mayer explained that he had just bought the film for her at an outrageous price and had signed Howard Keel to support her in the production. No expenses would be spared.

Judy was very interested in doing the film and told Mayer so. She had been looking forward to the possibility since first seeing Ethel Merman in *Annie* on Broadway. She told Mayer that she would look forward to starting work but that first she really needed this vacation.

He agreed, and gave her a $5,000 bonus. Then he told her he had a little favor to ask. Having taken the bonus, Judy decided that she couldn't turn Mayer down so she asked him what it was.

After beating around the bush for awhile, Mayer asked her to record one song from the score of *Annie Get Your Gun* so they could get started on the production while she was away. He said that it would only take one or two days. She agreed but felt it was a trick.

One song led to another, and one or two days led to two or three

Ibid.

81

weeks. After six weeks of recording, the score was completed. Soon she was led into rehearsals and then into the filming of the song sequences. Filming began. Judy was late or sometimes she just wasn't there. It was evident that she would be unable to finish the film at this rate, so MGM fired her. At a loss of over $1,000,000, they replaced her with Betty Hutton. At any rate, it was a monumental blunder to decide against waiting for Judy to regain her health.

Judy's score from the film included "Doin' What Comes Naturally," "The Girl That He Marries," "You Can't Get a Man With a Gun," "They Say It's Wonderful," "My Defenses Are Down," "There's No Business Like Show Business," "I'm An In'jun Too," "All That I Got," "Let's Go West," and "Anything You Can Do." It has never been released by Metro but the underground has gotten hold of it. Some privately made tapes and discs have been sold for as much as $75 each. Now, after Judy's death, when it's too late for her to get any credit for it, there are rumors that the record will be released. Each track, incidentally, is superb and there are no signs of Judy's illness in her voice.

Following her dismissal from *Annie Get Your Gun* Judy admitted herself into the Peter Brent Brigham Hospital in Boston and began undergoing care for nervous and emotional exhaustion. Her story of the breakdown and following events is one of the most heartbreaking in her life. She gave all the details in her 1964 *McCalls* article:

> Before I could tell them that I was very ill, they told me they had purchased Irving Berlin's "Annie Get Your Gun" for a fabulous sum of money. I was going to star in it. Before I knew it, Irving Berlin was in Hollywood. Everyone was taking pictures, the press was full of Judy and rehearsals began.
>
> I knew I wasn't good. In the first place, my head wouldn't stop aching. I was so very, very sick. I'd begged them to postpone the starting date, but they wouldn't. I wanted to do that part so badly. I'd seen the show on Broadway, and I'd had my heart set on doing it, and here I was in the middle of it and I knew I wasn't going to make it. I hadn't slept one night in fourteen.
>
> Then I noticed that my hair was falling out, and I was really terrified. I guess this is the dread of all women. Anyhow, I was in the picture and trying to go ahead. The first thing I had to do was learn to shoot a gun. Well, I've always been terrified of guns. I just couldn't do it. Then I had to learn an accent. I couldn't learn anything. All my life I've learned accents, lyrics, parodies, speeches but I couldn't learn that accent. I was just up there making strange noises. Here I was, in the middle of a million dollar wardrobe, and a million eyes on me, and I was in a complete daze. I knew it and everyone around me knew it. But I tried desperately to go on. I knew that if I didn't finish this one it was the finish of me. So I kept on, I was there on time every day, but it was like a dream. Nothing came out right.

So one day it happened again. This time, they sent me a note. Some stooge delivered it. I was in my dressing room in costume for the "I'm An In'jun Too" number and I was wearing war paint, moccasins, and a lot of Indian beads and the feathers. The note said "Your services are no longer required."

I was so mad the only thing I could say was: "You can't do this to me. With this make-up on I don't even know what tribe I belong to. What reservation do I go to?"

The man didn't say a word.

"Let me get this war paint off and this feather out of my head and get my nice dress on—then fire me. But don't fire me as a Navajo or whatever I'm supposed to be," I pleaded.

The man didn't even laugh.

I saw the humor of the situation but even humor can't cure what I was going through. One day, I made up my mind that I was sick and that I must get well—not in a mental institution or a sanitarium but in a legitimate hospital, away from Hollywood. Far, far away where I could be treated like a plain sick human being.

A doctor friend suggested that the Peter Brent Brigham Hospital in Boston was the perfect place. I was put on a diet of three great meals a day and lights out at nine o'clock at night, whether I slept or not. After word got around that I was there, I asked permission to visit the mentally retarded children in an adjoining hospital.

If I was cured at Peter Brent Brigham, it was only because of those children. Many had been there for twelve or thirteen years. All I can remember is their eyes. I went through the wards and finally got down to the young ones, about four or five years old. They were so friendly. They all waved at me from their little cribs and hollered out, "Hi! Judy!" After I had talked to each one and asked their names, I came to a little dark haired girl in the corner. When I walked up she withdrew completely, curled up and turned her head away. I asked the nurse about her and was told that she was five. She had come from a poor, ignorant family in which there were five brothers and sisters, all very healthy except her. They had hated her for her weakness, rejected her completely, and one day she stopped talking. She hadn't said one word in two years. I walked over to her, sat down on her bed, and made a point not to ask her a lot of questions. I just talked to her. About myself, where I came from, my little girl, anything that came to my mind. Finally, I said good-bye and went along to the next bed.

I stayed in Boston for about twelve weeks, and eventually Joseph Pasternak called and said he wanted me for a new picture, "Summer Stock."

After talking to those children every day for ten or eleven weeks, the day came for me to leave. Word got around that I was coming to say good-bye. I walked into the wards, and there they were—the older ones with lipstick on, their hair done up, their faces scrubbed, and each child holding a bouquet of flowers. I kissed them all good-bye, took my flowers, made them promise to write. Finally, I arrived at the last ward, where my little silent child was. The whole ward was watching me, holding my hands and clinging to me. I was so grateful to them, because they really had made me well again. They really had. I walked over to the corner and sat down on the bed with my little silent friend. She just looked at me with her great, beautiful, heartbreaking eyes.

I tried to be as casual as possible. "Well my friend, I'm going now, and I want to thank you for all you've done for me. I'm going to miss you. Be a good girl, and take care of yourself, and if you need anything, don't forget to write." I started to lean over to kiss her.

Suddenly she sprung forward on her knees and screamed at the top of her lungs, "Judy!" The first sound that had come out of her mouth in years. Then she threw her arms around my neck and started to talk and talk and talk. What she said didn't make a bit of sense: "My mother—don't leave—Judy—going away." Wild talk, just everything. She kept saying, "Don't leave, don't leave!" I was holding onto her neck and rocking her. The other children were crying. I was crying. The nurses were crying.

We missed the train. I sat with her for a couple of hours and she never stopped talking. It all came out of her like a torrent. Finally, she calmed down. They gave her a mild sedative, and she became quiet. I told her, "I have to leave, because I have to go back and make a movie, but you must promise me something." She kept saying, "I love you, I love you." I said, "If you love me, you must promise me you'll talk to the nurses, because they love you very much too." The nurses came over, and I made her talk to each one of them. I waited until she fell asleep. When we got to the car I looked up, and there they were, hanging out the windows, waving good-bye.

I guess I had a few gratifying moments in my life, but nothing will ever approach what I felt in my heart when that silent little girl screamed, "Judy!"*

Judy arrived in Hollywood ready for *Summer Stock* but once again she had gained weight and needed to take it off. During rehearsals she had to put herself back on a strict diet—too strict.

The production went slowly because Judy was weakened again by the diet and soon she began coming in late and sometimes just not coming in at all. Once, she reached the gates of the studio and thought she saw the words, "This will be the day," carved in the archway. She turned around and headed for the beach to think things out. She thought it an omen that the day would be the one when everyone pointed at her and criticized her work. Charles Walters remembers Judy sitting on the tractor between takes of the "Happy Harvest" number and asking: "What am I doing here? Would someone get Vincente to take me home."

In addition, her migraine headaches were returning. She'd suffered with these headaches throughout her life. They were unusual in the respect that they could come and go surprisingly quickly. Once, she was

*Judy Garland, "There'll Always Be Another Encore," *McCalls Magazine*, January-February, 1964.

watching the day's rushes in a dark projection room. When the lights were turned on she was on the floor writhing in pain. Another time she was being rushed to the hospital with the same kind of headache. Suddenly it was gone. She had the ambulance return home.

Summer Stock turned out to be a good film although it was never one of Judy's favorites. I quote again Douglas McVay:

> Distinctly the superior of the Walters pictures, though, is "Summer Stock." This unfairly forgotten piece, reuniting her with Gene Kelly, was the last completed before her 1950 breakdown and four year retirement from celluloid. One might accordingly anticipate signs of stress, but what signs there may be dovetail so nicely with the harassed nature of the role that they are hidden; the sole noticeable feature is how much plumper she looks in the opening scenes than in the rest, and this is trivial.
>
> In "Summer Stock" she plays a female farmer who lets out a barn to a passing road show, and unexpectedly becomes the star owing to the leading lady's default. The mingling of two worlds results in some beguiling sequences; the proposal to her by show producer Kelly just before curtain rises on the first night ("You people are crazy," she whispers shakily as he presents her with a good luck bouquet) but in particular an earlier episode where she wanders stage struck under the winking pastel hued arc lights and Kelly speaks to her of enslavement by greasepaint.
>
> This perceptively written, perfectly acted passage has Kelly making a very personal statement, and also a delicious irony in Garland's supposed ignorance of show biz. The relaxed, leisurely, mutually affectionate song and dance "You Wonderful You" which closes the conversation is repeated during the climatic revue, with the partners executing a shorter arrangement in likeable St. Louis-ish get up (rather akin in atmosphere to their record "When You Wore a Tulip").
>
> Judy's other numbers ranged from the opening song—"If You Feel Like Singing, Sing" (taken at a carefree tal-la-la while beneath the shower) and "Happy Harvest" (invigoratingly caroled as she drives a tractor towards a camera tracking away from her, shifting into a final close-up on a huge sustained last note when she makes fun of her vocal exhaustion with popping eyes), to the sentimental soliloquy "Friendly Star" (close-ups and close-shots), in which she transcends unremarkable material.
>
> But I have a weakness for the disruption of the staid local Historical Society by the visiting company, when Kelly gradually induces her to surrender to the rhythms of a jazzed up "Portland Fancy." She keeps pace with him throughout an electrically fast routine, and can never have danced better. Non-musically, her performance was most cherished for its flashes of comic temper. Saddled with a weedy fiancé who declared himself during bouts of Dutch courage to be "a young bull" when roused, she eventually blows her top, unleashes a blistering tirade, and flashes off "And you can tell that to the young bull!" Or else

—ordered by taskmaster Kelly to practice a tap number for the ump-teenth time—she retorts, weary, stiff and sore: "All right. ALL RIGHT!" . . . During its second half with its scenes of busily painstaking rehearsals and performance, "Summer Stock" often appears a sort of trailer to the production with which, in 1954, Judy was to return to Hollywood—"A Star Is Born."*

After making *Summer Stock* Judy was ill again and suffering from exhaustion. Metro promised her another vacation and she left for Carmel "just to play a little golf."

Well, before she could reach the eighteenth hole Metro called again. It seems June Allyson was going to have another baby and they needed someone to replace her in *Royal Wedding* with Fred Astaire and Peter Lawford. Judy fought—she didn't want to do it. But Metro bribed her with the promise of a longer vacation afterwards.

She decided to make the film and do her best in it. She was on time for all the rehearsals and she recorded the songs (including "How Could You Believe Me When I Said I Loved You When You Know I've Been a Liar All My Life?"). Filming began, but after a few days she became ill—she'd been on another diet. Metro was furious—they wouldn't admit it was their own fault, so they suspended her.

They never thought of what she had given them—the millions of dollars she had made for them—the way she and Mickey Rooney had practically kept the studio alive during the early forties—what they had taken from her and what they had helped do to her.

On June 20, 1950, after having an argument with Vincente Minnelli and her agent Carleton Alsop, Judy ran into the bathroom. She drank a glass of water and then just stared at the glass. Suddenly she broke the glass and with a piece of it tried to slash her wrist. (The accounts vary—some claim that it was her neck she tried to cut, others her wrist. The latter is more likely.) The cuts were so minor they could have been made with a pin. Actually the wound was more like a scratch, but it proved that there was definitely something wrong. The next morning the "suicide attempt" was all over the papers—on the front page.

Minnelli had rushed Judy to the hospital.

Judy Garland was a very sick girl and the papers said so, but they didn't tell the public why she was so sick, or who had done the damage. Why should a twenty-seven-year-old woman with the love of millions of people, a husband, and a loving daughter have tried to kill herself? Why?

*Douglas McVay, *Films and Filming*.

Judy (top left) in scenes from *Ziegfeld Follies*. (Courtesy of Metro-Goldwyn-Mayer) Judy and Charles Walters (top right) on the set of *Easter Parade*. (Courtesy of Metro-Goldwyn-Mayer) Judy and Fred Astaire (bottom left) singing "Snooky Ookums" in *Easter Parade*. (Courtesy of Metro-Goldwyn-Mayer) Judy (bottom right) in costume as Manuela for *The Pirate*. (Courtesy of Metro-Goldwyn-Mayer)

Judy and Fred Astaire (top left) singing and dancing "When the Midnight Choo Choo Leaves for Alabam" in *Easter Parade*. (Courtesy of Metro-Goldwyn-Mayer) Judy and Mickey Rooney (top right) singing "I Wish I Were in Love Again" in *Words and Music*. (Courtesy of Metro-Goldwyn-Mayer) Judy and Mickey Rooney (middle left) singing "I Wish I Were in Love Again" in *Words and Music*. (Courtesy of Metro-Goldwyn-Mayer) Judy and Van Johnson (middle right) in a scene from *In the Good Old Summertime*. (Courtesy of Metro-Goldwyn-Mayer) Spring Byington, S. Z. Sakall, Judy, and Buster Keaton (bottom) in a scene from *In the Good Old Summertime*. (Courtesy of Metro-Goldwyn-Mayer)

Judy and Van Johnson (top) in a scene from *In the Good Old Summertime.* (Courtesy of Metro-Goldwyn-Mayer) Judy, Phil Silvers, Hans Conreid, and Gloria DeHaven (bottom left) in a scene from *Summer Stock.* (Courtesy of Metro-Goldwyn-Mayer) Judy (bottom right) in a rare publicity photo from *Annie Get Your Gun.* (Courtesy of Metro-Goldwyn-Mayer)

Judy singing "Friendly Star" in *Summer Stock*. (Courtesy of Metro-Goldwyn-Mayer)

Judy, singing a song and wearing a costume that would be forever identified with her—the "Get Happy" number from *Summer Stock*. (Courtesy of Metro-Gold-wyn-Mayer)

Judy (top left), singing "Swanee" during the "Born in a Trunk" sequence from *A Star Is Born*. (Courtesy of Warner Brothers) Judy and Tommy Noonan (top right) in a scene from *A Star Is Born*. (Courtesy of Warner Brothers) James Mason, Judy, and Charles Bickford (bottom) in a scene from *A Star Is Born*. (Courtesy of Warner Brothers)

Richard Widmark and Judy (top) in a scene from *Judgment at Nuremberg*. (Courtesy of United Artists) Judy and Burt Lancaster (middle left) in a scene from *A Child Is Waiting*. (Courtesy of United Artists) Judy and James Mason (middle right) in a scene from *A Star Is Born*. (Courtesy of Warner Brothers) Judy (bottom), as Irene Hoffman in *Judgment at Nuremberg*. (Courtesy of United Artists)

Gregory Phillips and Judy (top) in a scene from *I Could Go On Singing*. (Courtesy of United Artists) Judy (bottom left), singing "I Could Go on Singing" onstage at the London Palladium in a sequence from *I Could Go on Singing*. (Courtesy of United Artists) Judy (bottom right), singing "It Never Was You" in *I Could Go on Singing*. (Courtesy of United Artists)

JUDY GARLAND-Metro Goldwyn-Mayer

Judy in one of her first MGM portraits, circa 1935. (Courtesy of Metro-Goldwyn-Mayer)

Judy, circa 1937. (Courtesy of Metro-Goldwyn-Mayer)

6

Luckily, *Summer Stock* was released after Judy's suicide attempt and it gave her career a boost when it needed it most. The public flocked to the neighborhood theatres to see Judy in her latest film. They were glad to have her back—in anything. There was one spot in the film, however, that really presented what was to be the new Garland. She was never again to act the wistful child parts of former days, never again to be "Dorothy adorable," her own term for those earlier roles. In "Get Happy" she showed us what a powerful entertainer she really was and what a beautiful pair of legs she possessed.

Because Judy appeared so plump throughout the rest of the film, many people claimed that "Get Happy" was a stock shot—a song taped for an earlier film but never used. This wasn't so.

Before starting *Royal Wedding*, Charles Walters decided that Judy needed another number in the film and she choose "Get Happy," written by Harold Arlen. By this time she was much thinner. "Get Happy" was actually the last footage taken of Garland on the Metro lot—she left there with a *bang!*

Wanda Hale of the *New York Daily News* gave the film the following review:

> If audience reaction is an indication, "Summer Stock," the new Judy Garland–Gene Kelly film, will give the year's best musical comedies lively competition.
>
> Judy and Gene are in fine form. Their singing and dancing, alone and together, brought hearty applause from enthusiastic spectators attending the first showing of the MGM technicolor picture at the Capitol Theatre . . . Both are able players, which makes it as much a pleasure to see them act as it is to hear them sing or watch them dance.*

*Reprinted by permission of the *New York Daily News*.

When Metro previewed the film outside of Los Angeles, Judy attended. At the appearance of Judy's name on the screen the audience burst into spontaneous applause. The same reaction followed each of Judy's songs in the film.

Shortly after she attempted to take her life, Judy filed suit for divorce against Vincente. She was granted the divorce and was also given custody of Liza. Meanwhile, her name was kept in front of the public through numerous radio appearances. Judy had had a very active career on the radio throughout the forties. In January of 1941 she did a play for "Lux Radio Theatre." She had written the play, *Love's Own Sweet Song*, herself. In December, 1942, also on "Lux Radio Theatre," she starred in *A Star Is Born* with Walter Pidgeon and Adolphe Menjou. Her performance in this is said to have been more powerful than her performance twelve years later in the screen version. In the early forties Judy also starred with Mickey Rooney in radio treatments of *Strike Up the Band* and *Merton of the Movies* and with John Payne and Adolphe Menjou in *Morning Glory*. Beside those mentioned, Judy did numerous other radio plays. On February 15, 1945, she participated in a satire called *Dick Tracy in b Flat or Is He Ever Going to Marry Tess Trueheart?* The others in the cast were Bing Crosby (Dick Tracy), Bob Hope, Jimmy Durante, Frank Sinatra, the Andrews Sisters, Dinah Shore, Jerry Colonna, Frank Morgan, Cass Daley, and Harry Von Zell.

Throughout the war years, Judy did dozens of shows for the Armed Forces Radio Network. Sometimes she would act as hostess on one of the variety shows or would be a guest; other times she would participate in plays. Often she would answer some of her mail from GI's over the radio. Seldom did a week go by that she wasn't on the radio in one show or another. In the late forties her radio appearances consisted mainly of guest spots on "The Bing Crosby Show." She and Bing made a great team and judging by the number of appearances she made on his show they must have gotten along well together. There were times when she appeared on the show three weeks in a row. This gave Judy and Bing the chance to do many humorous comedy routines and to sing some very funny parodies, not to mention many beautiful duets. With the two of them blending so well with each other, I can't help but wonder why they never made a film together.

The Crosby shows helped Judy, especially in the latter part of 1950 and throughout 1951 and 1952. When Crosby's wife Dixie Lee was dying, Judy, in appreciation of the help Crosby had given her, took over his show for the week so that Bing could remain with his wife.

Besides the Crosby show, she appeared on "The Bob Hope Chesterfield Show" and "The Al Jolson Show." In 1950, Judy also appeared in a radio version of Booth Tarkington's *Alice Adams*. Her performance as Alice ranked with the best of her career. In December of that year she appeared in the radio version of *The Wizard of Oz*. The following year she was heard in the "Lux Radio Theatre" version of *Cinderella*—the entire script was written in verse.

Judy's greatest radio appearance of all took place in February of 1953. She starred in *Lady in the Dark* and gave a superb performance in the role Gertrude Lawrence had immortalized on Broadway.

Around this time Judy met Sid Luft at a cocktail party given by Jackie Gleason and they began going out together. Sid was a former test pilot who had once been married to actress Lynn Bari. Judy found she could talk easily to Sid and she told him that she felt she would be happiest just singing in live shows. She wanted to feel the immediate response of her audience and she didn't want to have to worry about keeping her weight down for the camera. Luft told her he would try and arrange it.

Sid talked to officials at the London Palladium and they signed Judy for a vaudeville run at their theatre. Roger Edens agreed to write Judy's act.

Well, she rehearsed and rehearsed and as the day for her departure for London approached she began to get more and more nervous. A couple of days before Judy was to leave she was upstairs packing her luggage. Suddenly she heard a voice at the door yelling "Where is she?" It turned out to be Fannie Brice.

Judy called down to Fannie and before she knew it, the famous comedienne was storming up the stairs. Soon Fannie was yelling at Judy. "Now you listen to me, Judy Garland! You're going to go over there and with the voice and talent God gave you you're going to make everyone proud of you. It's time you stopped pampering yourself. Good Lord, girl, do you think you're the only person on earth who has problems? We all have things we can't face. I knew every heartbreak in the book, but I never gave up—and you're not going to either! Now you keep your head up and your sights on tomorrow—and the hell with yesterday!" Fannie turned and left, leaving behind a well-shaken Judy.

Then it dawned on Judy: "Fannie is right. The past is dead and gone and tomorrow is what I make it."

On April 9, 1951 Judy walked onto the stage at the London Palladium for the first time and, in the middle of her opening dance number, fell flat on her backside! The audience, to build up her confidence, began applauding and yelling for her to sing. Sid Luft was standing in one of the boxes above the stage and he began yelling: "I love you. Sing! I love you." With the help of her pianist, she got up and gave a truly memorable performance, much like the one she was to give in the States some months later. Judy took her show through England, Scotland, and Wales and received standing ovations everywhere. Closing night in Edinburgh her audience sang "Auld Lang Syne" to her. She had won these countries over and they would remain hers for the remainder of her career. She loved England, especially London, and she often referred to it as "home." When she left for the United States, she promised that she would be back.

Robert Donat was always one of Judy's idols and during her engagement at the Palladium she received two dozen roses from him with a card that read: "May I come and visit you?" Judy was thrilled and told Mr. Donat's chauffeur that she would like to see him as soon as possible. A short while later she received a telegram: "Impossible to see you tonight but will see you Saturday night." Saturday came and went and no visit. Another wire: "Hold on. Will be there." Judy and Sid looked into it and found out that Donat was in a sanitarium for a mental breakdown and had heard that she was suffering from the same thing—that's why he urged her to "hold on." She did—for eighteen more years.

Finally, the big day came. On October 16, 1951 Garland reopened the Palace Theatre in New York City. The theatre hadn't presented a live act in over ten years and indeed, for that while, vaudeville had been dead because the Palace was the heartbeat of vaudeville. Well, on that memorable October Eve, Judy Garland revived vaudeville and the two-a-day.

On opening night Judy played to an audience that included Martha Raye, Sophie Tucker, and Marlene Dietrich. The show opened with the usual stand-up comedians and acrobats. After a fifteen-minute intermission, Judy appeared with her group of chorus boys, singing an original song written for her by Roger Edens, entitled "Call the Papers—We're Going on the Town." Next, she sang a medley of numbers dedicated to great ladies who had played the Palace. In this she sang "My Man" for Fannie Brice, "Shine on Harvest Moon" for Nora Bayes, "Some of These Days" for Sophie Tucker and "I Don't Care" for Eva Tanquay. This was followed by "Rockabye Your Baby" with a few words about Al Jolson and then by a medley of her own hits including . . ." "You Made Me Love You," "For Me and My Gal," "The Boy Next Door," and "The Trolley Song." This same medley, minus "The Boy Next Door," was to remain a permanent part of Judy's repertoire until her death. After this number she went backstage and changed into a black dancing outfit similar to the one she had worn in *Summer Stock*, then came out and sang "Get Happy." Then she changed into her tramp costume and teamed with one of the chorus boys to sing "We're a Couple of Swells."

But the greatest moment of any evening came when, after singing "Swells" and while still in her tattered tramp outfit, she sat on the edge of the stage with just a tiny spotlight on her face, and sang "Over the Rainbow." By the end of the song there were tears streaming down her face. After this there wasn't a dry eye in the Palace. Her encores were usually made up of tunes like "Love," "A Pretty Girl," and "Liza." On opening night Judy's partner in "Couple of Swells" was Charles Walters (the same Charles Walters who had directed her in films and had now staged her comeback at the Palladium and the Palace.)

For her opening and throughout her run Judy got excellent reviews. She broke all existing records at the Palace, beating such greats as Burns and Allen, Eddie Cantor, and Kate Smith.

The strain of doing eleven shows a week, however, caught up with her. Towards the end of the run Judy became ill. It was believed that she had heart trouble. A doctor found nothing wrong with her but gave her some pills to remove the pain temporarily. The pills knocked her out completely. When she regained consciousness she insisted on going on with the performance. She later described herself as feeling "halfway between the floor and the sky." She got through the performance but forgot many lyrics—her accompanist, Hugh Martin, had to throw them to her. It was only through pure instinct that she made it to the end of the show. When she was about to stagger back onto the stage for an encore she was grabbed and rushed into a waiting ambulance. As she was carried out the stage door she said to a crowd of gathered fans, "Don't worry, I'll be back." She was, within a few days. Meanwhile, Vivian Blaine (of *Guys and Dolls*) replaced her.

Closing night was the greatest of them all. It was some nineteen weeks after Judy had opened in October and there was a definite air of excitement all around the theatre. After singing her heart out, Judy introduced the man who was to open at the Palace the next week, Lauritz Melchior. The two of them joked together for a while onstage, then Melchior said he hoped that the next time he saw Judy he would be able to say he had made a success at the Palace so that she would be proud of him. That's all Judy needed; she started to cry and Melchior went back to his seat.

"Well, I think I'd better go now," she told the audience. They shouted "No," but she said that she thought it "would be better all around." Melchior suggested that the audience sing to Judy and Judy overheard the remark. She was thrilled by the idea: "Sing me a song? You want to sing me a song? All right. Come on, sing me a song. I'm tired of singing, come on." At this point Melchior stood up and Hugh Martin began to play "Auld Lang Syne" and the whole audience was on its feet singing with the orchestra. And there stood Judy, onstage, her arms full of flowers and gifts, crying like a baby. The ovation was tremendous.

That night, the legend of Judy Garland was born. That night, she established her immortality.

Variety reported:

> Judy Garland's closing performance at the Palace will remain one of the more memorable experiences in the history of a two-a-day. A loaded house in a sentimental mood sent Judy off stage in tears with the mass singing of "Auld Lang Syne." It was one of the warmest tributes even given a headliner in New York.
>
> Miss Garland's Palace run made show business history firstly by proving that two-a-day can be a top box office medium and that the Palace name is still an important landmark. It needed a Judy Garland to prove that vaudeville can still be sold at $4.80 and that a performer of Miss Garland's magnitude can run indefinitely on that basis. It's

generally conceded that Miss Garland could have remained another nineteen weeks had she so desired. The bill grossed approximately $750,000 in that run of which $50,000 came the final week with 11 performances. It's more than was ever grossed by any other vaude bill.

The Sunday night show presented a peculiar parlay of circumstances. In the first place, more than 50% of the house had seen the show before. House contained many black ties and the audience included Joe Louis, Phil Silvers, Barry Gray, Faye Emerson, Skitch Henderson, Shelley Winters and Ben Blue.

The prevailing sentiment seemed to be lachrymose. After the audience got through cheering Miss Garland, both manually and vocally, she did her first encore, "Over the Rainbow" in her tramp costume used in "Couple of Swells." There were moments when tears came to Miss Garland during its rendition. The effect was similar on many members of the audience. Speeches and three extra numbers didn't suffice. The crowd just didn't move although most knew that she had already done three numbers more than in her usual shows. There were requests from all over the house. A voice in the direction of her manager-fiance Sid Luft apparently suggested that the audience sing to her. Miss Garland took up the suggestion, stood back and waited. In short order, maestro Jack Cathcart maestroed "Auld Lang Syne." Halfway through the number, Melchior stood up, and the rest of the house followed suit. It had sufficient emotional wallop to bring tears.

Miss Garland has set a pattern that will be hard for anybody to follow. At her opening, the public seemed to sense that she needed to make good on this engagement if her career was to continue. Theatregoers knew that she was a sick kid, and there was a collective feeling that they would give her the security she needed. Her public may well have contributed considerable therapy to her physical and mental comeback. Her professional status was never in doubt.

During her engagement at the Palace, Judy received a special Antoinette Perry Award (Tony) for her appearances on Broadway. Other winners that year were Gertrude Lawrence and Yul Brynner.

Judy took her act to Los Angeles and San Francisco. The response to Judy's show at the Los Angeles Philharmonic Hall was unbelievable. There were more stars in attendance than ever before and Jinx Falkenburg was there to interview all of them. When they were asked if there was any special reason why they were at the show, Lucille Ball and Desi Arnaz (then in the first season of "I Love Lucy") replied: "Yes, a very special reason, because we love Judy and we're glad to have her back." And that was the feeling all over Los Angeles: they were glad to have Judy back.

While appearing at the Curran Theatre in San Francisco Judy married Sid Luft. In *McCalls* in 1964 she had this to say about the beginning of their marriage:

102

In early 1952, Sid and I were married, while I was appearing in San Francisco. We slipped away for the ceremony at the ranch of his friends. I spent my wedding night back in San Francisco doing my show. That was a preview of our marriage.

The birth of our daughter Lorna, was the only bright spot in the first year of our marriage. From the beginning Sid and I weren't happy. I don't know why. I really don't. For me it was work, work, work and I didn't see much of Sid. He was always dashing off to places, lining up my appearances. I wasn't made any happier looking into mirrors, seeing myself balloon out of shape from liquids trapped in my body. The doctors said it was caused by metabolic imbalance, brought on by all those crash diets and nervous strain.*

Lorna was born in November, 1952. The same year, the Friars honored Judy with a testimonial dinner. The guests included Mickey Rooney, Frank Sinatra, Ezio Pinza, and George Jessel. Homer Dickens commented in *Film Careers* magazine:

> Frank Sinatra paraphrased her "Dear Mr. Gable" hit, singing "Dear Miss Garland, you made us love you." The list of celebrities who honored Judy that night is long enough to fill the Beverly Hills telephone book. A stunned Judy sat tearfaced listening to each tribute that let her know she was admired and loved by her fellow professionals.**

By this time Judy was having a lot of trouble with her mother. Mrs. Gumm, now Mrs. William Gilmore, had married a man with whom Judy didn't get along. After this there was a severe break between her and Judy when Judy decided that she was no longer responsible for Mrs. Gilmore's support. Within a few years Mrs. Gilmore moved to San Antonio, Texas and after that she seldom saw Judy. She returned to Los Angeles in 1950 after Judy's "suicide attempt" and got a job at the Douglas Aircraft Factory. In the summer of 1952 Mrs. William Gilmore went to court to complain that her daughter, Judy Garland Luft, would not support her. Mrs. Gilmore lost the case. Not many months later Judy's mother was found dead in the parking lot of the factory where she worked. The cause had been a heart attack.

Judy collapsed when she was told the news. She blamed herself for her mother's death.

In 1953, Judy and Sid decided to form a production company and produce a film starring Judy. They felt it was time she was seen on the screen again. The company was formed and called Transcona Enterprises (shortened from Transcontinental). They choose *A Star Is Born* as the film

*Judy Garland, "There'll Always Be Another Encore," *McCalls Magazine*, January-February, 1964.
**Homer Dickens, *Film Careers Magazine*, 1964.

and an arrangement was made with Warner Brothers to take care of studios, equipment, and distribution. The budget for *A Star Is Born* was set for an estimated $1,800,000. As it turned out, this was an extremely modest, not to mention naive, estimate.

James Mason was paid $125,000 for the first twelve weeks and $12,500 a week after that. He worked a total of twenty-two weeks, receiving a salary of $250,000. (It is a little known fact that Cary Grant was originally chosen to play the role of Norman Maine, but backed out after a few strenuous rehearsals.)

The film took five months to shoot and went way over budget. Jack Warner never complained. He had faith in Judy's talent. By the completion of the picture the budget had hit $5,000,000.

Judy worked exceptionally hard during the production of *A Star Is Born*. As one observer on the set exclaimed, "That girl should do just one take a day and then catch an ambulance home."

During the production Judy found that she just couldn't work well in the daytime. Her old sleeping habits were still with her, but now, after having revived vaudeville and all of vaudeville's glories, she was suffering the curse of one of vaudeville's woes—the bad hours. The schedule was revised and many of her scenes were shot in the evening. The day that Judy recorded the soundtrack for *A Star Is Born* her friend Humphrey Bogart was on the set. As a good-luck gesture for Judy he dubbed in the voice of a drunk in a brief sequence in a cafe. His voice can be heard calling for her to "sing Melancholy Baby." A stand-in was used in the actual filming but Bogart's voice remained!

Judy's performance in *A Star Is Born* was nothing short of sensational. It was, without a doubt, the best of her career. She laughed, cried, sang, and danced. She was the old Judy and yet at the same time a new Judy. If there was ever a piece of work that she could be totally proud of it was *A Star Is Born*. There had been talk of temper tantrums on the set and this talk may have been founded on truth, but evidently if Judy created any problems on the set she must have known what she was doing. When she fought for a point it was usually because she knew she was right. What many people have failed to realize, and this is no exaggeration, is that Judy was a show business genius. She didn't just sing. She danced. She acted. She could be tragic and yet she could be a great comedienne. She knew everything about makeup, lights, sound systems, and almost all other phases of production. If something was wrong she knew instinctively where the fault lay.

Concluding Douglas McVay's coverage of Judy's film career, I print here the passages on *A Star Is Born:*

> In "Meet Me in St. Louis" she was Esther Smith, in "A Star Is Born," Esther Blodgett. Esther has certainly been a lucky name for her. Cukor's picture beheld her triumph from first to last; vivacious in

"Gotta Have Me Go With You"; her voice faltering in breathless disconcerted amusement during the final lines as Norman Maine (James Mason) drunkenly interrupts her act; radiating an intense yet controlled blues power in "The Man That Got Away," where she seems at moments quite to dominate the screen; loving and gentle in "It's a New World," Esther's song of grateful fulfillment to Maine on their honeymoon, and one of the film's most moving sequences. But needless to say, what one primarily recalls are two mammoth set pieces.

"Born in a Trunk" gave us her humble and homely drooping emphasis on the first syllable of "Pocatello," Esther's birthplace; the trouper's pride that rings through her declaration "the show must go on"; and, in the brilliant series of numbers built around the title song, the delicate quiet of "I'll Get By" and "Melancholy Baby," the full throated exuberance of "Swanee." Yet it is in "Someone at Last" that the instincts of satiric mimicry inherited from "Ziegfeld Follies" and "The Pirate" attain definitive expression. "He wears a lamp-shade for a hat" she complained on a track of "The Letter" lp, "The Worst Kind of Man"; yet here she does precisely that at one juncture, impersonating a Chinese. More than once during this thoroughly infectious monologue I have felt the audience hypnotized by the elusive phenomenon, star quality; and Mason's hilarity as he sits watching and listening to her is as genuine, we would be prepared to swear, as that of Garland and Kelly in the "Be a Clown" shenanigans. Judy may not be a great actress. (Ideally the part required one, but none I've ever known could have tackled it, for it called for an as yet unincarnated amalgam of "straight" and "musical" capabilities.) But while a great actress in the role might have moved us more, the playing of this warm-hearted human being supplied—to put it mildly—an ample substitute.*

Bosley Crowther's *New York Times* review of the film read:

> Those who have blissful recollections of David O. Selznick's "A Star Is Born" . . . may get set for a new experience . . . one of the grandest heartbreak dramas that has drenched the screen in years. A sweet and touching love story that Moss Hart has smoothly . . . modernized . . . Cukor gets performances from Miss Garland and Mr. Mason that make the heart flutter and bleed. Miss Garland is excellent in all things, but most winningly perhaps in the song "Someone at Last" wherein she dances, sings and pantomines the universal endeavors of the lady to capture the man . . . It is something to see, this "A Star Is Born."**

When *A Star Is Born* was completed it was 180 minutes long. Until that time, it was the longest motion picture ever made by Warner Brothers. However, in 1954 films weren't shown on a first-run, reserved-seat basis as they are now—not even very big films. The average length of a

*Douglas McVay, *Films and Filming*.
**© 1954, the New York Times Company. Reprinted by permission.

film had to be about 100 minutes since almost all films were shown on a double-feature bill. When *A Star Is Born* was "sneak-previewed" almost everyone agreed that it was a fine motion picture, but there were some complaints that it was too long to sit through. (Now, of course, the public is used to such films, thanks to *Ben Hur, Funny Girl,* and *The Sound of Music.*) Director George Cukor offered to cut the film to a shorter length and he felt that it was possible to do it in such a way that the film would still run smoothly. Warner Brothers, however, insisted that the film be shown in its full length. Then, at the last minute, they decided that it should be cut. Instead of asking Cukor to do it, they gave it to their own editor. As a result, Warner Brothers' hands had blood on them from the severest butchering job Hollywood has ever seen. They cut the film down to 150 minutes in length and did so by omitting two of Judy's songs and some of her best scenes. George Cukor is sure that this is why she didn't win the Academy Award she so richly deserved.

Not long ago, before the film was released to television, Warner Brothers was planning to re-release it in theatres around the country with all of its formerly omitted scenes intact. When they went to put it together, however, they found that they had lost the edited material entirely. A search was made immediately after Judy's death but to no avail, Warners still couldn't find the footage. Now, however, it has been found and the film is being restored in the hope of re-releasing it. Garland, referring to the film shortly before her death said: "They didn't edit the film, Harry [referring to Harry Warner, one of the founding brothers, then in his seventies] gummed it to pieces!"

Judy was nominated for the Academy Award and her running mates were Grace Kelly, Dorothy Dandridge, Jane Wyman, and Audrey Hepburn. Shortly before the ceremonies Judy was rushed to the hospital for the birth of her son, Joe. The night of the ceremonies found Judy the mother of three (not counting Luft's boy, Johnny, who sometimes lived with them). Cameras were brought into her hospital room and arrangements were made for Lauren Bacall to rush to her side with the award, should she win.

Wires were strung up Judy's night gown and hidden under the feathers that encircled her neckline. A nurse was put in charge of raising the window shade to let the television apparatus set up outside pick up Judy's image, and a friend of Judy's was hidden from view under the bed. The whole situation struck Judy as hilarious, and on her television series, later, she said: "After all that I was ready to say 'Hi, Bob' [to Bob Hope], whether I won or not!" Suddenly the moment came and as the envelope was opened Judy and the hospital staff prepared for their moment of glory. She had decided that with all the trouble the television crew had gone to, they must have been sure that she'd win.

"And the winner is . . . Grace Kelly for *The Country Girl.*" The television engineers in Judy's room immediately began disassembling their equipment—never saying a word to Judy. Although Judy was disappointed she was firm in her belief that God had given her a special award of her own, her son Joe. Nevertheless, this was another mistake on the Academy's part. Grace Kelly's performance was tremendous (it's interesting, also, to note the similarities in the stories of *The Country Girl* and *A Star Is Born*), but she was not more deserving of the award than Judy. The Academy's taboo on musical actresses was becoming more and more ludicrous. The award should have been given to both Kelly and Garland (just as it was to Hepburn and Streisand more recently).

The morning following the awards Judy received a telegram from Groucho Marx: "Judy—That was the greatest robbery since Brinks."

A Star Is Born was given two very elaborate premieres. The first was in Hollywood. The second and biggest was in New York City. The latter was a dual-theatre premiere with *Star* opening simultaneously at two theatres on Times Square. Judy appeared at both the Hollywood and New York premieres. In New York, George Jessel was on hand for the event to tell everyone how he had named Judy. Both Judy and the thousands of fans gathered in the square "ohed and ahed" as millions of gold stars cascaded down on them. Seeing the Palace across the street she sighed: "Oh, I'm home now!"

Even though she didn't win the Oscar that year she won every other conceivable award, including the *Box Office, Film Daily,* and the *Look* awards.

7

Following Garland's triumph in *A Star Is Born* and the birth of her son, Joe, in 1955, she decided to accept one of the many television offers that were flooding her agent's office. She signed a contract with the Columbia Broadcasting System (CBS) to star in the first "Ford Star Jubilee." The show, her television debut, was to be done in color—a rarity in those days. She was paid $100,000 for her services. The show's budget was $250,000. David Wayne was signed to do the hosting chores and to fill in a few gaps while Judy would be changing her costumes. As was the custom then, the show was telecast live.

The show was done from a Long Beach theatre and record-breaking crowds were turned away. The date of the telecast was September 25, 1955. The next day *Variety* reviewed the show as follows:

> CBS-TV dished up a "double-decker" of more than passing significance Saturday night, the occasion being the TV premiere of Judy Garland as one of the last hold outs among top-flight stars, and also marking the initial entry of Columbia into the realm of spectaculars in following the pattern incepted by rival NBC a year ago. Thus the bow of "Ford Star Jubilee" as CBS' Ford-sponsored one-a-month 9:30 to 11:00 salute to the big, big, big program concept was, on both counts, an eagerly awaited event. Though unquestionably a personal triumph for Miss Garland, it was not the show it should have been. CBS has a lot to learn in penetrating the 90-minute upper programming frequencies. What should have been a milestone in the fabulous career of one of the great artists in show business, to be remembered as a fitting companion piece to her now storied Palace, N.Y., two-a-day engagement of a few years back, was dissipated by CBS' inability to cope with a major show case. Whether it's called a spec or a "jubilee," it takes know-how and plenty of experience to put on a super show. In mood, pace, tempo, lighting, timing, and overall cohesion (and even color

109

definition) the deficiencies reflected CBS' year behind status. This is in no way to detract from Miss Garland's talents. When she was on camera, and particularly in the closing thirty minutes when it was her show, that ol' black magic and magnetism came through in all its treasured nuances. But unfortunately, this wasn't a thirty minute show, and the preceding hour was punctuated with so many stage waits of lacklustre and uninspired material as to destroy a lot of Jubilee's overall impact. More's the pity, because out of the closing half hour or so, when Miss Garland took over, with a fine assist from the eight Escorts, came something long to be remembered. Here the spectacular—and rightly so—went out the window. It didn't need color, nor for that matter any production furbelows. Just the close-up camera shot as Miss Garland was given the spot light and the chance to go to work. First, atop a piano, in a sentimental mood, with "While We're Young," then into a whole medley of standards—"But Not for Me," "For Me and My Gal," (in duet with David Wayne, who emceed and did some specials of his own), "The Boy Next Door," "The Trolley Song," and an unforgettable rendition of "Rockabye Your Baby." Then into her trademarked tramp act (partnered with Wayne) but with some of the remembered lustre somehow lacking. Finale was the inevitable and surefire "Over the Rainbow." What to the average viewer appeared to be an over studied and over emotional rendition was revealed later as genuine tears provoked by a case of laryngitis. (Some of the tunes were prerecorded.) Seemingly there were any number of less fortunate elements competing with Miss Garland and it's a tribute to the star that nothing else mattered when she was on and her vibrant personality took hold of things. Her costumer, Irene Shariff, for one, was certainly not in her corner, for she bedecked Miss Garland in a manner that not only failed to slim down a paunchy Judy but actually appeared to accentuate her embonpoint. Sid Luft, Miss Garland's husband, who helmed the star through her recent show biz years, including last season's "A Star Is Born" entry, also produced this TV spec (with Paul Harrison doubling from director into an associate producer status) and it's perhaps as much Luft's fault as anyone's that the show as a whole fell apart in too many places. Turning over so much of the bill to the Goofers, a zany combo, was a mistake. Perhaps in the right place the quintet would be recognized for their talents in making with the funny business as they ride herd with their instruments on trapeze, pogo stick, see-saw, etc. And the drummer's monkey-face bit is, in its way, a little gem in panto. But showcased smack in the middle of the Garland show, it had the effect of throwing the whole tempo of the production out of kilter. It was even jarring on the nerves. Wayne's contribution to the show, both as emcee, in company with Miss Garland, and with his own material, is perhaps a matter of taste. It wasn't this corner's dish of tea. True, as a threesome on "It's Delightful" with Miss Garland and Mitsuko Sawamure, a moppet songstress with a flair for some Nipponese nipups on vocalizing, he hit a gait and ease that complemented Miss Garland's style and sureness. He fit in step, too, as he played and sang the tramp vis-a-vis. But his overall emcee de-

110

meanor; his long, long recap of the old Palace days with accompanying exhibition on memorabilia slowed the show down to a walk. (Memo to show's researchers: neither Al Jolson nor Sir Harry Lauder ever played the Palace.) And his own "archie and mehitabel" sequence seemed a forced and contrived bit. The regrettable "memory lane" turn did have its compensations in a sequel, for it served as an intro to Miss Garland's grand tribute to the two-a-day in a reprise of her "playing the Palace" which she did in her vaudeville engagement. Conjuring up "Shine on Harvest Moon," "Some of these Days," "My Man," and "I Don't Care," it was one of the few redeeming portions of the first hour. The show opened with Miss Garland getting into "Swanee" strike. Had they let her stay right through with an assist from her fine group of singing and dancing "escorts," this could have been a show of shows.*

As it turned out, the show was one of the highest-rated shows on television that season. Judy later confessed to having been scared to death during her performance. She had never worked on television before and was frightened by the fact that whatever she did in front of the camera was exactly what was going to be seen by the public—there were no retakes, no second chances. As she said during the show: "I always wondered if the people on television could see those watching them on their sets. Well, now I know they can't cause I can't see anything!"

Prior to her "Ford Star Jubilee" outing Judy signed a recording contract with Capitol Records. Her first album, entitled *Miss Show Business*, was released the day after the special and it contained songs that Judy had sung the night before. The reviews were generally good.

On October 15, 1955 it was announced that Judy had signed a contract with CBS that called for her to star in three television specials in the next three years. The first of these shows was televised in April, 1956.

This one was a thirty-minute special for General Electric and it was a one-woman show. On April 9, 1956 *Variety* reported:

> Judy Garland wasn't at her singing best Sunday night (April 8). Not even sheer determination and hard work, of which she gave plenty, could bring this half hour up to the standards of her full capability. Possibly because she was doing some new songs, not very good ones either, her voice had a rough quality, especially in the higher registers. In one of her early numbers, her voice distinctly broke and her verve and showmanlike flair couldn't cover that up. She was more effective with familiar tunes, such as "Life Is Just a Bowl of Cherries," ably backed by jazz pianist Joe Pushkin, and she was winsomely plaintive in "April Showers." Show's biggest number was a new song done with a small instrumental group, but it proved over-busy. Director Ralph Nelson erred in allowing too many close-ups of Miss Garland while she was belting the song, the views of her contorted mouth and working

* *Variety*, September 26, 1955.

tonsils being hardly flattering to her distinctive beauty. However, he paced the show very well, keeping things moving at a lively clip. Settings by Richard Avedon were effectively confined to simple drapes. On the other hand, the costuming of Miss Garland was so-so. Production by Sid Luft was simple.

The following week, Capitol released an album largely comprised of songs from Judy's latest television special. It was entitled *Judy* and it is one of the most beautiful packages Judy recorded for them during her many years with the Tower.

In July, 1956 Judy was booked into the New Frontier in Las Vegas for the highest sum of money ever paid a nightclub entertainer until that time —$55,000. This was her nightclub debut and her act was a tremendous success. Years later the show biz world would be a-buzz over Barbra Streisand being paid $1,000,000 for a nightclub appearance at the International Hotel in Las Vegas. Judy had been offered that sum years before by an obviously eccentric millionaire who wanted her to do a concert in his home. The only catch was that he would be the only person in the audience. She declined as she couldn't see herself giving a show for one person!

Judy returned to the Palace Theatre in New York in September, 1956. She had put together a totally new act, which included such songs as "Happiness Is Just a Thing Called Joe," "New York, New York It's a Wonderful Town," and "Be a Clown." The show was a success, the reviews were good, and the run lasted seventeen weeks—second only to her own record of nineteen weeks in 1952.

During Judy's run at the Palace she revealed a small part of her technique to members of her chorus. She insisted that they smile while they were singing even though they were behind the curtain and couldn't be seen by the audience. "If you smile while your singing it sounds like you're happy" she insisted. The group found it difficult to smile on cue while staring at a blank curtain so until her time to on stage Judy would stand in front of them making funny faces. It worked!

On December 26, 1956, while Judy was still appearing at the Palace, *Variety* announced that she would do another ninety-minute special on CBS, this time for Buick. The date of the show was to be either February 25 or March 4, 1957.

As it turned out, Judy never did the show. She and CBS had problems agreeing on a script. CBS submitted one, but it was rejected, then Freddie Fields submitted one and it was rejected also. Soon CBS announced that they were terminating Judy's contract.

On March 20 of that same year Judy filed a libel suit and a breach of contract suit against CBS, seeking damages totaling $1,393,333. Judy charged that CBS was responsible for such statements as "She's known for a highly developed inferiority complex," "She doesn't want to work because something is bothering her," and "I don't know, but I wouldn't be surprised if she thinks she's terribly fat." Judy stated that because of these statements her reputation and character, as well as her ability to obtain employment, had been impaired. At the same time, it was announced that Judy's contract with CBS called for her to receive $83,333 a year for the first three years, $90,000 for the fourth year, and $95,000 for the fifth year. The statements had been made by a CBS executive to Marie Torre, a newspaper reporter. Mrs. Torre reported them in her column and that is when Judy first heard of them. The court ordered Mrs. Torre to disclose the name of the executive who made the remarks and she refused to. She was jailed for contempt of court. Meanwhile, the nation's newspapers all played up the angle that Judy Garland had had this woman put in jail, a woman whose young children were now without a mother! Judy Garland didn't have anyone jailed. Mrs. Torre took it upon herself to refuse to answer the court's question as to who the executive was. Although the case was settled some four years later the CBS executive's name was never revealed. (Mrs. Torre served a jail sentance of ten days and this case is now considered one of the most important in journalistic history. It's unfortunate, however, that Judy had to be involved as the whole thing was blown out of proportion because of her name.)

In 1957, Judy made a return visit to London (as she had promised). While there she appeared at the Dominion Theatre. The shows were very successful and she was asked to make a command performance for the Royal Family. After the show the Queen told Judy: "We missed you. Don't stay away so long next time." Prince Philip echoed the Queen's feelings: "We enjoyed it very much. Come back soon." "I'm sorry you weren't allowed to sing another song," said the Queen Mother.

Isidore Green, in the *London Record Mirror*, said of Judy during her stay in England:

> You cannot take it away from her. She is a superb artist, a born trouper, an entertainer, a performer in every sense of the term. The quality of stardom emanates from her every movement, her every gesture . . .
>
> . . . It is such a pleasure to write about someone who represents all that is best, all that is genuine in this great big world of entertainment—a pleasure to draw away, for a change, from certain other ballyhooed headliners of today who, on the basis of merit alone, still have to journey a million miles and learn a lot more before they can get anywhere near challenging distance of this well and truly named "Miss Show Business."

As was her custom, Judy's children had traveled with her to Europe. Since her marriage to Sid and the complete revamping of her career, Judy had been more and more inclined to travel great distances between engagements. She was determined to be with her children as much as possi-

113

ble, though, and took them with her everywhere until school got in the way.

In the summer of 1957, Judy appeared at the Greek Theatre in Los Angeles. The engagement was extremely successful and although Judy still didn't look well, her voice was getting better and better.

March of 1958 found Judy in hot water. She had opened to very good reviews at the Town and Country Club (one reviewer claimed: "Judy Garland opened at The Town and Country Club last night and showed everyone why she is considered the greatest singer in the business.") and the engagement had been going well. Then, one night, she appeared on stage and sang two songs in a poor voice. Then, she said to the audience, "I'm sorry. I have terrible laryngitis but it doesn't matter because I have just been fired." With that she walked off stage. She was sued for breach of contract.

Judy admitted that she was broke. She was arrested by New York State agents claiming that she owed $8,763 in back taxes. A $10,000 bond was set but Judy couldn't raise the money, so the state took custody of her jewels and costumes, which were worth an estimated $55,000.

Judy appeared in another successful engagement in Chicago in September of 1958. She did a week of concerts at Orchestra Hall and broke all kinds of records. She was signed to come back to Chicago soon. Following Judy's sell-out week in Chicago, Harry Zelzer, the impresario who had brought her there, compared her to Bach and Beethoven. This brought a rise out of a classical music buff to which Zelzer replied: "Could Bach or Beethoven sell out Orchestra Hall at $7.70?" Local Chicago press reported that "at no time during her stay in Chicago did Miss Garland display either tantrums or temperament. In fact, the newspaper photographers called her the most cooperative they've worked with."

She also made her debut at the Coconut Grove in Los Angeles. Capitol recorded the show and it was released as Judy's first live album. The show began with an overture of Garland hits by Freddie Martin and his orchestra. Then Judy walked out and opened with "When You're Smiling." She followed this with "Zing! Went the Strings of My Heart," "The Purple People-Eater," "You Made Me Love You," "For Me and My Gal," "The Trolley Song," "When the Sun Comes Out," "Rockabye Your Baby," and "Over the Rainbow." "After You've Gone," "Swanee," and "A Pretty Girl" were her encores. That month, Louella Parsons reported:

> Judy Garland's opening at the Coconut Grove was the party of the month. In the years I've been covering this town I've never seen such a turnout of stars, nor have I felt under one roof such an outpouring of affection and love as greeted Judy, the home town girl, when she appeared at the top of the stairs in her cute "Lady Tuxedo" garb.
> There was so much love going 'round—I even saw Jerry Lewis and Dean Martin patting each other on the back and exchanging laughs!

What a show—what a night, when Judy giving back all that affection by singing her heart out.

I think we all realized we were enjoying an event that has seldom been equaled and will hardly ever be topped.

The Pat Boones sat at the table with Hope and Don Murray . . . Pat said only Judy could get him to put on dinner clothes on a hot night.

Lana Turner, so thin and svelte in pale pink, had a table of young people, friends of Cheryl's. It was Cheryl's birthday and Lana had planned a party for her at home. But when Cheryl caught a bad cold and had to go to bed, rather than disappoint the girls Lana hosted a table for them at the Grove—and did they love it!

I saw the Henry Fondas and the Jimmy Stewarts at a table for four and Jimmy kept jumping up to applaud Judy so often you'd have thought she hired him! Very unusual for the quiet Mr. S.

Frank Sinatra was at a large table at one end of the Grove and Lauren Bacall at a large table at the other end—which was convenient. They still don't speak. And make oh such a to-do about avoiding each other—particularly at Judy's private party in the Embassy Room of the Ambassador Hotel later on.

Everybody waited to greet her and tell her how wonderful she was. Judy had changed from her tux to a Chinese dress of rich brocade when she joined us after the show.

She had taken the time to see her daughter Liza Minnelli off for home before seeing her friends.

I told Judy that I had tears in my eyes when little Liza joined her mother on the stage and sang a number with her.

"So did I," whispered Judy; "tears of pride. Isn't she wonderful?"

Most of the time she kept her hand linked in Sid Luft's.

These two seem happy again and maybe that is really the best news of that whole, wonderful, unforgettable evening of Judy's opening.*

It's true that Judy sounded good that night, but she certainly didn't look very good. Her face and body were severely bloated. At the time she was told that it was just another of her many weight problems.

As Louella Parsons implied in the above article, Judy and Sid had been having some problems. They had come near divorce a couple of times and once Judy had filed for it but then quickly changed her mind. They were still living in Holmby Hills, in the home they had bought after they married. They had many close friends in Hollywood and were members of the original "rat pack," which had been held together by Humphrey Bogart. Indeed, Bogart and his wife Lauren Bacall were among Judy's closest friends and were godparents to Lorna. Judy remained close to Bacall until her death.

Late in 1958 The Masquers honored Judy with a tribute attended by

*Louella Parsons, 1957.

George Jessel, Sammy Davis, Jr., James and Pamela Mason, Allan Jones, Jeff Chandler, Janet Leigh, Tony Curtis and Louella Parsons. Judy glowed with happiness as these and many other friends stood and cheered her entrance.

But for Judy, 1958 ended up on an unhappy note. She was appearing at the Flamingo Hotel in Las Vegas on New Year's Eve. In her *McCalls* article she recalled:

> The audience was celebrating and a lot of people were stoned. After my fifth song, a woman yelled, "Get outta here. You're too over-weight, and we don't want to hear you anyway!" A thing like that makes it rather hard to go into a song like "You Made Me Love You." I was trying to finish my act, until two women climbed over the foot-lights and began to dance. That was too much. I walked off, straight into a lawsuit for breach of contract—which I won.*

*Judy Garland, "There'll Always Be Another Encore," *McCalls Magazine*, January-February, 1964.

Judy, circa 1938. (Courtesy of Metro-Goldwyn-Mayer)

Judy, circa 1940. (Courtesy of Metro-Goldwyn-Mayer)

Judy, 1943. (Courtesy of Metro-Goldwyn-Mayer)

Judy, 1945. (Courtesy of Metro-Goldwyn-Mayer)

UDY GARLAND - Metro *Goldwyn* Mayer

Judy, circa 1948. (Courtesy of Metro-Goldwyn-Mayer)

Judy, 1954. (Courtesy of Warner Brothers)

86-680

Judy, 1954. (Courtesy of Warner Brothers)

Judy, 1962.

Judy, 1962.

Judy, Virginia, and Suzanne (top), circa 1925. Judy (bottom left), years before MGM would ever sign her to a contract. Judy, Virginia, and Suzanne (bottom right) —The Gumm Sisters, circa 1933.

8

Judy's recording career in the fifties left much to be desired. She had continued to record for Capitol since her initial release for them in 1955 and her albums were selling well, but for some reason Capitol never saw fit to release any single recordings by Judy aimed at the popular market. Throughout the fifties, singers like Peggy Lee, Frank Sinatra, and Nat King Cole, all recording for Capitol, had a constant stream of new discs appearing on the singles charts while Judy was constantly re-recording "Rockabye Your Baby," "Somewhere Over the Rainbow," and "A Pretty Girl." I agree that these are great songs and Judy's recordings of them were always beautiful, but why record them over and over? Looking back over her recording career, one notices a history of re-releases. For example, since 1939 "Over the Rainbow" has been heard on at least twenty albums! Yet Garland never recorded songs that were obviously suited to her talents. Imagine what treasures she could have made out of "Everything's Coming Up Roses," "If He Walked into My Life," "This Dream," "The Impossible Dream," "My Way," "It's Today," and "Before the Parade Passes By." Now, it's too late.

The highlight of Judy's recordings between 1955 and 1960 was an album entitled *The Letter* (later re-released as *Our Love Letter*). This album employed an original technique also used by Gordon Jenkins in such albums as *Manhattan Tower* and the more recent *What It Was Was Love*. *The Letter* told a love story set to music. In this album Judy introduced such classics as "The Worst Kind of Man," "That's All There Is, There Isn't Any More," and "The Red Balloon." The highly dramatic "Come Back," with which the story ended, was one of the most beautiful songs Judy ever recorded.

Gordon Jenkins, incidentally, was a great admirer of Judy's. Recently, on a late-night talk show, he spoke extensively on how much he loved working with her and said that he cried at every one of her concerts. The host of the show asked Jenkins if he would take two Barbra Streisands for one Judy Garland. He replied: "I wouldn't take two of anybody for a Judy Garland."

He also said, repeatedly, that he always looked forward to working with Judy and that he would look at his watch all day waiting for the performance. This should help dispel the rumors of Judy having been difficult at concerts and recording sessions.

Other Garland LP's of this period included *Judy in Love, Alone,* and *That's Entertainment.*

Soon Judy was signed for a week of appearances at the Metropolitan Opera House in New York City. She was to be the second "popular" performer to appear there in the history of the Met—the first was Sir Harry Lauder. Again, she routined a new act. It was tried out in Baltimore and was an enormous success.

Dancer John Bubbles and comedian Alan King were signed as Judy's opening acts. When the show premiered in Baltimore, 18,000 fans packed the Stanley Theatre. Sid Luft, with whom Judy had reconciled, remarked, "It's a new career for Judy and we're going to make a go of it."

A tour was planned to follow her Met performances and she was signed to sing at both the Chicago and San Francisco opera houses. She chose the largest theatres in each city she was going to play. She knew she could fill them.

During rehearsals, Judy admitted: "You know I've never been to the opera, though I like Puccini's 'Tosca' and 'La Boheme.' I haven't met Rudolph Bing and I don't really know what he'd think of the show." At that time, Bing was on the road with the Met's touring company. Consequently he wasn't present when the very heavy Judy bounced on to the stage and began her show with a piece of special material entitled, "What's Going On at the Opera . . . Did Mr. Bing Make Up With Maria Callas?" Her voice was in good shape. Other songs in Judy's new act were "A Wonderful Guy" (from *South Pacific*), "Almost Like Being in Love," "This Can't Be Love," and "I Happen to Like New York." She also included a shortened version of Gordon Jenkins's "The Letter." Jenkins, incidentally, was her conductor on this tour.

This was a new Judy. During her week of rehearsals she announced: "I'm going to do things I want to do from now on. I think I'm finished with the nightclub racket. It's too much for one performer." Sid Luft agreed: "After an early show in Vegas it's too much for a performer like Judy to give a late show, too. The new Met format allows Judy to give her audience her best."

This was actually the beginning of the Garland concerts. Although she had a few vaudeville acts on this tour, there was only one show a night, and she was to stick to this schedule throughout the rest of her career, even when she did play in nightclubs. It was only after she did away with the second show that she was able to lengthen her concerts. Her first real

128

concert, however (other than the 1943 outing in Philadelphia), wasn't to take place until the summer of 1960.

The proceeds from Judy's week of shows at the Met went to charity. As announced, she brought her show to Chicago and San Francisco. She also appeared in Los Angeles.

There's an interesting story about Judy that would fit in here. It was 1959 and Judy was driving through New York on her way to a show. The weather was miserable with rain coming down in buckets and Judy spotted a little girl, about twelve years old, standing in the rain with her cat clutched tightly to her. She was waiting for a bus. Judy and her driver pulled up alongside the young girl and Judy told her to get in the car. "There's no bus in sight. We'll take you where you want to go," she added. The little girl shook her head. She knew she couldn't get in the car as much as she would have liked to as she wasn't allowed to talk to strangers. Finally, Judy hopped out of the car and asked the young girl where she lived. The girl took Judy to her apartment. The girl's mother was astounded when she opened the door: "Judy Garland! I must be dreaming. What are you doing here with my Deborah?" "Your little girl looked so forlorn and lost," Judy replied. "She reminded me of myself because I so often feel just the way Deborah looked standing in the rain—like a little girl lost. I wanted to drive her where she wanted to go but she wouldn't let me. Tell her it's all right." Judy did take the little girl where she wanted to go—to the vet to take her cat for an examination. When she returned the little girl home, she told her "Don't ever forget me, you're a sweet little girl" and then she gave her a kiss and a hug while Deborah whispered in her ear, "I'll never forget you."

Today Deborah recalls, "Judy Garland never forgot me either. Everytime I knew she was in New York, I would go over to Manhattan to see her. Sometimes I got in and sometimes I didn't. The times I didn't though, she always sent me a message to come back again. She always remembered that I was the kid with the sick kitten."

Judy's stint at the Chicago Opera House went fine and most critics agreed that she was still a great performer (although a few commented that the show was too much of a production). Bently Stegner of the *Chicago Tribune* reviewed the show as follows:

> A little girl who was born in a trunk stretched a rainbow from wall to wall of the cavernous Chicago Opera House Monday night.
>
> The personality of Judy Garland ranged from the tiara crowned opera goer she impersonated in her first number to the waif in tattered tramp's clothes in her last.
>
> But from the beginning to the end, from dowager to hobo, she carried the crowd over the rainbow on the strains of her soaring, throbbing voice.
>
> She was John Bubbles' shadow in a "Me and My Shadow" bit, but

the shadow outshone the man who cast it. Alan King started out as her partner in the tramp sketch, but Judy ended it going alone.

Applause brought her back to sing most of the numbers that made her famous—"You Made Me Love You," "The Trolley Song," "The Man That Got Away," "For Me and My Gal," "When You're Smiling."

The audience wouldn't let her escape after what should have been her finale—"Over the Rainbow."

She threw them farewell kisses, but they brought her back to sing "Rockabye Your Baby."

She was weighted down with bouquets, but she set them aside for a go at "Chicago."

The spectators sat in their seats and cheered until the asbestos curtain finally convinced them that Miss Show Business was really through for the night.*

After Judy's opening-night performance in Chicago, hundreds of fans waited at her dressing room door in the hope of getting a glimpse of her or perhaps touching her. Judy could have avoided them by leaving through the back exit but she didn't. She signed as many autographs and shook as many hands as possible, then she went to the party being held in her honor at the Cafe de Paris. The Opera House took in a total of $100,000 during Judy's one-week stay (half in advance sales).

In July, 1959 Judy appeared at the Los Angeles Shrine Auditorium. Mike Connolly reported:

Judy Garland, hands-a-tremble, took over the vast Los Angeles Shrine Auditorium with her big voice and her big personality and made it her living room.

Introducing one of her songs, Judy said, "I like to salute each city with a song about itself. I was safe in Chicago and San Francisco, but there aren't any songs about Los Angeles so this'll have to do." Then she cut loose with that rousing Roger Edens arrangement of that burning-ember song-to-remember, "Chicago" and tore the roof off!

Little Liza and her father were in the audience and they went backstage to see Judy after the show. Judy was conversing with Luft but looked up to Vincente: "How nice of you to come and see me and I'm so proud of you!"

Then Liza kissed both her parents and drew them together so that Judy could kiss Vincente on the cheek. Sid Luft just looked the other way!

By late November of 1959 Judy had blown up to tremendous proportions. She was too heavy to sit or bend. She went to a doctor, who sent her to a weight farm. She brought the kids along and they had fun but the diet only made her get heavier. So, after a while, she left the farm. She refused to see any more doctors. Sid invited a doctor friend of his to the house but

*Reprinted courtesy of the *Chicago Tribune.*

didn't tell Judy who he was. After dinner, the doctor went up to Sid and told him that Judy was seriously ill. He said that he had touched her shoulder while speaking to her and found that she was full of fluids. Sid again mentioned doctors to Judy but she became furious—she wouldn't hear another word about it.

It was imperative that Judy get to a hospital. She had always liked New York's Doctors' Hospital and the physicians there, so Sid put together an elaborate plan to get her there. He told her that Elsa Maxwell and Aly Khan wanted to give her a party in New York. Judy was pleased but frightened. Nevertheless, she flew to New York with Sid and attended the party. She had been wearing nothing but bathrobes and men's slippers and when it came time to dress she had to split the seams of a dress and fasten them with large safety pins. She wore the men's slippers on her feet. Everyone at the party was wonderful to her and no one mentioned her weight but it was very depressing for her. After the party Judy realized just how sick she really was. Sid didn't have to wait much longer before she finally let him take her to Doctor's Hospital.

She was put on the critical list immediately and Luft was told that his wife had a seriously infected liver. She could go into a hepatomic coma any minute. If she went into such a coma she might never come out of it.

Over a period of one month, the doctor's drained off twenty-eight quarts of fluids from Judy's body. Meanwhile, all her fans held their breath as Judy brushed with death daily. At last, though, Judy was taken off the critical list and started up the road to recovery. She was told that she would be a semi-invalid for the rest of her life. She would never be able to work again.

Judy was glad just to be alive and took the news cheerfully. She liked the idea of having nothing to do but relax for a while. As she put it: "I've been working too damn long anyway!"

Her fans called her at the hospital and even tried to see her. She took all calls and saw all visitors. It was a miracle that she was alive. She had been walking around with that infected liver for three years without knowing it. Now, fifty pounds thinner, she was getting better and looking forward to a new kind of life.

9

After three months in Doctors' Hospital, Judy decided it was time to go home. She wasn't helpless and she was tired of being catered to. Besides that, there were rumors going around that she had been in the hospital taking a cure for alcoholism. This wasn't true and she felt she had to prove it. She decided to take the children to London so she could get away from everything waiting for her in the States and just "think." She had to straighten her life out. She told herself that she was "a halfway intelligent woman" and all that she needed was some time to herself. (In actuality, those who knew her well considered her an extremely intelligent woman. She was a constant reader and could speak on a wide variety of subjects. She was always well informed about current events and usually knew both sides of the story. As one of her acquaintances once said, "She could knock anyone down intellectually.")

Judy set up a household in London with Sid and the kids (in a house loaned to them by Sir Carol Reed). She spent seven happy months there. She was no longer Judy Garland. She was Mrs. Frances Gumm Luft. She did all her own marketing and probably lived the most normal months of her life.

Soon the rent had to be paid, however, so she decided to do a concert. It was arranged that she would appear for one night at the London Palladium, the scene of a previous Garland triumph.

Until this time, Judy wasn't even sure she still had a voice. But one day, while in the shower, she suddenly realized that it was still there and began singing, and singing, and singing. She filled the bathroom with steam and stayed in there singing her heart out. That same day, while still in the shower, she outlined the program for her concerts! Then, in August, she did her new show at the Palladium. Dan Slater of the *Daily Herald* reported:

They stood in the aisles. They stood at the back. They stood anywhere last night to hear Judy Garland. Garland the Great. Her reception at the London Palladium shook stagehands hardened by years of hysterical audience reaction. Even I had a lump in my throat. And Judy, the girl who found happiness through tears as audiences all over the world wept and laughed with her, gave them all she had. Three hours on stage. Thirty-one numbers. Tremendous applause followed every song. The audience reacted to every sigh, every smile, every emotion the 38 year old trouper gave them. And stage door keeper Dick Winters gasped: "I haven't heard a reception like that since Nora Bayes, the American singer, was here in 1923."

In Judy's own words: "It was a pistol!"

Judy did another concert at the Palladium that month, but still tried to keep her home life as calm (could anything about Judy Garland ever be calm?) and "normal" as possible. Whenever she needed some money she did another show. On October 5 and 7, Judy did concerts in Paris and was an enormous success. The Duke and Duchess of Windsor hosted a party in her honor. Among the guests were Yul Brynner, Maurice Chevalier, Yves Montand, and ex-queen Soraya.

While in Europe, Judy did some campaigning for John Kennedy, then in the middle of his campaign for the Presidency. She did concerts in Germany and while there held up Kennedy for President posters. In November, after speaking to the newly elected President of the United States on the phone from Washington, Judy announced to all those in hearing distance, "Call Me Madam."

She was called for another command performance in the presence of the Queen Mother. The *Record Mirror* reported:

> What is there left to say in praise of Judy Garland? I thought I had exhausted every superlative when I described both her "one-woman" performances (each of two and half hours) at this same theatre earlier this year. I can't think of many new ones to describe her performance tonight in the presence of the Queen Mother (who, when Judy was presented to her after the show, said: "I am always on the verge of tears when I hear Over the Rainbow"). If I report that Judy was as great as she was on those memorable Sunday nights at the London Palladium of August this year, then I am reporting the fact that she was absolutely brilliant . . .

Sid came up with the idea of having Freddie Fields, who had just established his own management agency—CMA (Creative Management Associates)—manage Judy's career. Judy signed with the Fields agency and did some more shows in Europe. Among them were two tremendously successful concerts at the Olympia in Paris and a concert in Amsterdam, which was broadcast complete over the radio. In the latter, she went through her entire repertoire and still got demands for more encores so she closed with a rare item in a Garland concert, "It's a Great Day for the Irish."

Judy returned to America on New Year's Eve, 1960. When she returned Fields told her: "If you want to weigh 140 or 155, fine. I'll get you the best parts—the best 150-pound parts—because you're the best 150 pounds in the business." Said Judy, "His care and intelligence and his practical business sense were good for me."

January, 1961 brought about a separation between Judy and Luft. She recalled in "There'll Always Be Another Encore," her 1964 *McCalls* article:

> At that time, I was $375,000 in debt. I hadn't realized just how much I had been in the red, nor had it dawned on me that I'd fallen out of love. Sid and I had separated on our return to New York that winter, and during that awful blizzard of January, 1961, I went out for a walk in the snow one night. I thought I was the blizzard. Suddenly, I realized I didn't give a damn about him.
>
> And that's like part of you dying. Because sick love, wrong love, or whatever—takes up a lot of space in your life just the same. Then, when you don't care and part of you dies you start to get healthy. But for a few hours there it was difficult—like being shot out of a cannon. It was really terrifying.*

One winter night, Judy attended Sammy Davis, Jr.'s closing-night performance at the Copa in New York. The nightclub was filled with celebrities and when Sammy's show was over everyone expected him to introduce the famed people in the audience, but instead Sammy said: "Ladies and gentlemen, I would like to dispense with show business tradition and just introduce two great ladies in the audience. The first is my mother." Mrs. Davis stood and was applauded. "The second great lady has just returned from London, where she has been recovering from a serious illness. Her name is Judy Garland."

The audience was silent for a moment then burst into riotous applause. A small spotlight picked up Judy sitting at a side table. She was dressed simply in a white blouse and black skirt. Suddenly, everyone in the room was on their feet shouting, "Sing! Sing!" The audience wept, the musicians wept, and Judy wept. Before anyone realized what was happening the orchestra was playing "Over the Rainbow" and Judy was singing it. She was singing before an American audience for the first time in a year. The room was totally hushed, and one woman was heard praying softly, "Please, please let her make it." She finished the song beautifully and the

*Judy Garland, "There'll Always Be Another Encore," *McCalls Magazine*, January-February, 1964.

135

audience got to their feet again calling for an encore, which she didn't attempt. She did, however, take seven bows!

After that Judy and Freddie Fields organized a concert tour that took her all over the continental United States. Just a few of the cities she appeared in are Detroit, Atlantic City, Boston, Cleveland, Chicago, Houston, Los Angeles, Miami, Haddonfield, Forest Hills, Newport, and Charlotte. All together she did a total of forty-eight concerts in forty-eight cities. She climaxed the concert tour on that memorable night in April, 1961 at Carnegie Hall. I have so many reviews from this tour that I find it hard to decide just which ones to use. Here are a few:

> Judy Garland is a smash hit. Judy's performance and song styling were tops . . .
>
> *Miami Herald**

> A night to remember. In my memory there's never been such a demonstration of hero worship in this staid old city. And she earned and deserved every bit of it. Lets hope it happens again.
>
> *Rochester Union Times***

> Another sensational evening with Judy. They gave her the kind of flamboyant ovation that most stars never dream of.
>
> *San Francisco Examiner*†

> Judy Garland songfest draws capacity crowd. A little and loveable Judy Garland wove a magic spell over the audience with songs of yesterday as she carried her listeners far out "Over the Rainbow" in another of her unforgettable performances here Friday night. Who else had the magic to draw 5,000 people up two flights of stairs to pack the Auditorium Ballroom in a town that is loaded with entertainment? Curtain calls—Judy could have answered them until dawn.
>
> *Atlantic City Press*‡

Judy's concert at the Hollywood Bowl is the best example of just how compelling her magic really was. Twenty-eight thousand people sat in the rain waiting for Garland to perform—not one of them let rain chase them away—they simply remained seated until the moment when Mort Lindsey's orchestra gave Judy her cue and she walked out onto the stage. The whole story is told in this review from the *Los Angeles Citizen News:*

Judy Smash Hit at Bowl
Did you ever watch Judy Garland singing in the rain? Well, I did last Saturday night at the Hollywood Bowl with about 18,000 other people

*The *Miami Herald*, 1961.
**The *Rochester-Union Times*, 1961.
†The *Atlantic City Press*, August, 1961.
‡The *Los Angeles Citizen News*, 1961.

(actually 28,000 people). It was a most unusual night in Hollywood: a light and sometimes heavy mist was falling for "Garland at the Hollywood Bowl," and I had picked this night for my first visit to the famed Bowl. In all my golden years in Hollywood, I had avoided the place. The Garland temptation was too much. I'm a Garland fan from way back! From the Sunday night at the Trocadero when she sang "Dear Mr. Gable" and from her first movie "Pigskin Parade" and right up to her latest album, "Judy at Carnegie Hall," the greatest! All Hollywood filled the Bowl, from Jimmy McHugh to Harold Arlen, from Vic Damone to Polly Bergen. They were all there, the guys and dolls and the "sixth man" sitting in the drizzle which continued throughout the concert. I sat in this huge outdoor stadium, bundled in my overcoat. I sat in this huge outdoor stadium, bundled in my overcoat. I took my arms out of my pocket only to applaud. Some people used bright colored umbrellas as a shield, others had transparent plastic raincaps over their heads. Hours that many of the attractive chicks—Marilyn Maxwell, Stella Stevens, Joan Staley, Carol Lynley—had spent at their favorite hairdresser were washed away. There weren't any complaints, Judy was worth it! Judy sang on the platform in front of the musicians who were protected from the rain by the large fanlike backdrop, which is always there, a permanent backing to throw the sound forward to the last row of seats high in the Hollywood Hills. Judy sang on this platform and then, hand mike in hand, would continue singing as she walked the long runway which stretched across a lagoon to the front of the box seats. The flags were waving in the wind from right to left. I thought for a moment that I was in Candlestick Park for a baseball game. But no! It was Judy in her hometown, singing in the wind and the rain, proving in person that she wasn't washed up. Judy wore a tight black skirt and a sequinned jacket as she sang "That's Entertainment," "If Love Were All," and "San Francisco," and her backdrop was the thin rain which made small circles as it hit the water in the lagoon. Occasionally there was the sound of thunder and a streak of lightning. The big sound, however, was the voice of Judy Garland. She was the voice heard throughout the mountains this night, and nothing could stop her—neither rain, nor wind, nor lightning, nor thunder could stop this courier of songs. I was worried however, that she might fall off the runway and into the lagoon. Judy said to the audience: "You know, I might get to like these runways." And on the runway Judy sang "Rockabye Your Baby." It was Jolson's runway and I thought of the night when I went with Al to the Carthay Circle to see Garland and Mickey Rooney in a musical. I don't remember the name of the film, but more important I remember what Jolson said: "She's the greatest female singer I ever heard. What she is now is nothing. She's going to be one of the all time greats." And there was Judy on Al's runway singing a Jolson song and proving him right. In fact the only two other performers I can visualize doing this to an audience when the game should have been called because of rain, are Jolson and Sinatra. And Judy is the only singer I ever heard sing "Stormy

137

Weather" during stormy weather. For the second half of the concert Judy returned wearing slacks and a blouse. "I was a little afraid of the lagoon," she later told me. Judy sang and sang. The orchestra would play the introductory bars and the entire audience would applaud, stopping only when Judy would start to sing. She sang "The Trolley Song," and I remember her doing it for the movie "Meet Me in St. Louis," only then she said it four or five times to get it right. Now, playing for keeps, Judy sang it better than right the first time out of her mouth. Judy sang "Come Rain or Come Shine," "The Man That Got Away," and her carefully combed hair was completely uncombed and her white blouse was soaking wet. Yet after "Over the Rainbow" the standing, water-soaked audience applauded until Judy came back and sang three more songs. The guys and gals and "sixth man" wanted more. Judy said: "You've heard every other song I've rehearsed with the orchestra. We don't know any more. If you want, I'll sing one I've already done." The audience waited. Judy sang "San Francisco" again. I've never seen this before—redoing a song! It was now a quarter to eleven. As I walked out of the Hollywood Bowl, the rain stopped. The rainbow came after Judy Garland finished singing. It was like bright applause.*

In the middle of the concert tour, *Life* magazine did a story on Judy. She told Shana Alexander:

> You stand there in the wings, and sometimes you want to yell because the band sounds so good. Then you walk out and if it's a really great audience, a very strange set of emotions can come over you. You don't know what to do. It's a combination of feeling like Queen Victoria and an absolute ass. Sometimes a great reception—though God knows I've had some great receptions and I ought to be prepared for it by now—can really throw you. It kind of shatters you so that you can lose control of your voice and it takes two or three numbers to get back into your stride. I lift my hand in a big gesture in the middle of my first number and if I see it's not trembling then I know I haven't lost my control.
>
> A really great reception makes me feel like I have a great big warm heating pad all over me. People en masse have always been wonderful to me. I truly have a great love for an audience, and I used to want to prove it by giving them blood. But I have a funny new thing now, a real determination to make people enjoy the show. I want to give them two hours of just POW!**

At Carnegie Hall on April 23, 1961 Judy's audience was again filled with celebrities. Among those in attendance were Phil Silvers, Rock Hudson, Harold Arlen, Polly Bergen (Mrs. Freddie Fields), Jule Styne, Betty

*The *Los Angeles Citizen News*, 1961.
**© 1961, Shana Alexander, *Life*, Time-Life, Inc.

Comden, Adolph Green, Myrna Loy, Richard Burton, Arthur Schwartz, Dore Schary, Carol Channing, Henry Fonda, Julie Andrews, Merv Griffin, Anthony Perkins, and Maurice Chevalier. Judy called this night the most exciting of her entire career. The critics agreed:

There was an extra bonus at Carnegie Hall last night, Judy Garland sang.

New York Herald Tribune*

Judy Garland's concert at Carnegie Hall will go down in show business history.

Long Island Press**

This kid is still a killer.

New York World Telegram†

Last night the magnetism was circulating from the moment she stepped on stage.

New York Post‡

New York's Carnegie Hall was supercharged on both sides of the footlights Sunday evening . . . Pandemonium broke loose and a standing ovation stalled the song fest for several moments. After her twenty-fourth number of the evening, she halted the tumultous applause demanding still another encore . . . Few singers can get as much out of a song as Miss Garland. When she's singing the happy rounds like "When You're Smiling," "It's Almost Like Being in Love," "The Trolley Song," and "Zing! Went the Strings of My Heart" or the quiet "You're Nearer," "A Foggy Day," and "If Love Were All" to an intimate piano accomp, or a jazz styled "Who Cares?", "Puttin' on the Ritz," and "How Long Has This Been Going On" or the blues fashioned "Come Rain or Come Shine," and "Stormy Weather," everything she's got goes into them and she's got plenty. The tones are clear, the phrasing is meaningful and the vocal passion is catching. In fact, the audience couldn't resist anything she did. The aisles were jammed during the encores . . . she followed with two additional numbers "After You've Gone" and "Chicago" which brought her song bag for the evening up to twenty-six numbers.

Variety§

That night, after her performance at Carnegie Hall, Judy was given a party at Luchow's. Guests included (besides those friends mentioned as having

*Judith Christ, the *New York Herald Tribune*, April 24, 1964.
**The *Long Island Press*, 1961.
†The *New York World Telegram*.
‡Reprinted by permission of the *New York Post*. © 1961, New York Post Corporation.
§*Variety*, April 24, 1961.

attended the performance) the Eli Wallachs (Anne Jackson), the Bennett Cerfs, Tammy Grimes, Mike Nichols, Nancy Walker, Shirley Booth, Natalie Schaffer, Lauren Bacall, and Jason Robards.

Wherever Judy went during the concert tour she was remembered. In one small town, the stationmaster at the railroad station from which Judy was to depart complained that he was having a bad time with his throat. Judy solved his problem: "You're probably not using your voice right. Take a deep breathe and I'll show you." He did and Judy pushed hard at his stomach as he did. "Feel it? That's where your power comes from. And be very careful of those loud eee sounds. They'll give you a bleeding throat unless you keep your teeth open."

In one city, right in the middle of "Swanee," several men in the orchestra were so astounded by Judy's power that they stopped playing and just listened.

Another time, in Buffalo, a musician rose in the middle of a number, and took out a camera that was hidden under his jacket. He snapped a picture and sat down again in time to get back to work!

The biggest surprise must have come when, while she was singing "Over the Rainbow" to 8,000 people, a large moth flew into Judy's mouth. She tucked the moth into her cheek with her tongue (she couldn't spit it out—it would ruin her spell, there were thousands of crying fans waiting for the next word) and finished the remaining twenty-eight bars. Then the spotlights went out and she spit and coughed out the moth. When the lights came on again, she was just sitting there smiling through her tears.

Judy made hundreds of thousands of dollars in 1961 and paid off all her bills. Capitol released a two-record set of her whole Carnegie Hall concert and the album won both the Record of the Year and the Grammy awards. Judy also got a gold record for this album. To this day there hasn't been a two-record set that has out-sold *Judy at Carnegie Hall*. It has continued to be a best-seller in record stores throughout the country, even after her death.

Judy, singing "Dear Mr. Gable" to the King himself at his birthday party on the set of *Parnell*. (Courtesy of Metro-Goldwyn-Mayer)

Judy spent hours in the photographer's studio during her early days at Metro, modeling clothes from her films.

Hedda Hopper, David Rose, and Judy (top), 1941. Judy and Bing Crosby (bottom) going over the lyrics to a song before recording it, circa 1943.

Judy and Vincente Minnelli, circa 1946.

Judy and Fred Astaire rehearsing a number at Metro, circa 1948.

"Instant cancer," muttered Judy (top) as she lit up. "Well we'll all go with you," remarked a reporter. Judy: "Oh no, I always do a solo." Houston press conference, December 15, 1965 (with Mark Herron). Judy (middle), shooting pool with Alpha Theta fraternity brothers at Dartmouth College, Hanover, New Hampshire, January, 1967. (Photo courtesy of the *Dartmouth*) Judy, Lorna, and Joe (bottom) arriving for Liza's marriage to Peter Allen. In New York, March, 1967.

RIGHT PAGE
Judy (top left), leaving Peter Lawford's home following a press conference on the morning of November 22, 1963—President Kennedy had just been assassinated. "It's too much," she told reporters. "It's just too much." Joey, Judy, Lorna, and Liza (middle left) at Kennedy International Airport on December 30, 1964. Judy and Mark Herron (bottom left), 1964. Judy (top right), onstage at the Diplomat Hotel in Florida, 1966. (Photo courtesy of Nancy Barr) Judy (bottom right), onstage at the Arie Crown Theatre in Chicago, May, 1965. (Photo courtesy of Nancy Barr)

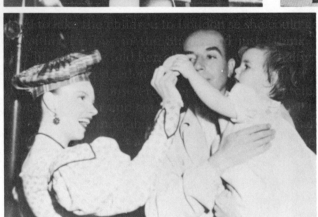

Judy (top left), onstage at the Newport Jazz Festival, 1961. Joey, Lorna, Liza, Sid, and Judy (top right), April, 1963. Judy, Vincente, and Liza (bottom left) on the set of *The Pirate*, 1948. Judy and Liza (bottom right) at the party following Judy's opening at the Coconut Grove, 1957.

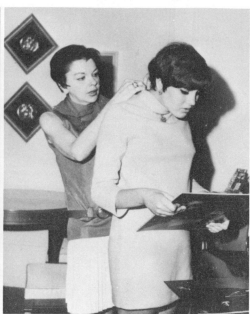

Judy (top left) at the reception following Liza's marriage, March, 1967. (Courtesy of Nancy Barr) Judy and Lorna (top right) in their hotel suite at The Warwick in Philadelphia prior to the concert at Kennedy Stadium, July 20, 1968. Judy (bottom left) at a press conference announcing her contract for *Valley of the Dolls*, March, 1967.

IO

In 1961 Judy Garland made her first motion picture in seven years. No one is quite sure why she held out so long (probably her weight problem). She had been offered some of the biggest parts in the biggest films of the fifties. She was asked to do the role of Nellie Forbush in *South Pacific* but Mitzi Gaynor ended up doing it. Then she and Frank Sinatra were wanted for the leads in *Carousel,* but neither of them made it. And what a pity. It would have been such a fantastic film. Much more of a delight than it ended up with Gordon MacRae and the beautiful and talented Shirley Jones. Many people felt that the part of Julie Jordan in *Carousel* would have brought Judy the long-awaited Oscar. She was also offered the lead in *The Helen Morgan Story* with Paul Newman, but she turned it down claiming, "There won't be any more sad endings for me."

In the late fifties she turned down the role of Eve in *The Three Faces of Eve* because she couldn't get her asking price—Joanne Woodward went on to win an Oscar for her performance in the role. (And some years later Judy was asked to appear in Mike Nichols's film *The Graduate* as Mrs. Robinson. Nothing ever came of it.)

Judy had also bought the rights to a film entitled *Born in Wedlock* about a widow and her three children, but for some reason the rights were never exercised.

Both Gertrude Lawrence and Fannie Brice expressed the wish that she play them in their biographies, if they were ever put on film. Both movies were made—much later—but without Judy.

In 1961, however, Stanley Kramer offered her a role in his epic-length motion picture, *Judgment at Nuremberg.* It was only a small part but it was important to the story and it gave Judy a chance to really sink her teeth into the character. She played the part of Irene Hoffman, a German housewife who had suffered mistreatment from the Nazis during World War II. The role required a very good actress. It gave Judy the opportunity

151

to show that she was not only a very good actress but a great one and one who had been greatly underrated for years. All in all, she wasn't on the screen for more than fifteen minutes, but her characterization was imbedded into the audience's mind for the remainder of the film.

When Judy arrived on the set on the first day of shooting, the technicians immediately burst into applause—their tribute to a great artist. Judy was happy again, and back in the movies!

> It's exciting to be back again. Actually pictures aren't my favorite working area. But there's such excitement and camaraderie making films that it's good to get back to them now and then. But I'd forgotten how hard we have to work. Movie making from dawn to dusk is quite a shock after years of concert dates, when you just sing your heart out for a couple of hours and then go home.
>
> People on the set are wonderful. But picture making is never really satisfying to me because you are doing it in little bits and pieces. On the stage, at the end of a concert, the audience reaction is to your total effort for the evening—and it's a better and more exhilarating gauge as to how well you've done.

One night, Spencer Tracy, Stanley Kramer, and Montgomery Clift were alone in a small projection room watching the "rushes" of that day's scenes. When Judy's scenes were over, the men found themselves giving her screen image a standing ovation. When Judy was told, she cried. After she completed her work in *Nuremberg* Stanley Kramer presented Judy with her wardrobe from the film—$6.98 worth of rags. She thanked him and the crew and said, "I shall treasure this as if Dior had done it."

When the film was premiered in San Francisco (the United Artists Theatre) and New York (the Palace Theatre) the audiences greeted the names of the other stars in the film with silence. But when Judy's name appeared on the screen it was met with thunderous applause. Before the film opened at the Pantages Theatre in Hollywood, three six-foot photographs of Garland were stolen.

Judy received an Academy Award nomination as Best Supporting Actress in 1961 for her performance in *Judgment at Nuremberg*, but Rita Moreno won for *West Side Story*. Because of her success in *Judgment at Nuremberg* Judy was once again a much-sought-after actress. Every day she was rumored to have been signed or offered this movie or that. Some of the more serious possibilities were Billy Wilder's *Irma la Douce* (which would have meant, obviously, changing the main character from a dancing prostitute to a singing one), Stanley Kramer's *It's a Mad, Mad, Mad, Mad World*, a musical production of *Hold Back the Dawn*, and a film with Bing Crosby entitled *By the Beautiful Sea*. She was also very much wanted for the role of Molly Brown in *The Unsinkable Molly Brown* and for a musical to be written by Richard Rodgers (with a story by Abby Mann).

For years rumors would follow her that she was going to appear in biographies of both Edith Piaf and Aimee Semple McPherson (she is supposed to have owned the script for the latter.)

At the Golden Globe Awards in 1962, Judy received the Cecil B. DeMille Award for her "outstanding contribution to the world through show business."

Freddie Fields and his partner David Begelman, settled Judy's differences with CBS and Judy signed to do two more television specials for them.

By January of 1962 Judy had brought her weight down to 120 pounds and the first of the two shows was taped. Her guests on the show, for which she was paid $100,000, were Frank Sinatra and Dean Martin. Norman Jewison directed. Jewison seemed to know exactly what was right for Judy. He opened with the famous Garland overture and then Judy came down a long runway singing "Just in Time." She followed this by singing "You Do Something to Me" as an introduction to her guests. The show closed after some twelve more songs with her rousing rendition of "San Francisco."

Judy herself was proud of the show:

> Dean Martin and Frank Sinatra are my guests. I think we have a terribly good show. I don't usually say this, but the show is beautifully produced and designed. I didn't think it was right that we should just stand around and tell jokes. I sing eight or nine songs alone and two numbers with the boys.

Every television critic in the country searched through his thesaurus for superlatives to describe Judy's special. Here are some excerpts:

> The orchestra begins the old song "I Can't Give You Anything But Love." She begins to sing. That warm full voice. The voice could belong to no one but Judy Garland.
>
> Cecil Smith, *Los Angeles Times**

> Judy Garland re-embraced the TV medium and lit up the spectrum with one of the entertainment delights of the season. It was a classy presentation, electric in its total impact on the viewer, with always the "punch by Judy" as the high voltage pay-off.
>
> *Variety***

The show was televised on February 25, 1962 and repeated on September 19 of the same year. It received an Emmy nomination but did not win.

With one success following the other so quickly, Judy had a much

*Cecil Smith, the *Los Angeles Times*, February 25, 1962.
** *Variety*, February 25, 1962.

more secure and confident feeling about her talents and career than ever before. Friends found her calmer and more self-assured. She was, generally, a happy, successful woman with a career she could be proud of. She was at this point, and would remain, the greatest singer-actress-comedienne in the business and one of the most sought after by producers around the world. Never again would a year go by when she wouldn't receive offers from all the major television networks. She confided to her friends and fans:

"I love my career. I want to say this because I'm always being painted a more tragic figure than I am, and I get awfully bored with myself as a tragic figure. I wouldn't have been anything but an entertainer. With all the troubles, with the stumbling and falling on the way, the rewards are still so great. If you happen to be a success, you meet writers, politicians, people in the arts, people with stimulating ideas in many places. It's a marvelous opportunity to lead a broad existence. As a performer I love the enthusiasm audiences have shown me. You can't blame me—we all want to prove ourselves, and I've had appreciation shown to me in the most inspiring, spontaneous ways."

Stanley Kramer was so pleased with Judy's performance in *Judgment at Nuremberg*, and with her behavior during the film's production, that he signed her for another motion picture, *A Child Is Waiting*.

In *A Child Is Waiting* Judy played the part of a woman who was trying to find a place for herself in the world. In her search for a home she came upon an institution for mentally retarded children. There, she got a job as a music teacher. Burt Lancaster portrayed her superior and their relationship provided most of the plot for the film. The two of them disagreed about the way a particular child should be handled and this led to the many complications that kept the film running.

Child was filmed on location at a home for the mentally retarded in California. Except for the most important child, played by Bruce Ritchey, actual retarded children were used in the film. When Judy was filming a scene in which she and the children are gathered together, a very touching thing happened. As soon as the director (John Cassavetes) called "Cut," all the children crowded around Judy and held out little slips of paper. They wanted her autograph. She signed the papers and then ran off the set in tears. Throughout the filming, Judy's handling of the children was remarkable and full of love.

Judy was thinner for her role in this film and she looked much healthier than she had in years. Once again she didn't sing a note. The critics hailed her performance as "the greatest thing she'll ever do!" Because of its subject matter, however, the film didn't go over very well with the public.

The *Saturday Review* wrote:

> Wonderful . . . is the way Judy Garland and Burt Lancaster work
> along with the children. Miss Garland and Lancaster radiate a warmth
> so genuine that one is certain the children are responding directly to
> them, not merely following some vaguely comprehended script.

On April 29, 1962 Judy made headlines again. She had filed for divorce against Sid again and they were just beginning a custody case that was to go on until 1966. Luft was threatening to have Judy branded as an unfit mother. He was threatening to take away the children. On the spur of the moment on April 28, 1962 Judy and the children had to flee the country so that she could keep them. The trip was so sudden that Liza had to carry dresses and slips over her arm—she didn't have time to pack. Three detectives joined Judy and the children as they went to Idlewild (now Kennedy) Airport and boarded a plane for London. As soon as they reached London, Judy had the children declared wards of the court.

Since her comeback in the United States Judy had been living in Scarsdale, New York. Scarsdale is considered by many to be one of the most beautiful residential sections in the country and its inhabitants are some of the richest. Its winding roads are lined with beautiful trees and exquisite homes. While residing there Judy tried to live as close to a normal life as possible. She often did her own shopping. Once, she was shopping in a men's store in Scarsdale Village. This was shortly after the Carnegie Hall concert. The proprietor of the store thought he recognized Judy as he waited on her but he never dreamed that it was the same woman he had seen onstage not long before. Finally, as he was ringing up the sale, it dawned on him. As Judy reached the front door of the shop he called out, "Aren't you Judy Garland?" "I thought you'd never ask!" she called back and flashed him her best smile.

Before leaving for London Judy had a public recording session at the Manhattan Center. The audience was full of celebrities. I won't list them all, but I will note that Hank Fonda was present—he seems to have been a constant attendant of Judy's shows! During this session Judy sang such songs as "Sail Away," "Hey Look Me Over," "Something's Coming," "Never, Never Will I Marry," and "Joey, Joey, Joey." The album was never released while Judy was alive, although some people, including myself, have managed to get a tape of the show. Judy's performance was top rate but she claimed that she had a cold and requested that the album not be released. Now, however, there are rumors that it will be released soon.

Judy's sudden trip to England wasn't all that radical as she had been scheduled to leave for London in a week anyway, to begin work on a new film entitled *The Lonely Stage*. Soon after arriving in London, Judy found herself in a recording studio again, this time working on the soundtrack for *The Lonely Stage*.

Judy's co-star in the new film was Dirk Bogarde, an old friend. They

155

had met years before at what Bogarde has referred to as a very boring cocktail party in New York. He particularly remembered the meeting because he had burned a hole right through Judy's dress with his cigarette. Since then they had been close friends and had been seeking a film to do together.

In the film, Judy played a famous American entertainer who had had an illegitimate child thirteen years before and had given custody of the child to the father (who married and legally adopted him). Now, however, she wanted her son back. Other members of the cast were Aline MacMahon, Jack Klugman, and Gregory Phillips. This was Judy's last screen appearance.

Before its release the title of the film was changed to *I Could Go on Singing*. Harold Arlen ("Over the Rainbow," "The Man That Got Away," etc.) wrote the title song. Although the film was often called a soap opera and wasn't considered very worthwhile, Judy's performance got good reviews. Here are a few excerpts:

> Judy Garland is back on the screen in a role that might have been custom tailored for her particular talents. A new song "I Could Go on Singing" provides her with a little clowning, a chance to be gay, a time for wistfulness, an occasion for tears. She and Dirk Bogarde play wonderfully together . . .
>
> *New York Daily News**

> A soulful performance is etched by Miss Garland who gives more than she gets from the script.
>
> *Variety***

> "I Could Go on Singing" is a showcase for Judy Garland's latter day singing and emoting. There are good scenes in London, also good personal scenes, with steam provided by Judy Garland and icy courtesy by Dirk Bogarde. The entertainment rests solely and heavily on the very theatrical shoulders of Judy Garland.
>
> *New York Post†*

In September, 1962 Judy went to Lake Tahoe, Nevada, to establish residence for a divorce. While there, she fasted to lose weight. She ate nothing all day and only allowed herself two cups of coffee (no cream or sugar). She didn't limit the number of cigarettes she was allowed to smoke. This went on for almost thirty days. Soon she had her figure back and it was one that any chorus girl would envy, but she hadn't been under a doctor's care and she wound up with a very serious kidney infection. She

*Reprinted by permission of the *New York Daily News*.
** *Variety*.
†Reprinted by permission of the *New York Post*. © 1963, the New York Post Corporation.

later described the pain: "Having children is a pleasure compared to it."

She was rushed to the hospital and was released just in time to open her new nightclub act at the Sahara in Las Vegas. One newspaper reported:

> Only four days out of a hospital and a few weeks away from a divorce, Judy Garland lived up to show business tradition last night— and the show went on at The Sahara Hotel here in Las Vegas.
>
> Judy sang fourteen numbers to a crowd that was standing room only. The show was sensational and the audience rewarded Judy with a standing ovation that lasted over two minutes.
>
> She opened with "Hello Bluebird" and closed, one hour and five minutes later, with an arrangement of "Chicago" that was just not to be believed.
>
> On stage with Miss Garland was a 37-piece orchestra. Judy will do only one show a night. Ray Bolger will fill the other spot.
>
> Celebrities in the audience included Ray Bolger, Spike Jones, Ed Sullivan, George Burns, Henry Fonda, Carol Channing and Carol Burnett.

Judy's divorce didn't go smoothly. Sid Luft countersued in California and all of Judy's efforts in Nevada were in vain. As it turned out there were almost three years to go before the case would be settled.

II

Judy spent the Christmas of 1962 in Los Angeles and signed with CBS-TV to do a one-hour weekly television series. Needless to say, this was the greatest news heard all through the planning for the new television season.

That month, Judy was Jack Paar's guest on his late-night television show. This was her first television "guest" appearance. Robert Goulet was also on hand. Judy and Goulet had just finished dubbing the voices for an animated feature-length film about two French cats who were in love. It was entitled *Gay Purr-ee*. Judy played the heroine, a cat named Mewsette, and Robert Goulet was the voice of Robespierre, her lover. Harold Arlen and Yip Harburg worked on the score (they had teamed on the *Oz* score among many others) and wrote six new songs for Judy, two of which Judy sang on the Paar show. She chatted amiably with Paar and told many humorous anecdotes about her friends in Hollywood. She also made no bones about hiding her feelings about Bob Goulet ("I think he's dreamy"). Earlier she had dubbed him "an eight-by-ten glossy photo." Many people have taken credit for this remark about Goulet but it was Judy who said it first! She sang two solos from *Gay Purr-ee* and she and Goulet closed the show with "Mewsette," one of their duets from the film. The show ended in gales of laughter when Jack Paar switched the cue cards on Judy and Goulet as they were singing. But Jack did find time, before signing off, to thank Judy for being there, saying, "I don't even belong on the same stage with you." The show was telecast on December 7 and was one of the best television appearances of Judy's career.

On December 8 John Horn of The *New York Herald Tribune* reported:

> Judy Garland, seldom looking or sounding better, worked with a
> new team last night in most congenial surroundings. The upshot was

a happy hour of spontaneous fun and joyous song . . . but the night and storytelling honors, thanks to the host's catalytic prompting, belonged to Miss Garland. She revealed herself an engaging raconteur with an irrepressible urge to act out her stories, a gift for a telling phrase, and a large store of show business yarns. Her songs, new ones, sung with intensity and vibrance, were the kind of ballads she does best. In her performance, much of the child she was still glowed in the older woman.

Very early in 1963, Judy taped her second special for CBS. Her guests on this one were Robert Goulet and Phil Silvers. The show was telecast on March 19, 1963 and received good reviews. The show opened with Judy, Goulet, and Silvers singing "Hello Bluebird" and after many skits (including one about muggings in Central Park that had Judy yelling, "A masher, a masher!") and many songs, Judy closed the show with "I Could Go on Singing."

In the spring of 1963 Judy returned to England to take part in the festivities involving the premiere of *I Could Go on Singing.* While there she appeared on "Sunday Night at the Palladium," a weekly television show comparable to "The Hollywood Palace." Judy sang four songs and her performance was very well received even though she stopped the orchestra three times at the beginning of "Comes Once in a Lifetime," saying that they weren't playing it right. It was all done in good fun, though, and the show went well. Portions of this telecast were later shown on "The Ed Sullivan Show" and this was actually Judy's first performance on the long running granddaddy of American variety television. Six months after Judy's death, when recapping the year's events, Ed Sullivan reran a segment of Judy's performance from this show. People all over the country shed tears as they listened to her tell them to "Light up your face with gladness, hide every trace of sadness. Although a tear may be ever so near . . ." in Charlie Chaplin's song, "Smile."

Soon, Judy was home in America and ready to go to work on her television series. She bought a beautiful home in Brentwood, California, and began preparing herself.

No one really thought that Judy would be a success on the show. They didn't even think she would show up for work after the first few tapings. Newspaper writers and "those in the know" in California were sure she wouldn't make it while hundreds of thousands of fans all over the country never doubted her.

It was unfair that Judy should be branded as "unreliable" at this point in her career. She had done very well during the first tour in 1951 and 1952. She again did well in 1955 and 1956. Although she missed some performances in Philadelphia and Washington in the late fifties, her record was still fairly good. Then, in 1960, 1961, and 1962 she was as reliable as anyone could be. She had done a tremendously long string of concerts

160

without any nasty headlines. What more did she have to do to prove that she was reliable? The press only wanted to believe the worst.

In Las Vegas, hundreds of dollars were being wagered that Judy wouldn't complete the first three shows. In late May, Judy, her agents, and CBS decided that it was time to prove to the CBS affiliates that Judy was ready for the ordeal of a series. It was arranged for them to have a chance to see Judy, in person, at a meeting in New York City. This was to be Judy's only chance to "prove herself."

The night before the meeting, Judy and David Begelman, her manager, wrote special lyrics to the music of "Call Me Irresponsible." The next night, at the meeting-banquet, Judy stepped onto the ballroom stage beautifully dressed, with her gorgeous new shape and sang: "Call me irresponsible, call me unreliable, but it's undeniably true, I'm irrevocably signed to you." That was it! She had won them over! The whole room full of CBS executives went out of their minds applauding her!

CBS really gave Judy the star treatment. A forty-by-ten-foot house-trailer was hoisted to a second-floor ramp and converted to her dressing room. Inside, it was decorated to represent a miniature version of Judy's home. It had air-conditioning, wall-to-wall carpeting, antique marble tables, indirect pink lighting, a piano, a stereophonic sound system, a tape-recorder, and a bar. Outside it was painted with red and white stripes.

Almost $100,000 was spent on studio facilities. The stage was raised and a separate revolving stage was built into it and camera crews were outfitted with brand new Marconi television cameras. (They mysteriously hide facial wrinkles.) Meanwhile, a yellow brick road was painted from the door of the trailer to the door of the set.

Soon tapings began and Judy was having a ball. As her first guest she signed Mickey Rooney. She knew she would be tense for the first show and felt that he would manage to keep her calm. He did. They did a good show and everything went along fine. The highlight was a little skit about their early films from the forties. At one point during the taping (though this was not seen on the show) Mickey called out: "Hey, Legend. We should have made 'The Days of Wine and Roses' together." After the taping, the audience gave them a tremendous ovation. Taking Judy's hand, Mickey said: "This is the love of my life, there isn't any adjective in the world to express my love for Judy. She's Judy and that's all there is to say." Judy couldn't say anything at all. She was crying.

Afterwards a party was given to celebrate. All the celebrities who had been in the audience attended. Included were Nick Adams, Jack Benny, Lucille Ball, Max Baer, Clint Eastwood, Van Heflin, Glynis Johns, Nancy Kulp, Sheldon Leonard, Dick Martin, Ross Martin, Roddy McDowall, Jimmy McHugh, Gary Morton, Irene Ryan, Dick Van Dyke, Anne Francis, Cara Williams, and Natalie Wood.

After the first three shows were taped, George Schlatter, the producer (later to head "Laugh-In") got the surprising news that CBS wasn't satisfied. The CBS execs thought the programs lacked a feeling of pattern. Vice President Hunt Stromberg, Jr. commented: "Any weekly show has to be formatted. There have to be standard compartments that audiences look forward to like Garry Moore's 'That Wonderful Year.'" He also claimed that Judy had a lack of contact with her viewers. He said she was "too unreachable." There may have been a lack of contact between Judy and CBS but not between Judy and her audience. That had always been one of the greatest things about her, there was nothing that could prevent her from reaching the hearts of those watching her perform.

Schlatter disagreed with CBS. He explained: "Since Garland is one of the giants I felt her show required a different kind of television. I wanted each show to be a special event and to tape it as a live theatrical presentation. I couldn't do a show with tracing paper."

Nevertheless, an order is an order, and Schlatter had to follow orders. In the fourth show he added a segment where Judy sat at a tea table with one of her guests, in this case Terry-Thomas, and chatted with him as the orchestra softly played "Tea for Two." He also added a "Born in a Trunk" episode at the end of each show. In this episode, Judy pulled objects from a trunk and reminisced about her past. This led into her closing song or songs.

Meanwhile, CBS was running a series of tests across the country to get the public's opinion of the series, which as yet had not been shown on the air. People were recruited at random and taken into darkened studios where they were shown the programs on giant screens. Well, the public didn't judge the shows, they judged what they had read about Judy in the newspapers. A sampling of the comment cards revealed statements like, "I don't like her, she's nervous," "She seems unhappy," "She drinks," and "She was mean to her mother." The CBS execs studied these reactions, and, concerned about the network's investment, decided to lower the boom. First to go was Schlatter, whose only mistake was in producing a show too original for the network's and, perhaps, the public's taste. Three writers and a choreographer were also dismissed. So far, only five shows had been completed.

Judy later recalled:

> Everybody went. I thought I was going, too. They swept out a whole bunch of people and whoever got caught up in that whisk of the broom was out. I wish somebody would have warned me in advance —maybe I could have avoided anyone's being decapitated. I was stunned and bewildered. It came as a shock.

Writers Arne Sultan and Marvin Worth were hired at $10,000 a week and told to give the show a complete revamping. Norman Jewison, who had directed the widely acclaimed Garland special in 1962 (and later was to direct the award-winning film *In the Heat of the Night*) was hired at $12,500 a week as executive producer. Before long, the show's budget went from $155,000 to $200,000 per program.

First, Jewison decided that the audience had to "get to know Judy Garland." A series of one-liners was added to the show. Judy would say things like, "I used to be fat . . . not fat, obese . . . O'Bese, that's O'Henry's cousin." Imagine Judy Garland saying lines like that! It was like giving Katharine Hepburn a first-grade reader to recite!

Production was stopped for five weeks to lessen the momentum that had built up during the first five shows and to give the new staff time to put their heads together. Three weeks after the slow-down, Judy entered Cedars of Lebanon Hospital briefly for what was described as "her yearly check-up." When she reported to the set after production resumed, those working on the show noticed a change in her.

The first show Jewison did was with June Allyson and Steve Lawrence. It turned out to be a mixed up hodgepodge of Judy and June singing "the old songs." The only good moment in the whole show was Judy and Steve Lawrence singing "Be My Guest." The show was made even worse by the constant reappearance of Jerry Van Dyke, who had been signed as the resident comedian. His material was no better than Garland's.

On September 29, 1963 Judy's show made its network debut. The first show televised was not the one with Mickey Rooney (as originally planned). Instead, a less deserving segment with Donald O'Connor was shown. Publicly, the series was off to a bad start. Judy opened the show with her "Call Me Irresponsible" parody and then did another medley of "old songs," such as "Yacka Hicky Hoola Doola" with O'Connor. Then we listened to Jerry Van Dyke's skit about the Lone Ranger and watched O'Connor sing and dance to "Sing You Sinners." There were occasional moments when Judy's magic shone through—for example, in any of her solo numbers. But these weren't enough to counterbalance the lack of creativity on the show.

In spite of this, the next day Judy received a telegram: "Congratulations on a wonderful show last night. Know it will be a big hit in the coming season. John F. Kennedy."

The show went somewhat better the next week, when Judy had Barbra Streisand and the Smothers Brothers as her guests. Judy and Barbra did a number of medleys together and chatted during the "Tea for Two" segment. Ethel Merman made a surprise entrance during this. Then Judy, Barbra, and Ethel did a rousing rendition of "There's No Business Like Show Business."

Some months later, when Emmy time rolled around, there was a sticky situation at hand. Judy was nominated for an award and Barbra was also nominated in the same category for her appearance on Judy's show. The Emmy Awards obviously needed to be reorganized! How could a woman who worked all season on a series be nominated in the same category as one who had worked for a week on one segment of that series? It was a very unfair system.

Soon there were rumors that Judy was missing rehearsals. Judy denied them: "I haven't missed any rehearsals—if I had, I wouldn't have been able to do the show. There's just no time to indulge yourself on weekly television—you don't even have time to get a headache or catch a cold." Jewison's response to the rumors was this: "Look, if you want somebody who's gonna be right on time and attend every rehearsal, go work with Dinah Shore. I admit that Judy isn't known for arriving on time. She'll always be there a little late. But I have never met anyone in my life who can pick up a routine as quickly." Years later, there were no nasty remarks made about Dean Martin not arriving for his rehearsals. As a matter of fact, it was accepted as "par for the course." Both Judy and Dean (both are Geminis) didn't feel they needed to be there all the time. They could easily learn a routine and just step in during the dress rehearsal. The finished product of Judy's show never suffered from her absence at rehearsals.

Many people began writing in and complaining that Judy fingered her guests too much. They said that she moved her hands nervously. The complaints began getting more and more ridiculous. Soon Judy had to defend herself again: "I don't see anything objectionable about it [her touching her guests]. If I think someone is funny, I'll laugh and touch them. I'm not the type of performer who can relax and put her feet up and get paid all that money. It's not nerves. Maybe it's just a kind of exuberance, which I've always had." Nevertheless, CBS asked her to try and control her movements. She agreed to. However, the next show she filmed had Vic Damone and Zina Bethune as guests and they were both nervous so Judy ended up right back where she started.

Jerry Van Dyke's role in the series was affected by CBS's efforts to "humanize" Judy. Originally his character had been that of a quiet likable type, but it was changed into a pushy, obnoxious personality. They liberally laced his dialogue with Judy with such comments as: "This isn't the original, this is the twelfth Judy Garland—the original went over the rainbow years ago." and "What's a nice little old lady like you doing on television?" Is it any wonder the show failed?!

After the tenth show, Van Dyke requested and received his walking papers. Judy was not shaken by the efforts to take her off her pedestal ("I don't know what humanizing or de-glamorizing is—I don't think I'm too glamorous or in-human"), but she was shaken by Van Dyke's departure. "I'm going to pretend it's just not happening," she told him. "I don't even want to talk about it. If I don't talk about it, I won't think about it."

Time after time, as the Nielsen ratings came in, Judy was beaten by "Bonanza." CBS had tried to make Judy into a combination of Perry

164

Como, Garry Moore, and Dinah Shore but the recipe hadn't turned out right. The public was looking for the old, original Judy Garland.

After the thirteenth show, director Bill Hobin decided he'd had enough and left. Soon afterward, Jewison left (having completed only eight shows) to direct a Doris Day film.

And at home, the public were seeing the last month's work on their television sets. The shows were inconsistent. Some were great and some lacked any kind of impact at all. They weren't bad, they just weren't good.

Judy did some very good shows with Peggy Lee, Vic Damone, Bobby Darin, and Count Basie. Her Christmas show, with Jack Jones, Mel Torme, Liza, Lorna, and Joe was beautiful. It's a pity that it isn't shown yearly as a Christmas special. Throughout the series Judy's songs were well chosen (usually by Mel Torme) and most of her guest stars were fitting companions to the Garland humor. But what, I ask, were Zina Bethune and Soupy Sales doing on the Judy Garland show? They may be good entertainers but they just didn't fit in. Neither did the Dillards, a group of hillbilly singers.

Judy had been fairly good friends with President John F. Kennedy. She had done a considerable amount of campaigning for him in the early sixties and she had a home next to his in Hyannis Port one summer. Her home, as a matter of fact, was the only one within the Kennedy Compound that did not belong to a Kennedy. She was also very close to Mr. and Mrs. Peter Lawford, the President's sister and brother-in-law. In an article in *Ladies' Home Journal* she recalled:

> One of the best friends I ever had was President John F. Kennedy. When I was doing my TV series, there were times when I didn't think I was getting the right advice. So I would telephone the President or his secretary, Mrs. Evelyn Lincoln, and I could hear the operator tell another, that "Judy Garland has flipped again—she thinks Lincoln is still in the White House!"
>
> I remember that Mr. Kennedy was in a meeting when I called one evening but he came to the phone anyway.
>
> "Hi, theah," he said. "How's the television show going?"
>
> I told him that I had some problems, but I said that I knew he was busy and I certainly didn't want to take up his time. He said, "That's not important! You're just as important to me as this meeting. We love your show and we've changed the White House dinner hour on Sundays so we can watch you. Now what's the matter?"
>
> I told him, "Norman Jewison is coming to direct the show for $12,500 a week and I don't think I can afford him."
>
> "Do you want Jewison?" the President asked.
>
> "I don't mind him," I replied, adding that it was CBS's expensive idea.

165

"Well then," Mr. Kennedy said, "CBS should pay for him—and they will. You see that they do. Don't you put one cent out."

When I told him I would try to follow his advice, he said: "All right, now sing me the last eight bars of 'Over the Rainbow.' Make my day a little easier."*

When Judy heard about Kennedy's death she decided that the show she was working on would have to be put off so she could do one dedicated to him. Producer Bill Colleran once told what happened that week:

> She locked herself in her room and cried all day. When she finally pulled herself together she called me up and said "Bill, we've simply got to do something on our program. We've got to."
>
> We worked out an idea we thought was appropriate and then submitted it to CBS. The answer we got will be written across my memory forever. The idea was rejected and we were told—and I quote —that they (meaning the public) will want to forget about it by the Sunday show."
>
> This of course, didn't satisfy Judy, so what she did was to go through her regular show, ending it with the usual "Born in a Trunk" routine. When the audience thought she was through she walked back on stage, stood in the center of the long ramp, and without once mentioning President Kennedy's name, sang "The Battle Hymn of the Republic."
>
> I can still see that little four foot eleven inch gal standing there, her head going higher and higher, tears streaming down her face, as she sang her heart out.
>
> It's moments like this that make you forget the problems.

Judy's rendition of "The Battle Hymn of the Republic" was, without a doubt, the highlight of the entire series. There has never been a more movingly sung version by anyone—and she did it without publicity. She didn't go out and say, "I'm doing this for John Kennedy—he was my friend —and doesn't this show my love for him?" It was her personal prayer for her friend and his world. A prayer for a man who would have liked to make his country a "Camelot."

When Judy was told that her show was being canceled she decided to make one last try to get her ratings up. She put her foot down with CBS and insisted that she was going to do the remaining shows her own way. By this time they had completed about twenty shows and there were only six to go. The first thing she did was to get rid of the revolving stage (which, she claimed, had been making her dizzy since work on the series had begun) and she put the orchestra onstage behind her (she had wanted

*© 1967, Downe Publishing, Inc. Reprinted by special permission of the *Ladies Home Journal.*

them there from the beginning), but she was told that things weren't done like that on television. Judy decided to do four one-woman concerts on the air. After all, she figured, the basis of her recent surge in popularity had been her outstanding streak of concerts in 1960 and 1961 and someone must have liked them. She was right. These four shows are remembered by many as highlights in the history of television. The first of them was shown on February 9, 1964. It was one hour of pure music—Judy style. She sang "Give My Regards to Broadway," "That's Entertainment," "Make Someone Happy," and "Liza," among others, and closed the show with a moving rendition of "America the Beautiful." The show got rave reviews and the ratings began to go up.

Two more shows were completed and then it was time for the final show. Taping began on Friday afternoon and continued until 5:00 A.M. on Saturday. During that time Judy sang and taped enough numbers to make up the entire show. However, there was to be a very long number at the end in which Judy (dressed in a clown outfit she had designed herself) was to sing "Here's to Us" and "Born in a Trunk." When filming ended Saturday morning, everything but "Born in a Trunk" had been completed. CBS had plenty of material to put together an entire show (including a number entitled "Something Cool," which was new to Judy's repertoire). However, for some reason they chose to use only forty-five minutes of what Judy had done, completing the show with five numbers from previous shows. A great deal of Judy's other work on the series has never been seen, including songs like "Jamboree Jones" and "Witchcraft."

Why did the Garland show fail? The late President Kennedy felt that the show was ahead of its time. Someone else summed it up perfectly in a letter to *TV Guide:* "Fine art will never be for the masses."

After her show went off the air, Judy went to Australia to do a few concerts. She didn't bring her children with her because they were in the middle of a semester and she didn't want them to have to switch schools again. She felt that their lives had included enough private tutors. Her first stop was Sydney. She gave a sensational show and got rave reviews. However, no one warned her that if they praise you in Sydney, they'll kill you in Melbourne. Her next stop was . . . Melbourne.

At this time Judy's traveling entourage included her conductor, Mort Lindsey (who had been with her since her Carnegie Hall days and throughout the concert series), David Begelmen and his wife Lana Wood (sister to Natalie), and Mark Herron, a young man Judy had met in Los Angeles.

The Melbourne concert didn't go well at all.

The afternoon before the show Judy was at the stadium rehearsing. The manager came over to her and said something cruel and thoughtless. Judy's face went white, then she asked him to repeat what he had said. Judy slapped his face and walked out. She went back to the hotel to sleep but was too nervous and had to take sleeping pills. Soon it was time for her to get ready for that night's performance. Herron had a hard time waking her. She was ninety minutes late.

When she arrived onstage, dressed in a short white dress trimmed in sequins, the audience was jeering and clapping. Some shouted "Have another brandy Judy" and "Get on with it." Nevertheless, she went on with the show, explaining that she hadn't been able to get out of the hotel on time. She completed the first half of the show.

She was having difficulty with an overly long microphone cord and had to speak to her conductor (Lindsey) several times about what to sing next. She teased the orchestra as she always did, but the audience didn't appreciate her humor and later said that she had been "cruel" to the musicians!

At half-time she went offstage for an intermission and came back in half an hour. Her usual intermission is twenty minutes. She was dressed in slacks and a beaded top. The audience continued to heckle her. After singing "By Myself" she walked off the stage, leaving the orchestra to play "Over the Rainbow." A major portion of the 7,000 people in the audience asked for their money back. The press gave Judy the worst possible punishment. Almost all the papers wrote against her. Very few of them printed the whole story. (Perhaps very few of them *knew* the whole story.)

First, I'd like to say that I have read a first-hand report given by a woman who saw the concert and she admits that the show was destined, from the beginning, to have trouble. Judy tried to explain to the audience why she was late but they wouldn't let her speak. Her microphone was squeaking and the air-conditioner was drowning her out. Some people got up and walked out in the middle of the performance.

Judy left Melbourne the next day and returned to Sydney. She went immediately to her hotel. When leaving Melbourne she had talked to fans and was generally pleasant to them. The press reported that she had to be helped onto the plane but this wasn't true. Photos of Judy and Mark Herron walking through the airport and onto the plane show clearly that Mark was simply trying to help her through the crowds of fans that had mobbed the airport. He was not carrying her or supporting her—he was pushing her.

When asked what she thought of the show she replied, "I didn't like it, did you?"

An Australian radio station broadcast the following interview:

Question: Why have you been avoiding the press so long? We have been waiting for you all day.
Answer: Well, that's your problem.
Question: Do you think your performance last night was up to standard?
Answer: No.

Question:	Why?
Answer:	Well, I don't think I should sing anymore.
Question:	Do you think it's time you retired?
Answer:	I think so . . . I would like to do a play.
Question:	What type?
Answer:	I would like to do a comedy.
Question:	It has been said that you were suffering from laryngitis.
Answer:	Yes, that's true.
Question:	Would you like to apologize for being late the other night? [As mentioned earlier, Judy tried to apologize at the concert but the audience wouldn't let her.]
Answer:	Why? I thought I was rather good.

Analyzing the above interview, I must say that the first question was ridiculous. After the press blasted her and made every insinuation they could get away with, this character had the nerve to ask her why she had been avoiding them! Judy was understandably angry. One Australian headline had read: "Judy Bombed?" They weren't giving her any chance at all. Also, my first-hand witness says that Judy was not suffering from laryngitis and that her voice was as good as ever. As for Judy's comments on her impending retirement—they must have been made in anger. All in all, I feel it can be agreed that Judy was treated unfairly by the press. Other than the fact that Judy was doing a lot of talking during the show, there was nothing wrong with it.

On leaving Sydney for Hong Kong, a few days later, Judy said: "I shall be back." She also made it clear that she didn't like the treatment she had been given by the press. I wish I could print a few of the articles here from the Australian press but they are all too long and involved.

Judy's maid in Sydney recalled:

> I loved her and thought the world of her. I was shocked when I first saw her. I thought she looked very sick, thin, and frail. But whenever she called me she always looked happy and relaxed. She spent most of her time sitting in a chair looking at the view. She played some records too, and listened to the radio. She was mad about the view. She said it was like San Francisco. She gave me two tickets for the next show [her second show in Sydney, also a success]. I said I wouldn't be able to go, but she made me take the tickets anyway. When she got back from Melbourne she didn't seem upset. I helped her unpack her luggage on Friday morning. She said she couldn't decide whether to catch the plane then or at night. She was never tempermental. When I said goodbye she said she wanted to come back again and I felt she meant it.

If you evaluate the whole situation, there is only one possible conclusion—it was a very big misunderstanding. The kind of misunderstanding that only Judy Garland could get herself into.

169

On May 27, 1964, while still in Hong Kong, right in the middle of a violent storm, Judy Garland was rushed to the hospital. Many reasons were given. In the excitement following her admittance, doctors, nurses, friends, and family all offered different explanations—some claimed she'd had a heart attack, some that it was her kidneys, some that it was a stroke or another attack of hepatitis, and some that she had taken a whole bottle of sleeping pills. The experience in Melbourne had plunged her into the depths of insecurity again. She was unconscious and in very serious condition. In a telephone conversation reported in the *New York Journal American* on May 28, Mark Herron said:

> "Her condition is awful. She is very, very bad." Asked about the nature of her illness Herron replied, "I don't know. The doctors won't tell me anything." He continued, "The doctors saved her. They worked on her for two hours and they saved her life." Herron asked the Journal to contact Freddie Fields and ask him to call Herron as quickly as possible.

Two days later, Dr. Harry Colfax said that Judy was improving and was off the critical list. A hospital spokesman said that Miss Garland's personal physician, Dr. Lee Siegel, would fly to Hong Kong.

Judy's fans all over the world were praying for her recovery; meanwhile, in Las Vegas, her oldest sister, Sue Gumm Cathcart, had succumbed to a long and serious bout with cancer.

Judy came out of her twenty-four-hour coma and it was announced that she would have to rest for "a period of several days." It was also announced that she had received "mountains of flowers from well-wishers." Garland wanted to thank all of them but she didn't know how. She did, however, send a brief note to the president of her fan club and asked that she pass it along to her "registered" fans.

Soon, hospital aides were reporting that Judy was "chattering like a bird." She admitted that when she first came out of her coma she was afraid. She saw all the little Hong Kong nurses and thought, "Oh my, God made a mistake and sent me to Chinese heaven." She was sure she had died.

Back in New Hope, Pennsylvania, where she was appearing in a summer production of *Time Out for Ginger*, Liza said, "I am terribly worried and feel very badly." Meanwhile, Sid Luft, who was in California with the two smaller children, was reported to be "distraught and worried" and said he was doing everything possible to keep the news from the children. He was also reported as having said: "If I knew she wanted me, I'd rush to her side right now—after all, she's still the most wonderful woman in the world."

On June 1, 1964, Judy was released from the hospital.

On June 10 (her forty-second birthday), while at a Hong Kong nightclub, Judy announced: "Mark and I were married five days ago. I'm very happy." The next day, however, there was no record of the marriage at the marriage registry. Mark Herron gave the following confused interview.

American actor Mark Herron said today that he had married Judy Garland, the 41 year old singer, aboard a ship here, "six or seven days ago, but I cannot remember the exact date."

When he was shown a local paper report asking whether or not Miss Garland was on her honeymoon here, he commented: "I suppose so."

Herron said the captain of the ship—whom he thought was a Swede or a Norwegian—performed the ceremony.

"Word came through from Mexico that Judy had obtained a Mexican divorce from Sid Luft," he added.

"We found and hired a boat for the wedding. It is a fairly big ship, but I cannot remember its name."

Then beaming broadly, he said "I don't even remember what day it is today."

Meanwhile, in Hollywood, Mr. Freddie Fields, manager of Judy Garland, has branded as "impossible and erroneous" the report that the singer and Mark Herron are married. "She is not divorced from Sid Luft, yet," said Mr. Fields.

Judy and Mark left Hong Kong for Tokyo on June 12. While on board the liner *President Roosevelt,* Judy added yet another piece to the confusing puzzle surrounding her supposed marriage:

Judy Garland and her actor companion, Mr. Mark Herron, insisted last night that they were married. In fact, they said, they had been married twice in the past seven days.

Interviewed aboard the liner, President Roosevelt, before sailing to Japan, they said the first ceremony took place aboard a Norwegian ship "three miles out at sea" last Saturday.

Then, "because people began to ask questions," they went through a Chinese marriage ceremony at the Mandarin Hotel yesterday afternoon.

Miss Garland produced a Chinese marriage certificate.

She said the certificate for their first marriage, which was performed by Captain Norviik, master of the Norwegian ship, Bodo, was "locked away."

In high spirits last night aboard the liner, Miss Garland said she was "proud and happy."

Asked whether the marriage would be considered valid in the United States, Miss Garland said she had consulted lawyers in Hong Kong, Honolulu, Los Angeles, New York and other places. "I never do anything without consulting lawyers," she said.

Meanwhile, back in Hollywood, Garland's press agent, Guy McElwaine, stated, "I know it's a gag because I know the sense of humor involved."

When Dr. Lee Siegel left Hong Kong he reported that Judy, while under his care in the hospital, had gained twenty pounds, bringing her weight up to ninety-eight pounds. He added that "she's never looked better."

On June 19, Judy announced that she had not married Mark Herron. She said that they had been blessed in Hong Kong by a Buddhist priest for her recovery from the illness. At the same time she announced that she had had a tracheotomy during her critical days in the hospital and wouldn't be able to sing for several months. As it finally turned out it seems that the whole married-not married question resulted from a misunderstanding probably brought about by language-translation difficulties. Judy has emphatically stated to friends that she never told anyone she had married Mark Herron in Hong Kong or anywhere else until November, 1965 when the ceremony actually took place.

Judy left Tokyo on June 25, accompanied by her nurse, Mrs. Snowden Wu (Judy called her "Snowy") and Mark Herron. Her destination was Copenhagen. On the way, they stopped in Anchorage, Alaska. She arrived in Copenhagen on June 26. From there, she and Mark continued their tour to London. They arrived on June 30.

On July 20 Judy was back in the hospital. She had been moving into an apartment in London and while trying to open some trunks with a scissors she accidently injured one of her wrists. Judy left the hospital on July 23. She was scheduled to make a walk-on appearance at the "Night of 100 Stars" benefit at the Palladium. The show, however, didn't go as planned. The next reviews read:

> Judy Garland stopped London's biggest charity show of the year last night by singing "Over the Rainbow."
> The many other British entertainers, including The Beatles, who had participated in the show, faded into the shadows when Judy stepped on the stage of The Palladium and sang her famous song. She followed this by singing "Swanee." This, after being told by her doctors not to sing.
> The audience's applause was so enthusiastic that the final act— singer, Shirley Bassey—was cancelled.
> Miss Garland's triumph came just a few hours after she checked herself out of a London nursing home. Her escort for the evening was Mark Herron, her fiance.
> The Beatles, acting as Masters of Ceremonies, asked Judy to come to the stage toward the end of the show.
> The audience jumped to its feet, cheering and yelling, "Sing Judy, sing." Miss Garland smiled but she said that she couldn't sing. The

cheers went on as she waved and began to back away from the microphone.

Finally, she returned to the microphone and sang in a still beautiful
voice. At the completion of her second number, The Beatles and other
stars gathered around to congratulate her. A Palladium spokesman
commented, "I think if Judy hadn't sung there would have been a riot."

After she had finished her two songs Judy said: "It's nice to be home
again. It's left me speechless and so terribly grateful." As usual, Garland
bounced back when it was least expected. The London papers blazoned
with such headlines as "Judy Stops Show" and "Palladium Sizzles With
Judy." Most American papers ran the story on their front page.

Professionally, Judy was inactive during most of the summer but in
early August she recorded four songs from Lionel Bart's stage show, *Maggie May*. The records have never been released in America but they were
in England, where they received good reviews.

Meanwhile, back in America, Sid Luft was fighting for permanent
custody of the children. He claimed that Judy was "squandering the family
fortune" and that she was neglecting the children. A hearing was set for
October 28.

Liza arrived in London in early September for a short visit with her
mother, but she had to return to New York shortly afterward for talks
concerning a Broadway show. While in London she and Judy discussed
plans to do a concert together at the Palladium.

On September 23, after attending the opening of *Maggie May*, Judy
was admitted to a London hospital with an "acute abdominal condition."
She was released the next day.

Soon after it was announced that Judy and Liza would do a concert
at the London Palladium on November 8. It was to be a one-night-only
event but the house was sold out in only two days and the public demanded that a second show be scheduled. The ATV arranged to tape part
of the show for use as a television special and Capitol prepared to record
it for release as an album.

At the same time, Judy signed an Australian singing team, the Allen
Brothers, under her management. She had "discovered" them in Hong
Kong. She was particularly fond of Peter Allen and had decided that he
would be the perfect husband for her daughter Liza. She introduced them
and, as she had hoped, they took an immediate liking to each other.

In California, Luft wouldn't give up trying to get the children and he
was fighting his hardest. On October 27, Luft and his lawyer, Saul Bernard,
brought witnesses to court to state that Judy had once tried to jump out
of a Philadelphia hotel window while nude and that she frequently drank
in front of the children. Judy had witnesses present to testify that she was
a good mother to her children and that she didn't drink excessively.

173

Then Judy got a warrant out for Sid's arrest, claiming that he had unlawfully taken a TV set, liquor, and silver from her home. Sid didn't appear at a hearing to show cause why he should not be held in contempt for disregarding a restraining order that forbade him to enter Judy's home. A decision was reached on October 28 when the judge announced that Judy and Luft were to have temporary joint custody and that Luft had unlimited visiting rights. The only restriction on Luft was that he had to announce himself at Judy's home and while there he had to act as a guest.

The court also ruled that the children could not visit Judy in London. A divorce hearing was set for December when Judy was expected to be back in the States.

On November 8 Judy and Liza did their show at the Palladium and received good reviews. The second show, while just as successful financially, was not as good as the first. By the Judy got around to singing "Over the Rainbow" her voice had gone completely and she asked the audience to sing it for her. Some of her other songs were: "Just Once in a Lifetime," "Maggie May," "It's Yourself," "Smile," "Make Someone Happy," "The Music That Makes Me Dance," "What Now My Love," and "Never, Never Will I Marry." She also did many duets with Liza.

In late November, Liza announced that she and Peter Allen were engaged to be married. No date was set for the wedding.

Judy's first American television appearance since her series was on "The Jack Paar Show." In her fifteen-minute segment she opened with "Never, Never Will I Marry." and closed with "What Now My Love." In between she and Paar chatted and Judy told a few humorous anecdotes about herself and Marlene Dietrich. She looked marvelous and was wearing one of the many beautiful gowns Ray Agahayan had designed for her during the concert series. The reviews, however, were not good.

It was on this show, incidentally, that Judy revealed just how lonesome her life could be—even with all the love and adulation. Her remarks were brought on by a question that was to become standard in any Garland interview: "What's it like to be a living legend?" Judy replied: "Do you know that some nights I just sit by the phone waiting for it to ring. But it never does. They all say 'I don't want to bother her, she's too busy—so I just sit there!"

In preparation for her return to the United States, Judy asked that the children be allowed to meet her in New York since she had commitments that would keep her there until the middle of January. She wanted to spend Christmas with them.

The Palladium television special was shown on December 20, 1964. This was a condensed version of the second concert she and Liza had done together. It is surprising to see that the very show that got such good reviews as a concert could receive such unbelievably mixed reviews as a television program. This can probably be explained by the fact that although the whole show was filmed, the TV version was cut from the original 130 minutes to only 60 minutes. Some of Judy's best moments were omitted. Many people wrote in to newspapers complaining that Judy and Liza were "too mushy."

Judy was granted permission to have the children for the holidays but no one could find Lorna, Joe, or their father. Lorna, however, called home to inform those in charge that she and Joe were staying with their father at the home of a Miss Brigette Sommers. Miss Sommers's name had been brought up in the custody case and Luft testified that he had hired her to look after the children when they stayed with him. A warrant was sworn out for Luft's arrest.

Finally, on December 28, 1964, Judy and her children were reunited. The *New York Daily News* reported:

> Christmas Day came four days late this year for singer Judy Garland, but Santa Claus and all his reindeer, could not have brought her more joy than did a jet plane which dipped down at Kennedy Airport yesterday from Los Angeles.
>
> Aboard it were two of her children, Lorna, 12, and Joseph, 9, pawns in a bitter custody battle between Judy and her estranged husband, film producer Sid Luft. The youngsters should have been here for Christmas but were not.
>
> A warrant for Luft's arrest was issued last week in California when he failed to return the children to their Brentwood, California home so they could leave to spend Christmas with their mother.
>
> Then, on Monday, the children walked up to their governess, Mrs. Letitia Chapman, on a Beverly Hills street and asked to be taken to New York.
>
> (Luft said on the West Coast yesterday that he would "rather go to jail than to have missed Christmas with my children—it's the first Christmas in three years I spent with them, and it was a wholesome, happy, and delightful holiday.")
>
> When Lorna appeared on the plane ramp, Judy called to her: "Hello, beautiful." And to her son she said: "You grew nine feet."
>
> Mother and children, who had not seen each other since Judy embarked on a world tour in March, cried and kissed and hugged each other in the Trans-World Airlines waiting room. "We made it. We made it," shouted Lorna.
>
> Also on hand to join in the greetings were Liza Minnelli, Judy's daughter by a previous marriage; Liza's fiancé, Peter Allen, and Mark Herron, who accompanied Judy on her tour.
>
> Liza and the two youngsters staged an impromptu jig before they all departed in a limousine for Judy's suite at the Regency Hotel.
>
> "We haven't opened our Christmas presents yet," Judy said. "We're going to open them now, though."*

*Reprinted by permission of the *New York Daily News.*

Dean Martin, Judy, and Frank Sinatra (top left) rehearsing for her television spectacular, January, 1962. Judy (top right) in Philadelphia, July, 1968. Judy and Robert Goulet (bottom) on "The Jack Paar Show" ("The Tonight Show"), December, 1962. (Courtesy of National Broadcasting Company, Inc.)

Dean Martin, Judy, and Frank Sinatra in a publicity shot for her CBS television spectacular, January 1962.

Judy and Robert Goulet (top left) on her CBS television special, "Judy and Her Friends," April, 1963. Judy and Phil Silvers (top right) on her CBS television special, "Judy and Her Friends," April, 1963. Judy and Peggy Lee (bottom left) during the "I Like Men" medley on "The Judy Garland Show," October, 1963. Shelley Berman, Peter Gennaro, and Judy (bottom right) singing "Making Whoopee" on "The Judy Garland Show," January, 1964.

**Judy, onstage at the London Palladium in a segment of "The Ed Sullivan Show,"
April, 1963. (Courtesy of Ed Sullivan Enterprises)**

Judy (top left), singing "Jamboree Jones" on "The Judy Garland Show." This segment was cut out of the final print. Judy (top right), singing on "The Judy Garland Show." Lorna, Judy, and Joe (bottom left) on "The Judy Garland Show," December 22, 1963. Judy and Liza (bottom right) at rehearsals for "The Judy Garland Show," October, 1963.

Judy, lifting Joe out of the audience at the climax of her March 8, 1964 show. She had just sung "Be a Clown."

Judy and Liza singing "Two Lost Souls" on "The Judy Garland Show," October, 1963.

Judy (top left), onstage on "The Jack Paar Show," May, 1964. Judy (top right) on "On Broadway Tonight," January, 1965. Judy and Perry Como (bottom) during dress rehearsals for "The Perry Como Show," February, 1966. Note hair curlers. (Photo courtesy of National Broadcasting Company, Inc.)

Judy and Perry Como on "The Perry Como Show," February, 1966. (Photo courtesy of National Broadcasting Company, Inc.)

Judy and Sammy Davis on "The Sammy Davis Show," March, 1966. (Photo courtesy of National Broadcasting Company, Inc.)

Judy, singing "My Man" on "The Hollywood Palace," November, 1965.

Judy (top), on "The Sammy Davis Show," March, 1966. (Courtesy National Broadcasting Company, Inc.) Judy (middle left) in the "Mr. and Mrs. Clown" number on "The Hollywood Palace," May, 1966.

Judy (right) on "The Sammy Davis Show," March, 1966. (Photo courtesy of National Broadcasting Company, Inc.) Judy (bottom left) with Perry Como's nephew Vincent and Mark Herron on the set of "The Perry Como Show," February, 1966. Vincent had designed Judy's gown. (Courtesy of National Broadcasting Company, Inc.)

Judy and Mickey Deans in London, January, 1969. (Photo courtesy of Syndication International Ltd.)

LEFT PAGE
Judy, onstage, at "The Talk Of The Town" in London, March, 1969. (Photo courtesy of the *London People*)

Judy on "The Sammy Davis Show," March, 1966. (Photo courtesy of National Broadcasting Company Inc.)

Judy, onstage at Caesar's Palace, December, 1967. (Photo courtesy of The Las Vegas News Bureau)

12

In February of 1965, Judy went to Toronto, Canada, to do a week of concerts at the O'Keefe Center—the site of one of her 1961 triumphs.

Unfortunately, she was suffering from laryngitis and had to cancel two shows because of it. The reviews of the other shows weren't very good. It was generally said that Garland's voice wasn't what it used to be but that her spirit was still there. *Variety*'s headline, "Only a Touch of Judy Left in Singer's Pathetic Concert at Toronto Date," was a little overdramatic. There was nothing pathetic about the concert—Judy just wasn't as good as she could have been.

Judy's return, after the two canceled performances, showed a marked improvement over the first shows. While in Toronto, she gave two press conferences. The first was a brief one upon her arrival at the airport. When asked if her trip had been all right, she replied, "Yes, the trip was fine . . . except, as usual, I ate too much." Had she brought much luggage? "Only the usual 118 suitcases!"

The second conference was much more substantial. "My ambition is to be a good cook, a good mother, do a good show, and have some fun." And what does Judy Garland do when she gets tired? "Slap myself on the hip like an old pony!"

On Friday, February 5, a previously taped February 2 guest appearance by Judy was shown on "On Broadway Tonight." The reviews were fantastic and it was claimed that Judy's voice was now better than ever! The critics had nothing but praise for her.

Judy opened her engagement at the Fountainbleau Hotel in Miami on March 11. She was there until March 20. The reviews were fantastic. The *Miami Beach Sun* headlined: "She Had Them in Her Hands." The *Miami Herald* proclaimed: "Garland Belts Em Out in Best Form," and *Variety* reported: "Miss Garland scored a tour-de-force." Judy got standing ovations every night. One night, after finishing her show at the Fountainbleau, the supposedly unreliable Garland rushed over to the rival nitery, the Eden Roc, to sub for Debbie Reynolds, who had collapsed and could not go on.

On March 12, it was announced that Judy had signed to play the role of Jean Harlow's mother in the Electronovision version of *Harlow*. By March 25, however, Judy had bowed out of the production because of prior commitments. Some suspect that billing was also a problem.

On April 8, 1965 Garland appeared on the "Academy Awards" television broadcast to sing a tribute to the late Cole Porter. Gene Kelly introduced her by saying, "Our producer, Joseph Pasternak, has chosen a lady of monumental style herself, Miss Judy Garland." She came out, sang a medley of beautiful Porter songs in a fantastic voice, and got a standing ovation. The papers headlined: "Last Night Judy Rocked the Academy with Cole."

While she was staying in Honolulu for a brief vacation, Judy's small rented home on Diamond Head caught fire. Damage to the home was estimated at $2,000. The Honolulu papers carried photos of Judy clad in a two-piece bathing suit after having helped the firemen to put out the fire.

On March 23, Judy did a concert at the Charlotte Coliseum in Charlotte, North Carolina, for the Democratic Party. Unfortunately, she was having voice trouble and received poor reviews.

Early in May, Judy was granted a divorce from Luft. Outside the courtroom she was asked how much weight she had lost recently. "I just shed 186 pounds in there!" was her quip.

On May 7, 1965 Judy did a concert at the Arie Crown Theatre in Chicago. The reviews were good although Judy had confessed to having trouble with her voice that night. Her program was the same as the one she had been doing since February, including such numbers as "Swing Low, Sweet Chariot," "By Myself," and "As Long As He Needs Me." In Chicago her program changed again. She brought back many of the numbers she had sung at Carnegie Hall and added "My Kind of Town (Chicago Is)."

On Tuesday, May 11, Liza Minnelli opened on Broadway in *Flora the Red Menace*. The critics panned the show but gave Liza tremendous praise. For her performance in this show (the music and lyrics were by Fred Ebb and Johnny Kander) she received the Antoinette Perry (Tony) Award as the best musical actress. (This wasn't the first Tony Award in the family. In 1952 Judy had received a special Tony for her Palace show.)

At Ruby Foo's, following Liza's opening, Judy was asked for autographs. It was the first time she ever turned a fan down. "No, this is Liza's night," she said and then beamed broadly.

Judy's name, however, made headlines again on May 31 when she canceled the last half of a performance in Cincinnati. The *Cincinnati*

Enquirer printed two articles. One was a review of the concert itself. Its headline was, "Judy's Voice Brings 'Em to Their Feet." The other article covered the cancellation:

> Singer Judy Garland failed to finish a concert here Saturday night because of illness. Whether she'll come back and "sing for free" as she promised still was up in the air today.
>
> Approximately 4,500 people had paid a $7.50 top to hear Miss Garland and about 1,000 of them milled around her dressing room after the cancellation, demanding refunds.
>
> They didn't get refunds because half of the show had been completed. Dino J. Santangelo, producer of the show for local backers said that ticket stubs for Saturday's concert would be honored—if the singer comes back.
>
> Her personal press agent, however, said it would cost Miss Garland $8,000 just to return.
>
> The show ended after an intermission—after Miss Garland had sung a half-a-dozen songs. Three physicians were called to her dressing room. Two of them eventually led her back to the stage where she said she couldn't continue.
>
> The doctors said she had a virus infection and a temperature of 102.

On June 13, just three days after her forty-third birthday and three days before her scheduled opening at the Thunderbird Hotel in Las Vegas, Judy was admitted to the UCLA Neuropsychiatric Institute for treatment of an allergic reaction to a drug. Hospital spokesmen said she had a fever and a rash.

The next day it was announced that Judy was in satisfactory condition and doing well.

Surprising all her doubters, Judy opened on schedule at the Thunderbird. Ralph Pearl of the *Las Vegas Sun* headlined: "First Nighters Go Wild Over Judy: Wins Standing Ovations," and the *Las Vegas Review Journal* proclaimed: "Confident Judy Thrills Vegas." Judy got a standing ovation before even singing the first note of the evening—a rarity which was soon to become a custom at Garland concerts. It was claimed that she sang in "the distinctive Garland tones hoped for." And just think, only four months earlier her show had been called "pathetic."

On July 19, 1965 Judy did a concert at the Forest Hills Tennis Stadium in New York City and again got rave reviews. *Billboard* headlined: "Garland Displays Her Old Form at Concert." *Variety* reported that "the standing ovation was to be expected, and was, in this case, merited."

As Judy was being ushered to her limousine after the concert, a young fan called to her: "Say Judy, my name is Judy too. I don't have shoes to wear but I buy your records." Judy answered sympathetically, "Oh my . . . you should buy shoes."

On July 9th Judy had taped an appearance on "The Andy Williams Show" which was later shown in September.

On August 31, Judy opened at the Circle Star Theatre in San Carlos. Although the reviews of the opening night show carried headlines such as "Judy's Still Got Old Impact" and "Judy Gets Over Rainbow," her performances that week were not her best. For this reason, the San Carlos engagement is not mentioned much in discussions of Judy's career. The same week Judy and Mark announced their engagement. Now that was news?

An incident at a coffee shop in San Carlos gives a humorous insight into Judy. It occurred when Judy was semi-incognito during the period of rehearsals before her show began. She walked into the coffee shop and was recognized by a waitress, who swore, "I won't tell anybody you're here!" To this Judy replied, "Honey, bring me a hamburger and you can tell the world!"

Judy opened in Los Angeles at the Greek Theatre on September 13. The reviews were fantastic. The *Hollywood Reporter* exclaimed: "This was Judy back home in Hollywood, looking and sounding better than she did in her 1957 Greek appearance."

Variety reported:

"From the opening 'The Whole World in His Hands' to her much demanded 'Over the Rainbow,' Judy was in control all the way and had the packed house shouting for more."

But this engagement was not destined to go smoothly. After her first night's performance Judy broke her arm. The following night she went onstage and did her show with the help of her friends Martha Raye, Johnny Mathis, and Mickey Rooney. While the reviews were still good, Judy found it necessary to cancel the rest of the run.

On September 20 Judy's segment of "The Andy Williams Show" was telecast. Her main solo was a rocking rendition of "Get Happy." She also sang some duets with Williams and did a medley of her hits. The show got mixed reviews.

"On November 14, 1965 Judy Garland married Mark Herron for the first and only time." The ceremony was held in a small wedding chapel in Las Vegas. Her attendants were Mrs. Snowden Wu and Pamela Austin (wife of publicity director Guy McElwaine—but better known as the Dodge Rebellion Girl). The best man was Mr. McElwaine.

The same night Judy appeared—on videotape—as hostess of "The Hollywood Palace." She received excellent reviews and the producers of the show said that she was "a dream to work with."

On November 30 Judy opened at the Sahara Hotel in Las Vegas. The next day the *Las Vegas Sun* reported:

A radiant Judy Garland enchanted the opening night throng at the Hotel Sahara Tuesday night in a sensational return to the resort after two years.

The Garland magic was in full evidence as she deftly maneuvered her Congo Room audience to a nostalgic peak and then climaxed her performance with her immortal "Over the Rainbow." After a quiet pause, her fans gave her a standing ovation, which only the house lights could quell at last.

Judy looked like a school girl in her rose dress as she embraced the microphone and swung easily through fifteen old and new favorites. The house shook with applause when she delivered her version of the dramatic "What Now My Love."

Her husband of three weeks, Mark Herron, was at ringside. Judy strolled down a special runway built for her, leaned over and kissed him. "He sure is a doll," she sighed.

On December 17 Judy was the first artist to give a concert in the Houston Astrodome. The first half of the show was performed by the Supremes. Judy came on after intermission. The show was a success but the Dome was not. Those in attendance reported that its sound system was poor and so was its seating. For this show Judy added "Houston" to her repertoire and also did a specially rewritten number, "My Kind of Town (Houston Is)."

At one point during a press conference in Houston, Judy started to light a cigarette and mumbled something about "instant cancer."

"Well, we'll all go with you," remarked a reporter.

"Oh no . . . " responded Judy. "I always do a solo."

Garland opened at the Diplomat's Cafe Crystal in Hollywood, Florida, on February 3, 1966. Again, the reviews were good. The *Miami Herald* headlined: "Judy in Excellent Form in Her Cafe Crystal Show." Ted Crail summed it all up in *The Miami Beach Sun* when he asked his readers, "What would this century be without Judy Garland's singing?"

February also found Judy in New York taping a guest appearance on "The Perry Como Show" (a monthly special) and two appearances on "The Sammy Davis Show."

The Como show revolved around the theft of Judy's Maltese ring. It was a fictional thread of plot put together just to give Judy, Perry, and Bill Cosby something to joke about. Judy sang "What Now My Love," "Just in Time," and a short medley of some of her hits. The show went well.

On each of the Sammy Davis shows Judy sang a few solos and dueted with Sammy on long medleys of various songs. Of the songs Judy taped for the second show, two were cut from the final print: "I Can't Give You Anything But Love" and "If Love Were All."

Judy turned up on "The Hollywood Palace" as hostess again on May 7. The show had been taped on April 1. The same day the show was televised, it was announced that Judy and Mark Herron were separating.

197

Judy opened her "Palace" performance with Burt Bacharach's "What the World Needs Now," sang two other solos, and did a routine with Van Johnson, entitled "Mr. and Mrs. Clown."

Early in May, Judy participated in a benefit for the Judy Holiday Memorial Hospital and according to the papers she "stole the show." Among other songs she sang "The Party's Over," one of the many Comden and Green songs that had first been sung by Judy Holiday.

Here's an amusing story concerning Judy and her appearance at this benefit. The next week she was home when she received a letter from the dinner's chairman, Arnold Krakower, which read:

> Dear Miss Garland,
>   We are sorry you were unable to attend the Judy Holiday Memorial benefit.
>   We were fortunate enough to have been entertained by such outstanding talents as Judy Garland, Betty Comden, Adolph Green, etc.

Accompanying the letter was a photocopy of a *New York Post* article illustrated by a photo of Judy and Alan King taken at the event. Judy couldn't believe what she was reading and decided that she had finally "flipped out." She had her maid read it and after being reassured that she was not crazy she framed the letter and had it hung on her wall because "no one would ever believe me this time!"

On August 3, Mark Herron sued Judy for separate maintenance. Herron stated that he had not filed for divorce because he hoped a reconciliation was still possible. On August 5, Judy issued the following statement: "His public and private behavior, which has been distasteful and untenable makes any reconciliation impossible."

On August 16, Herron changed his plea and sued for divorce. Sid Luft, meanwhile, was still trying to get custody of the children.

In August, Judy made her Mexican singing debut at the El Patio Nightclub in Mexico City. She received sensational reviews but canceled after her second show due to laryngitis brought about by the change in altitude. Betty Hutton was brought in to replace her. Following is a translated review of Judy's opening night:

> Glorious, extraordinary, electrifying, and magnetic was the triumphant presentation of the great star of the world cinema, Judy Garland, the formidable show woman on the floor of the traditional cabaret, El Patio . . . She interprets her songs, and more than sings them—she acts them. She creates new meanings to the words of her songs. . . . She has enormous artistic proportions and apparently has ever since her early years . . . She has a large and devoted audience and during an act that included more than twenty songs one was not able to say less than that she was a great artist. When she finished her performance the tempest

of emotional applause continued until her diminutive figure was lost in a crowd of men, women and children that stood and threw flowers at her.

It was around this time that another man appeared in Judy's life. His name was Tom Green and he accompanied her on her trip to Mexico— as her publicity agent.

On September 12, 1966 Judy sought an annulment of her marriage to Herron, claiming that it had never been consummated. The annulment was not granted.

After her engagement in Mexico City, Judy was professionally inactive until March of 1967. During this time she rested at home. In December of 1966 she traveled east with Tom Green to spend the holidays with his family.

13

Although Judy was professionally inactive for quite a few months after the Mexican fiasco, she definitely did not keep herself under wraps.

She and Tom Green were dating steadily and were seen out often in the Los Angeles area.

Around this time, Janet Leigh and her husband Bob Brandt gave a party for Patricia Kennedy Lawford, then just divorced from Peter Lawford.

Judy, being a friend of both Mrs. Lawford and Mrs. Brandt, was invited. She attended with Tom and mingled with the other guests wandering around the Brandt mansion. Among them were Dean Martin, Steve McQueen, Ann Sothern, and Carol Channing.

Somehow, Judy felt that Pat Lawford was being a bit aloof and remarked, "What the hell is she so snippy about?" As the evening wore on, Judy became more and more bored and more aggravated at Mrs. Lawford's supposed "snippiness." Finally, she gracefully glided over to Pat's side and as she stood there, looking beautiful in pink sequins from head to toe, asked, "Is it true you've gone Republican?" Then, to complete the effect, she poured her ice cold vodka and tonic down the back of Pat's white lace original! She followed this by gracefully sweeping into the house and locking herself in the bathroom. Because she stayed in there quite a while, everyone began to worry that perhaps something disastrous was happening. (Many of Judy's rumored suicide attempts had taken place in bathrooms.) Meanwhile, she was thoroughly enjoying herself knowing that everyone was probably getting ulcers. She finally descended the stairs looking more beautiful and "ever-so-composed" and claimed that she had gotten interested in an issue of *Redbook* that she had found lying around. As she passed Dean Martin, he howled: "Don't forget to mark this date on your calendar, baby. We're gonna make it an annual affair. Not often you get to a great party like this one!" She had brightened up the party for a lot of people—and dampened it a bit for her good friend Pat Kennedy Lawford!

Another party Judy attended around the same time was one given by Sharman Douglas for Princess Margaret and Lord Snowden. Another guest was actress-singer Polly Bergen. Miss Bergen was the wife of Judy's former agent and manager, Freddie Fields, and Judy, for some reason, had never been very fond of her.

At the party, Miss Bergen was called upon to sing. I won't go into the details of what happened, but I will tell you that Judy swore it had been an accident that her high heel got caught in Miss Bergen's microphone wire and unplugged her in the middle of a song!

A little later, one of Miss Douglas's aides told Judy that the Princess desired her to sing. Judy snapped back: "Go and tell that nasty, rude little Princess that we've known each other long enough and gabbed in enough ladies rooms that she should skip that Royal routine and pop on over here and ask me herself. Tell her I'll sing if she christens a ship first!" Judy did sing before the party was over—but on her own terms. She had no time for snobbery, class-consciousness, or "one-upmanship."

Now, before I end this little session of Garland stories, I have one more to tell.

Cardinal Cushing of Boston was sponsoring his annual benefit for crippled and retarded children. Also involved was the late President's sister, Eunice Kennedy Shriver. Judy was asked to attend and entertain, and this being her favorite cause, did so gladly.

Well, she arrived early (which almost put everyone in shock) and joined the others waiting for the Cardinal. His Eminence finally arrived very late and gave a brief speech about the need for funds for this charity and his work in the parish. Then, passing by some fifty crippled children attending the rally, he returned to his air-conditioned car.

The money hadn't exactly been pouring in that afternoon and it was left to Judy, the last to perform, to build up the take.

She burst into a rendition of "Over the Rainbow" that sounded, as Tom Green later wrote, "as though God had blessed her vocal chords." The audience burst into applause and the children's faces lit up as they watched the love pour from Judy. Following this she went to each and every retarded or crippled girl and boy and chatted with, hugged, or kissed all of them.

Few entertainers of Judy's caliber or standing would have taken the time to speak to fifty retarded children who really couldn't do anything to help her career. Not a word of this appeared in the press.

In March of 1967, Liza and Peter Allen were married in New York. Guests at the small wedding included Tony Bennett, Walter Wanger, Phil Silvers, Polly Bergen, and Marissa Pavan. Naturally, both Liza's parents were present, as were Lorna and Joe. Judy looked extremely attractive in a yellow dress and a shimmering yellow and green striped coat. The outfit was of her own design.

While in New York, Judy appeared as the mystery guest on "What's My Line" and she also announced at a very large press conference that she had signed with Twentieth Century–Fox to appear as Helen Lawson in the film version of *Valley of the Dolls*. She mentioned her role in the film on "What's My Line" and said defiantly, "And I'm the only one in the book that *doesn't* take pills!" During her week in New York Judy gave many interviews. During one of them she said:

> If I'm such a legend, then why do I sit at home for hours staring at the damned telephone, hoping it's out of order? Let me tell you, legends are all very well if you've got somebody around who loves you, some man who's not afraid to be in love with Judy Garland!
>
> I mean I'm not in the munitions business! Why should I always be rejected? All right, so I'm Judy Garland. But I've been Judy Garland forever. Luft always knew this, and Minnelli knew it, and Mark Herron knew it, although Herron married me strictly for business reasons, for purposes of his own. He was not kind to me.
>
> But I bear them no malice. Sid Luft turned out to be a very nice man, and Vincente is also very nice. They've given me beautiful, talented children. I haven't made out so badly . . .
>
> [Speaking of her role in *Valley of the Dolls*]:
>
> So, I'm cast in the part of an older woman. Well I am an older woman. I'm not an ancient woman but I can't go on being Dorothy for the rest of my life, now can I? Besides, there are bills to be paid, groceries to be bought and children to feed. I'm delighted to be in "Valley of the Dolls," although my slanderous press already has me walking off the set! Mind you, the set hasn't even been built, but already they have me walking off it!
>
> It's this kind of ugly slander that keeps me out of work.

In no time, things were confused again. Judy recorded her one song for the movie, "I'll Plant My Own Tree," and was reported to be in very good voice. (I have a tape and can attest to the fact that she was.) Travilla designed some beautiful outfits for her to wear in the film. Judy appeared on the set on time and went through with two days of filming. The scene she was filming was one in which Patty Duke was to tear off Judy's wig and destroy it. Those on the set said that Judy had been agreeable and friendly.

Then, before anyone could tell what had happened, the cast was being informed that Judy was no longer in the film. The press said that Judy had walked out. Judy said that she had been fired. No one could get the truth out of anyone. Every story heard was different from the last. Not long ago, Tom Green reported that when Judy had seen the late Sharon Tate filming a nude scene for the film, she decided that she no longer wanted to be in it. She'd never made a movie like this one before. Before her death Judy did agree that the whole thing was "sort of a mutual agreement."

On April 11, 1967 Judy was granted a divorce from Mark Herron. She claimed that Mark drank excessively and that he had beaten and kicked her. When asked if he did indeed hit her, Herron replied, "I only hit her in self defense." "Self defense?!" shot back Judy, "Look at me, I'm only a little woman." At the same time she finally got around to having her stage name, Judy Garland, made her legal name. Up to that time she was Frances Ethel Gumm Rose Minnelli Luft Herron!

While in New York the month before, Judy had been interviewed by Barbara Walters for the "Today" show and around this time the interview was televised. In it Judy exclaimed:

> I'm sick and tired of being called "poor Judy Garland." Maybe this will distress a lot of people but I've got an awfully nice life, I really have. I like to laugh, I like to have a bag of popcorn, go on a roller-coaster now and then. I wouldn't have been able to learn a song if I'd been as sick as they've printed me all the time.

When asked what things made her happiest, Judy replied:

> Well, first of all, my two friends here [Lorna and Joe], myself, my oldest daughter, my son-in-law, my future, my past, and my audiences! And that ain't bad!

On May 7, 1967 Judy taped an appearance on a Jack Paar special entitled, "A Funny Thing Happened on the Way to Hollywood." I was present at the taping and I must honestly say that the final version of the show did not show Judy to her best advantage. It's true that she wasn't at her best that night, but her anecdotes and stories were so cut up in the final version that when viewed on television they seemed incoherent and didn't make much sense. At one point we even saw Jack Paar take off a pair of glasses that he had never had on! Judy didn't sing because of a dispute she was having with the musicians' union over payment that she owed a drummer. The show was certainly not well received by the press, except for Earl Wilson, who loyally exclaimed: "Judy Garland staged one more truly brilliant comeback last night . . . "

On June 1, Judy and Tom Green announced that they would be married sometime in August. That same month Judy signed to do three weeks of concerts. The first week was at the Westbury Music Fair. She opened on June 13. I quote here, in part, Jerry Talmer's review, which appeared in the *New York Post:*

. . . and then she did her third number, "Almost Like Being in Love." Second chorus, she waited, leaned back, hit it, let it ride, it was all there, it mounted, sailed. There were those listening who were torn with shudders, with tears, but mostly there were hundreds and hundreds on their feet, shouting—shouting love—the place was in an uproar.*

Twice during the week at Westbury Music Fair, Judy's voice gave her trouble. One night she was almost totally without a voice, but she went on with the show—determined that she wasn't going to have anyone acuse her of missing her performances. Generally, though, the week was successful. The headline in the *New York Times* read: "The Old Garland Throb Still Thrills the Faithful." Radie Harris reported in the *Hollywood Reporter:* "She never looked or sounded better."

Judy's week at the Storrowtown Music Fair (in Massachusetts) went even better. She had no voice trouble and the reviews were all good.

On July 10, Garland opened at the Camden County Music Fair in Haddonfield, New Jersey (fifteen minutes from Philadelphia). The *Philadelphia Inquirer*'s headlines reported: "Judy Garland Given Standing Ovation." The *Philadelphia Bulletin* said: "Judy Isn't Over the Rainbow Yet," and Charles Petzold of the *Camden Courier Post* said: "Judy's voice didn't crack once." All week long, Judy's shows were greeted by thunder along with thunderous applause. I attended the entire week of shows.

On July 14, it was announced that Judy would open at the Palace Theatre on July 31 and that her two youngest children would be joining her in her show there. The children had been appearing onstage with Judy in her tent concerts.

The first four of Judy's concerts in Haddonfield went smoothly. She received a standing ovation every night, even before singing, and an evening didn't go by when she didn't receive at least three more.

The fifth show, however, on Friday night, was a different story. Following the overture, Garland came out and again got an ovation before singing her first note. She immediately went into "I Feel a Song Comin' On" and although it didn't sound as good as the night before, no one would have noticed anything unless they had seen the previous shows. After finishing the song Judy announced, "I have great news for all of you tonight—I have no voice at all." She went on with the show and sang "Almost Like Being in Love," "This Can't Be Love," and "Just in Time." Then Lorna did two songs and Joey did a drum solo. Following this Judy and the two kids sang "Together." Then Judy asked if anyone in the audience would like to come up and sing. Two young men went onstage and each sang a song—during this time about thirty or forty people left the theatre. Judy noticed them but tried not to show how much it bothered her. Meanwhile, I sat there, amazed at the ignorance of those who

*Reprinted by permission of the *New York Post*. © 1967, New York Post Corporation.

left. Finally, Judy sang "Old Man River" and continued to give an enjoyable performance. She followed this with "That's Entertainment." Next came "San Francisco" and "Rockabye Your Baby." In both of these songs it was more than obvious that Judy was having voice problems. There were times when nothing would come out. At these times she would jokingly slap herself on the back and utter things like "Come on voice . . . come out dammit!" Nevertheless, she saved what power she did have and was able to finish both songs with something like the old Garland zing. The audience encouraged and applauded her. Lorna came on again and the two of them sang "Chicago." In this Judy suddenly sounded good again. Finally, "Rainbow" time was here. Judy sat cross-legged on the floor and began to talk-sing "Over the Rainbow." Suddenly, in the middle of the song, during a musical interlude, she put her head down and began to sob. She had trouble coming in on cue but finished the song in a burst of tears and wild applause.

After shaking about twenty hands she ran up the aisle that led to her dressing room but as she reached the fifth row and stood next to my seat, she turned to one of her entourage and said, "I can't leave them like this, I have to go back to them." She did go back onstage, and although she didn't sing anymore, she shook hands with hundreds of people. Backstage, she told a friend that she felt she had let her audience down.

The following night, all went well. My cousin, John, then seven years old, was at the show with me and he will certainly never forget that evening. At the end of the concert, he was standing in the aisle that led to Judy's dressing room and as she walked up it, shaking hands on all sides, she noticed him staring at her, with his mouth wide open. He couldn't believe he was so close to her. "Oh you little darling, you," she exclaimed, pinching his cheeks. Then, she disappeared behind the red curtains and her week at Camden County Music Fair was over.

Soon, pre-Palace interviews and rehearsals began. Before we knew it, it was her opening night and the *New York Daily News* was proclaiming:

Judy Soars as the Palace Roars

As any New York cabbie can tell you, Judy Garland has had her ups and downs in recent years. But what the cabbie and everyone else ought to know is that right now Judy is up—way up.

Judy opened a four week run at the Palace Theatre last night and one thing that came through, despite the audience's constant roar of adulation, is that she is as great a performer as they think she is. Her fans were out in force, crowding the sidewalk in front of the theatre and inside the house, wildly applauding at the mere suggestion of a song or at the first bars of overture played by the orchestra.

She looked slim, lovely, and vibrant, as she made a grand entrance down the aisle to the stage from the rear of the house. Her copper colored, multi-jeweled, mod slack suit sparkled in the spotlight as she stepped onto the stage and blew kisses to her friends while the hand-clapping and hoarse cheering rose in crescendo.

It seemed that she did not have to sing a note and the night was hers. But she did sing and her voice was richer, stronger, and truer than ever. And time, instead of taking its toll as they say, has given an even greater authority to her stage presence and a more dramatic quality to her vocal control.

The show is called "Judy Garland, at Home at the Palace" and she and her director, Richard Barstow, succeeded in maintaining a very informal atmosphere on a bare stage against a deep red backdrop. Only a spotlight was used for mood and this was used with restraint . . .*

The entire run at the Palace was a success. Everyone loved Judy— every review had something good to say. ABC Paramount released an album recorded on Judy's first three nights at the Palace. I was in the audience on Judy's closing night. The entire crowd sang "Auld Lang Syne" to her. This was not, however, until she had sung "Over the Rainbow." She added a special touch this time, though. In between the final verses she spoke to the audience. It went like this:

> Birds fly over the rainbow,
> Why then, oh why, can't I
> I don't think I have to ask that question anymore. I think I've made
>   it.
> If happy little bluebirds fly . . .
> I'll be back, come back and see me soon!
> Beyond the rainbow . . .
> I made it!
> Why, oh why, can't I?

The reaction of the audience was fantastic and touching. After a brief moment of silence they burst into wild, hysterical applause. We called her back for thirteen curtain calls and applauded her for over twenty minutes. Finally, after we had sung "Auld Lang Syne" to her, a tearful Judy told us: "You can't image what you've done for me tonight. This is very touching." The night was over but the melody will linger forever in the hearts and minds of some 2,000 people.

When Judy's Palace album was released in New York, a record store received a phone call from a woman who wanted to know if they had the album. They told her that they did and she asked if they would hold a copy for her. She gave her name as Mrs. Mark Herron. They replied that she could pick the album up any time.

A few hours later a very tiny woman, wearing a very large hat, walked up to the sales desk at the store and said she had a record being held for

*Reprinted by permission of the *New York Daily News*.

207

her. The clerk asked her name and she replied, "Mrs. Mark Herron." He went for the album and then, handing it to her, realized just who he was actually talking to. "Oh Miss Garland, you must let us *give* you this album. We couldn't possibly let you pay for it." "Oh no," Judy said, "For every album I sell I get residuals!" "But please," he begged, and begged, *and begged*. Still, a stubborn Judy refused to allow him to give it to her. Then, she thought of something! "You know what you could give me," she quipped, "a new copy of my Carnegie Hall album—mine is worn out!" Needless to say—she got the album.

On August 31, 1967 Judy did a free concert on the Boston Common. In attendance were 108,000 people! I'd like to point something out now. Barbra Streisand did a free concert in Central Park. New York has a population of 8,000,000 and Streisand got an attendance of 125,000. Boston, however, has a population of only 800,000, and with Judy getting 108,000 she pulled in one-eighth of the entire population, compared with Barbra's one-sixty-forth in New York! At one point in Judy's show the entire audience sang, "Hello Judy, well hello Judy, it's so nice to have you here where you belong . . ." The *Boston Globe* ran two headlines: "Boston Goes Big for Judy" and "Familiar Blockbuster Magic—Uncommonly Delightful."

While in Boston, Judy visited a veterans' hospital in the area. She went through the wards and "left patients with a song, a smile and a kiss." The *Boston Globe* of September 2 reported:

> The 44 year old singer planned to visit Michael J. Pallamary, a patient recovering from a hip injury. Pallamary's wife, Nancy, had worked with Miss Garland at the Palace years ago.
>
> As it turned out, she walked through several wards, talked with a few Vietnam veterans, shook hands, bussed cheeks, and sang some songs.
>
> "If we had more people like her in this country, we would have the war won in Vietnam," Pallamary said.
>
> With Francis J. McKenna of Melrose and Robert D. Fitzgerald of Dorchester, Miss Garland sang "Little Things Mean a Lot."
>
> "We got a boy down here who lost his arm in Vietnam," a hospital spokesman whispered to her.
>
> "I'd like to see him very much," she said softly.
>
> Albert Dionne of Dover, New Hampshire, lost his left arm and left eye in Phuc Vinh when he tried to toss back a hand grenade that had landed in his foxhole.
>
> "How is it over there, pretty grim?" asked Judy.
>
> "It wasn't so bad," replied Dionne.
>
> When photographers asked Miss Garland to kiss Dionne she replied, "ask the gentleman, please."
>
> He smiled. She kissed him.
>
> "Don't go back to the war," she warned him.

She returned to Pallamary's room to sing a song. "What do you want me to sing?" she asked.

"Over the Rainbow," someone suggested.

"I don't remember how it goes," she joked.

After she finished the song, John Collins of Dorchester told her, "I'm a single man."

"I'm a single girl," Judy shot back, "and when you get out we'll talk about it."

Later, in the hospital recreation room, Miss Garland sang "Just in Time," "Over the Rainbow," and "Bye, Bye Blackbird" to about fifty patients who had been watching a movie.

Officials said the last performer to visit the hospital was Jimmy Durante, eight years ago.*

While in Boston Judy took the children to Paragon Park, where her picture was snapped on all the amusements!

Now Judy brought her show on tour. She visited Chicago (September 14, 15, and 16), Columbia, Maryland (September 8 and 9), Cleveland (September 19), St. Louis (September 27), Detroit (September 29), Indianapolis (October 1 and 2), Columbus, Ohio (October 8), Hartford (October 20 and 21), and South Orange, New Jersey (November 3 and 4). The reviews ranged from very good to fair. Between June 13 and November 4, Judy Garland did sixty concerts. And yet, even after her death she was still being called unreliable by the press.

On November 30, 1967 Garland opened a three-week engagement at Caesar's Palace in Las Vegas. Her reviews were excellent but she did miss one show on the occasion of Bert Lahr's death. Lahr was the Cowardly Lion in *Oz*.

Judy was onstage the following night, giving her show. As usual there was a capacity audience, and at the end of her show many of them realized why Judy had been out the night before. She dedicated "Over the Rainbow" to "My Lovely Cowardly Lion." She hadn't been engaged in any "temper games" of a super-star; she was just too overcome with grief to perform.

A few nights later, Danny Thomas was in the audience. Judy invited him onstage to sing. He obliged, asking each person in the room to pick up a match, and requesting that all the lights be turned out except a small spotlight on Judy's face and his. Then Danny sang a song to Judy, "I'll See You in My Dreams"—and on the word *light* in the last part of the song, "They will light my way tonight," a thousand people struck matches and held their flames high in the air in tribute to Judy Garland. When he was finished, Danny simply said, "What you saw, all that light, is only an infinitesimal fraction of the brightness your loveliness has brought to the world."

*Reprinted from *The Boston Globe*, September 2, 1967. © 1967 Globe Newspaper Company.

That story never made the newspapers.

On Christmas Day, Judy opened the new Madison Square Garden's Felt Forum. The building was so new that it wasn't even finished. (I'll never forget an actress friend of mine making her big exit out of our limousine into a mud puddle in front of a construction fence!) We saw her performance on December 27 and although the show was superb it was evident that Judy was not feeling well. The opening night had gotten very good reviews. The night I saw her, her foot was bothering her so much that she had to wear bedroom slippers during the second half. Besides this she was catching a cold. Judy's whole program consisted of: "Give My Regards to Broadway," "Never, Never Will I Marry," "Just in Time," "How Insensitive," "For Once in My Life," "Do Re Mi," "Positive Thinking," "What Now My Love," "Zing, Went the Strings of My Heart," "The Man I Love," "Do I Love You," "Old Man River," "Battle Hymn of the Republic," "Rockabye Your Baby," "By Myself," "I Can't Give You Anything But Love," and "Over the Rainbow." It was the longest show she had done in a very long time.

On the way home after the performance, I predicted to my family that Judy wouldn't finish the scheduled week of shows. As it turned out, she did one more show and then it was announced that she was too ill to complete the engagement.

Judy's next concert was in Baltimore and it was a real fiasco. Her voice wasn't in good shape and she appeared drugged and shaky. She explained, however, that she was suffering from food poisoning. And columnist Earl Wilson announced that everyone who had eaten in the same restaurant had come down with the illness.

One week later, Judy appeared at Lincoln Center in New York City in a successful concert which somehow didn't get reviewed at all. I have first-hand accounts of the show and have heard a tape-recording of it and Judy was in very good voice.

In April, Judy brought charges against Tom Green, accusing him of stealing $100,000 worth of her jewelry and pawning it. A pawn ticket was found with his signature on it. Naturally, the marriage was called off (Judy denied that they'd ever been engaged) and the charges were soon dropped, but it left the public with the impression that there was a lot more than was told. However, no matter what differences Judy and Tom may have had, he was an enormous help and comfort to her when she needed him.

Around this time Judy was one of the leading contenders being considered to replace Angela Lansbury in *Mame* on Broadway. She had been considered for the role before Miss Lansbury was initially signed and was now very glad at the chance to "try again." She often stated that Jerry Herman's score for *Mame* was one of her special favorites (whereas his score from *Hello Dolly* was one of her least favorites). As the selection narrowed down to just Judy and a couple of other possibilities, she realized that at this point in her career there wasn't anything she wanted more than to star in this show. When Janis Paige was signed she was heartbroken. Friends cheered her up that night by taking her to see Liza, who was then appearing in New York with her fantastically successful nightclub act. She joined Liza onstage for a duet and seemed to be feeling very much better by the end of the evening. It has been said that the most important of the few reasons preventing Judy's getting the role of Mame was the fact that she refused to work matinees. She was afraid that doing the two or three matinees a week would drain her energy supply too much. Until her death, however, there were many rumors that she was *the* actress wanted most for the motion picture version (which, of course, has now been filmed starring Judy's good friend Lucille Ball).

On May 18, 1968 Earl Wilson reported that Judy had been evicted from the St. Moritz Hotel because of an unpaid bill of $1,800. She wasn't allowed back in and her belongings weren't allowed out. Judy claimed that because her costumes and orchestrations were locked up in the hotel she couldn't fulfill her contract to do two concerts at Boston's Back Bay Theatre.

Judy did do the first of the two concerts in Boston though, and she received very good reviews. She canceled the second show.

In June of 1968 Judy appeared on "The Johnny Carson Show" for the first time. The next week she opened at the Garden State Arts Center in Holmdel, New Jersey. I have only seen one review of this show and although it was favorable it was too insubstantial to quote from. It did, however, state that Judy was in good voice.

Judy collapsed onstage before completing her week of concerts. She was taken immediately to the Peter Brent Brigham Hospital in Boston.

Soon it was announced that Judy Garland would fulfill her concert commitment at the John F. Kennedy Stadium in Philadelphia. The show was set to take place on June 19.

Judy came to Philadelphia a week early and gave a large press conference. She looked good and was in good spirits. She said that she felt fine and was ready to perform. When asked what she had thought of the book *The Valley of the Dolls*, she said that it had been too boring and she hadn't finished reading it.

It rained on June 19, and the concert had to be called off because Kennedy Stadium is an outdoor stadium. The show was scheduled for the next evening.

I was in attendance that night, at what turned out to be one of the greatest concerts of Judy's whole career. Her voice was better than it had been for five years and she played to an audience of many thousands. Count Basie was also on the bill and she and the Count teamed up on "Strike Up the Band" and "The Sweetest Sounds." I can't possibly describe the greatness of Garland that night. Although she didn't know it then, that was the last concert she was ever to do in America. Incidentally, her first

211

American concert, the show in Philadelphia at the Robin Hood Dell, was in July of 1943—exactly twenty-five years before her show at Kennedy Stadium. The Philadelphia papers gave her unbelievably fantastic reviews. For example, the *Camden Courier Post* of June 21 reported:

> Judy Garland came to John F. Kennedy Stadium Saturday night and nearly started a riot.
>
> In her usual perverse manner, she proved every one of last week's newspaper interviewers right—she is indeed "alive and well in Philadelphia" as one of them put it—and full of all those vitamins and that energy she was talking about.
>
> Backed up by Count Basie's orchestra, plus an additional string section, she came on strong in her first number, "For Once in My Life." Her second song, "Almost Like Being in Love," was shaky, but her belting power stayed with her.
>
> And from that point on she had the audience with her too. Her musical highpoints had them on their feet screaming and her mistakes didn't seem to matter.
>
> She was best when she let out full blast with that famous voice in songs like "By Myself," "The Man That Got Away," and "What Now My Love."
>
> A newer number for her, "How Insensitive" was well done but failed to be "intimate" as she had hoped for. But then, how intimate can you be in a football stadium with over 20,000 people?
>
> By the time she was halfway through the show, she had the audience cheering at the end of each number, laughing at a few spontaneous wisecracks now and then, applauding through a medley with Count Basie at the piano and clapping in time with "Rockabye Your Baby."
>
> A bouquet plops on stage from out of nowhere. Then she drops the final clincher to make the whole show complete, "Over the Rainbow."
>
> "If happy little bluebirds fly, beyond the rainbow, why—I made it, I made it—why, oh why—thank you darlings, I made it all the way through, I didn't think I would—oh why, can't I."

Now here is an example of the way Judy was so often misquoted. She did not say those things during "Over the Rainbow." What she said was: "I finally made it over the rainbow thanks to all of you." Then she continued with the song, then she yelled, "We can all do it, you know." Then another phrase of the song, and finally, "Thank you. God bless you." And then, the end.

As usual, her words were twisted to show a totally insecure, neurotic woman. Why weren't her own words good enough?

While in Philadelphia Judy made an appearance on "The Mike Douglas Show." Her old friend Peter Lawford was also on the show and it was definitely one of Judy's best television appearances. But it did take some coaxing to get her on. Mike Douglas later told columnist Charles Petzold of the *Philadelphia Daily News:*

> We never hold the show for anyone, but we did for her. She was up in her dressing room giving them some kind of trouble and we held the show for over one hour. Finally, I went to her dressing room, knocked on the door and said, "Judy, we can't wait any longer. I'm going to start the show now. When I introduce you and say 'Here she is' I know you'll be there." And she was.
> Judy has it all. She had the audience in the palm of her hand. People talk about someone getting a standing ovation, but she's the only one who gets a standing ovation when they play the overture. It's incredible.

Her voice was simply beautiful as she sang "For Once in My Life," "How Insensitive," and "Over the Rainbow."

Except for modeling for a fur ad in the fall and an appearance at a tribute to Harold Arlen, Judy was inactive until December.

Then, in quick succession, she appeared on "The Dick Cavett Show," "The Johnny Carson Show," and "The Merv Griffin Show." For these performances, Judy sang four new songs written especially for her by Johnny Meyer. Her voice wasn't very good on the first show, but it kept improving. After her first appearance on the Griffin show, Merv announced that she would host one of his shows while he was on vacation. She did host it and did remarkably well—she was a gracious and surprisingly calm hostess. Judy also announced, following the first Griffin show, that she would soon be leaving for London to appear at the Talk of the Town nightclub and while there she would marry Mickey Deans (whose real name was Michael De Vinko). Deans had been associated with Arthur, Sybil Burton's New York nightclub.

Although not in her best form vocally on "The Dick Cavett Show," Judy's wit (she was known as Hollywood's wittiest woman) was as sharp as a razor's edge. At one point, Mr. Cavett turned to her and began "I have some questions . . ." Judy, expecting the standard living legend question broke in asking Cavett, "What's it like to be a living legend?" Even the brilliant, seldom-flustered Cavett was caught off guard. "At this moment, rotten!" was his reply as he broke up with laughter. Needless to say, Judy thoroughly enjoyed her joke. A little later, Mr. Cavett mentioned that Lee Marvin, another guest on the show that morning, had been a little late. "Good," exclaimed Judy. "I'm glad it wasn't me for a change!" The audience loved it. Mr. Marvin remarked to Judy, "Anytime you arrive—it's early."

When Judy arrived in London, she found that she couldn't marry Deans yet as she hadn't received her divorce papers from Herron.

213

She opened on schedule at the Talk of the Town and received generally good reviews. Then, one night she was late for a performance. The audience became very rowdy (she had given them an extra hour to imbibe) and when she appeared onstage they threw things at her (bread, rolls, crushed cigarette cartons, etc.). She tried to go on with the show until a man climbed onto the stage and started to shake her. She walked off.

She returned three nights later and got a very good reception. She completed the engagement without further misfortune. Contrary to what was reported in the press, Judy did not announce that she and Mickey had been married.

In March Judy and Mickey Deans were married at the Chelsea Registry Office with singer Johnnie Ray as their best man. After the ceremony they drove to the church of a friend of theirs, the Reverend Peter Delaney, and he blessed their marriage. The list of celebrities invited included Ginger Rogers, Bette Davis, Veronica Lake, James Mason, John Gielgud, Peter Finch, Albert Finney, Laurence Harvey, and Eva Gabor. None of them showed up.

Judy and Mickey rented a small house in London and set up a life for themselves there. They made many new friends and were known simply as Mr. and Mrs. Deans. Judy began seeing doctors to see if it would be possible to have a baby.

Soon, she and Johnnie Ray went on a short concert tour of Scandinavia. Judy's portion of the show garnered generally good reviews. The following is a review of her concert in Copenhagen on March 25, 1969:

> We found her last evening to be an enchanting entertainer, an exquisite artist in her field. Her confidence, her well-planned effects, reveal a skillful competency; added to this is the radiant personality so uniquely hers.
>
> . . . so there she stood, youthful against the large stage, slim as a boy, with a boy's long, thin arms—in constant movement. There was something infinitely fragile about her—almost touching in the first few minutes, as she with a type of curtsey advanced to the center of the stage and at once began "Get Happy."
>
> Clear, thin tones but compelling; they grow warmer and suddenly, the full tones pour forth . . . and out of this delicate little body emerges a surprising sound, surprising in its strength, in its power to fill the spacious hall . . .
>
> She left about 10 o'clock but as the thundering applause continued, came back in again. She seemed greatly amused by the Danish specialty of clapping in time . . . she sank to the floor and then sang "Over the Rainbow."
>
> A star was not only born, but reborn before our eyes. A star with a personal sweetness, with a style distinctly her own that allows her to shift from the somewhat surprising boyish expression to a convincing —and strongly erotic—femininity. Our experience with Judy Garland

served to reinforce the fact that she is one of the truly great in show business. She became a captivating experience—face-to-face.

While on the Scandinavian tour, Judy filmed a documentary television special entitled "A Day in the Life of Judy Garland." After Judy's death the special was telecast on Swedish television, under the new title of *"The Last Performance."* Critical response was unenthusiastic to say the least.

In London, Judy made an appearance on "Sunday Night at the Palladium" (replacing Lena Horne, who was ill) and sang three songs in a very good voice.

All in all, though she was not exceedingly busy with her career, Judy and Mickey seemed happy as they continued building a new life for themselves in England.

In late May Judy returned to America for what was to be a week but ended up three. It was a business trip, according to news releases, and Judy was seen around town eating lunch with old friends. Then, in June, she and Mickey returned to their new home in London.

14

On June 21, 1969 Judy and Mickey Deans were planning to go out to the theatre, but Mickey was coming down with a sore throat, so they decided to stay home and watch television. Sometime that evening, a friend of theirs, Philippe Roberge, stopped by and they watched a television documentary about the Royal Family together. Roberge left shortly after eleven and Judy decided that she wanted to go out for a drive. She was home by midnight.

The night before, Judy and Mickey had been guests at the home of the Reverend Peter Delaney. While there, Judy had her palms read by another guest. She was told, "You are about to find something you've been searching for for a long time." "I already have," she replied, pointing to Mickey. Gina Dangerfield was also at Delaney's that night and she later remarked that Judy was "cracking jokes and having a good time throughout the evening."

When Judy returned from her late-evening drive on the night of June 21, she still seemed to be in good spirits. She and Deans decided to go to bed. Mickey later told the press:

> When we went to bed, I wondered whether I should sleep in the same bed or not, with my sore throat. She pointed at her throat and I said: "Are you coming down with it now?" She put her feet up against me to keep warm as she always did, and went to sleep.

At about 11:00 A.M. (London Time) a long distance call came in for Judy from the United States. Mickey answered the phone. He turned to awaken Judy and found that she wasn't in bed.

He called her, but received no answer. He went to the bathroom door and found it locked. He called again but still didn't receive a reply. "It was good last night," he called, "What's the matter this morning?"

217

Not hearing any response, he looked over the wall of a dressing room that was being built. There, on the floor of the bathroom, was the body of Judy Garland, slumped over. She was pronounced dead by a doctor.

The news hit the American public early Sunday morning. The cause of death was "undetermined" but an autopsy was set for early in the week.

Sunday, at the same time that the media were reporting the news of Judy Garland's death they were reporting that tornados ("twisters") had hit Kansas late the night before. These tornados had, in fact, hit Kansas around the time Judy Garland was dying in London. And it had been in Kansas, some thirty years before, that tornados had first whisked Judy away to the land of super-stardom and super-sorrow.

There was still no decision after the autopsy but there were signs that death could have been caused by an accidental overdose of barbituates. Suicide was ruled out.

Meanwhile, here in America, Judy's family had been told of the news and her oldest daughter, Liza, was taking care of funeral arrangements. Liza Minnelli Allen released the following statement:

> It wasn't suicide, it wasn't sleeping pills, it wasn't cirrhosis. I think she was just tired, like a flower that blooms and gives joy and beauty to the world and then wilts away. I just want to send her off as she would have wanted to go . . . bright and lovely.
>
> My mother had that wild impatient streak to live. She loved Mickey. She was so happy with Mickey, she didn't want to work anymore, she just wanted to be with him. And I wish you would mention the joy she had for life. That's what she gave me. If she was the tragic figure they said she was, I would be a wreck, wouldn't I?
>
> It was her love of life that carried her through everything. The middle of the road was never for her. It bored her. She wanted the pinnacle of excitement. If she was happy she wasn't just happy, she was ecstatic. And when she was sad she was sadder than anyone.
>
> She had lived eight lives in one. And yet I thought she would outlive us all. She was a great talent and for the rest of my life I will be proud to be Judy Garland's daughter. She always told me I was living proof that she was a good woman and I intend to live up to that.

Judy's two younger children, Lorna and Joe, were staying in California with their father during Judy's travels in Europe. When told of their mother's death, they issued the following statement:

> The only thing that really comforts us now is the thought that nothing can destroy our love or disturb the legend that she created. To us that always was and always will remain a beautiful thing.

Liza announced that her mother's body would arrive in the States on Wednesday night but she would not disclose the arrival time. She also

218

announced that there would be a public viewing and that the casket would be open but enclosed in glass.

Judy had requested in her will that her former makeup man, Gene Hibbs, be permitted to perform the same service at her death. But the request went unfulfilled. Liza called Hibbs in Hollywood on Tuesday and begged him to come to New York to help prepare Judy's body. He told the press:

> I made Judy up for all her television shows. I would like to fly back to New York to put her final make-up on her, but that's impossible.

At the time Hibbs was working on the television series "Green Acres," doing Eva Gabor's makeup. A spokesman for the show said that it would cost $30,000 in lost time if Hibbs were to fly to New York. Producer Otto Preminger, a friend of Judy's and Liza's, called from New York in an effort convince the series producer to let Hibbs come but the answer was an absolute no.

By Wednesday, some of the greatest names in the business were making statements. One of the first to be heard from was Ray Bolger, who had appeared in *The Wizard of Oz* as the Scarecrow:

> I thought she was a dumpy little kid when she first walked on the set that day. The movie took nearly a year to make and we became almost a family, Judy, Bert Lahr, Jack Haley and me. When the kleig lights shone on her she was marked by a total lack of inhibition and an amazing intensity. She never had a minute to herself. I suppose MGM executives loved her and they adored her but she was still a commodity to them. She never had a childhood, never had a puberty. She went from child to marked woman in one shocking overnight experience. I last saw Judy when I was playing at the Waldorf. We had a Judy Garland tribute and I came on stage and said to her: "Tonight, the scarecrow comes to life for you again." I thought that maybe she didn't have very long to live.

Composer Jule Styne said:

> She was one of the great singing talents of all time, a forerunner of every young girl singer in the country. Most of them wanted to be like Judy, but they couldn't make it. It wasn't destined for them.

George Schlatter (producer of her CBS television series) said:

> I had a constant fight with CBS television because they wanted her to do a regular weekly series and look like "just folks" when she wasn't that. Judy, to me, was always bigger than life. Living up to that image

219

required an adjustment very few of us could make. It must have been very difficult for her.

Margaret Hamilton, the Wicked Witch, had this to say:

I did only one movie with Judy and found her delightful to work with. I feel very badly about what happened.

The director of *A Star Is Born*, George Cukor, stated:

Judy was obviously a very talented woman, but many people missed the great essence of Judy—which was that she was an extremely intelligent person. But all her wit and all her intelligence couldn't save her.

Television star Carol Burnett was deeply saddened. She made the following comment:

God bless her. I haven't felt like this since Marilyn Monroe died. There was just something she gave of herself. Who couldn't have loved her? Naturally I'm shocked. I knew Judy but I never worked with her.

Mark Robson, director of *Valley of the Dolls*, said:

She was certainly a great performer, one of the truly talented people of our time. We're all saddened by the tragic ending to a great career.

The fact that Hollywood and the entertainment world in general were saddened by the death of their Queen was shown many times in the weeks that immediately followed Judy's death. Many kind things were said about Judy, things that should have been said much earlier. I myself contacted over 200 of Judy's friends and associates but received replies from only a few. Gregory Peck wrote:

Judy always seemed tragic to me. She was scarred somehow early in life. She fought off her depression as long as she could by singing and dancing and pretending. She was gallant and she was one of a kind.

Janet Leigh's reply was most welcome. The blonde star of *Bye Bye Birdie*, *Psycho*, and *My Sister Eileen* wrote:

I would very much like to give a statement about Judy Garland.
Whenever I saw Judy Garland perform it was a special part of my life. She made me laugh, cry and feel. You're right, there will never be another Judy Garland.

I had written to Johnny Carson, asking for a statement, but instead received a letter which started:

> Dear Tonight Viewer:
> Thank you for your interest in the Tonight Show . . .

Louisette Levy-Soussan, secretary to Princess Grace of Monaco, wrote:

> The Princess feels it difficult to write a statement about Judy Garland, having only met her on two occasions, and therefore not knowing her very well.
> Her Highness certainly admired her talent in many films and she enjoyed her stage performances. Her untimely death, which brought to an end a successful career, was deeply regrettable.

I received a hand-written note from Betty Grable, which read:

> Judy Garland, to me, was not only a legend, but a beautiful warm lady. I shall miss her, along with her multitude of fans.

Douglas Fairbanks, Jr. wrote from London:

> There have been so many wonderful things said about Miss Judy Garland that I doubt if my own vocabulary would be able to successfully compete with the tributes paid to her. In any case, I was a great admirer of her incomparable gifts. I had known her since she was a child and just beginning her career, and would only wish to associate myself with her most fervent admirers, with whom I also share a profound sense of loss at her untimely passing.

John Cassavetes, director of *A Child Is Waiting*, found time for this reply:

> It would really be silly for me to comment about Miss Garland because I don't really know her. As an audience I'm a member of her vast admiration society and I thought she had the potential to be a really great actress. It's a pity and a shame she had such a short life.

I was extremely grateful for the following letter from Barbara Walters of the "Today" show:

> I remember that when I went to interview Judy Garland at her hotel in New York, she kept the film crew and me waiting for three hours. She knew about the appointment, but she was not able to pull herself together. Had it not been for the fact that I was such a fan of hers, I am sure I would have left.

221

But when she finally asked me into her very messy bedroom, and I found her there—frail and wearing a dress belonging to her fourteen year old daughter—I forgot the three hour wait . . . not just because I was touched by her but because she was so funny and warm and really delightful to be with. Her children were with her, and her love for them and theirs for her was a happy thing to see.

I liked Judy Garland. Her neuroses were hard to take, but her personality, when you were with her, made you forget all the faults.

Johnny Mercer, who has scored some of the greatest motion picture musicals of all time, including *Darling Lili* and *The Harvey Girls*, found the time to reply, even though he was very busy:

> I was a big fan of Judy's . . . loved her as many others did . . . but I'll be away for the summer, so perhaps you might try me again in the autumn when hopefully I'll be back in Los Angeles. Thanks for asking me. She was dear to me and was responsible for some of my big songs.

John Bubbles, the dancer and comedian who starred in *Porgy and Bess*, took the chance to reminisce about his days with Judy at the Palace:

> In regards to my most happy relations with Judy Garland, and the most pleasing artist that I had ever found such a pleasure for working with, and during our rehearsals for Judy at the Met, in 1959 with all the cast which was about six girls and six boys, also the stage director Richard Barstow, and his sister and Alan King, what fun we had, Miss Garland and I did two numbers together, "Shine On Your Shoes" and "Me and My Shadow." Judy was my shadow. When we were at the Palace Theatre in New York City she had two of her children, Lorna and Joey Luft working with us in the number "Me and My Shadow," I would sing the song, and go to one side of the stage, at the end of the chorus, and get Judy Garland, and she would follow behind me as my shadow, and we would do a chorus, and go to the opposite side of the stage at the end of the chorus and pick up Lorna who became the shadow of Judy Garland, and we three would do another chorus going to the other side of the stage and pick up Joey and he was the shadow of Lorna, then we all would do a dance; this number stopped the show every performance.
>
> And I am very pleased to know that I was the first negro to have worked with Judy Garland, also with her two children, and we all appreciated working together, and Liza Minnelli did a couple of shows with Judy at the Palace during our stay there. And I will never forget how wonderful she was at all times that I had the pleasure of working with her.
>
> Judy Garland was most magnetic and during my fifty years in the theatre I have never witnessed anyone to meet with such love from an audience and standing ovations. It is useless for me to wish for the return of such pleasures.

Mrs. Eunice Kennedy Shriver, sister of the late President and wife of Sargent Shriver, wrote:

> Generous. Generous. Generous. I remember her singing her heart out for three hours to a group of mentally retarded children. What could they do for her career? She did it because she had a great and generous heart.

Lastly, I must not omit the statement made to the press by one of the most important people in Judy's life, Mickey Rooney:

> I think everyone is a little late with their reactions to Judy. If they could have taken her to their hearts a little sooner she might still be alive today.
>
> It's a funny thing that people who knew she was ill over the many years couldn't come to her aid in the proper manner, but now she is —I'm sure at peace, and has found the rainbow. I'm sure she's with her father.

It was announced that Judy's body would be on view to the public from 11:00 A.M. till 10:00 P.M. on Thursday, June 26, and from 8:00 A.M. till 11:00 A.M. on Friday morning. The body was at Frank E. Campbell's Funeral Home on Madison Avenue and Eighty-first Street in New York City, where a private ceremony for family and friends would be held on Friday afternoon at 1:00.

That week, Mickey Rooney was performing at the Valley Forge Music Fair (just a ninety-minute drive from New York) in a production of *George M.* After the show he asked his audience to join him in a moment of prayer for Judy.

By 10:00 on Thursday morning there were 500 people gathered outside the funeral home. The opening was delayed (yes, Judy was late even at her viewing) until noon. When the doors were opened, there were 3,500 people waiting to see Judy Garland for the last time. And inside, in a white steel coffin, lay American show business.

By 5:00 P.M. the crowds were lined up as far back as Eighty-second Street and were beginning to stretch over to Fifth Avenue. There were 8,000 mourners waiting by then and they were entering the chapel at the rate of 1,500 an hour.

Judy was wearing her wedding band, in the French tradition, on the pinkie finger of her right hand, which rested on her left hand atop a prayer book. Around the waist of her high-necked, beige chiffon gown she wore a pearl-and-gold braided belt. On her feet were wide-buckled silver shoes.

The funeral chapel was crowded with floral pieces from such well-knowns as Fred Astaire, Myrna Loy, Tony Bennett, Otto Preminger, Ambassador and Mrs. Sargent Shriver, Prince Rainier and Princess Grace,

Frank Sinatra, Irving Berlin, Dirk Bogarde, Elizabeth Taylor and Richard Burton, and Van Johnson. There were also flowers from Tom Green and Mark Herron.

At 10:00 P.M., the time originally set for the closing of the chapel, there were still thousands of people waiting outside Campbell's, so Mickey Deans requested that the chapel remain open all night, and it did. Campbell's didn't close until 11:00 the following morning and then, only so that arrangements could be made for the private ceremony.

On Thursday, Deans issued the following statement:

> She wasn't Judy Garland to me. She was Gladys and I was George. That was what we called each other.
>
> That was the thing about our marriage, there was no star treatment. I don't know how people or husbands treated her before, but to me she was my wife and I expected her to behave as my wife and she knew it.
>
> It was beautiful and we had planned so much. We had discussed having a child and she was seeing a doctor to see if it was possible.
>
> I had Judy cutting down on sleeping pills. I said, "You don't need those damned things." That's why it came as such a shock.
>
> The most fun we had was not when Judy was doing concerts but in our little London house putting up lamps and me getting an electric shock. We were just like two eighteen year old kids starting a marriage, because she had never had it this way before. She always had servants doing everything and before it had been completely impersonal.
>
> They [Hollywood] didn't care. She was a property and they treated her as such. Everybody used her. The fans cared, but they were gone after a performance. They weren't with her. I won't allow her to be buried in Hollywood. I don't want people waking over her grave and pointing. She has given enough. If they are friends, they will come to New York.

The same day Mickey's statement was released, the outcome of the coroner's inquest was also made public.

The coroner said that Judy had died of "an incautious self-dosage of the sleeping drug Seconal." He said that the autopsy showed that Judy had been addicted to sleeping pills for years. He also made it clear that "there is absolutely no evidence that this was intentional."

Judy's doctor, John Traherne, said, "I don't think Miss Garland would have been able to sleep without Seconal."

Mickey Deans was also at the inquest. He testified: "She was not a heavy drinker in the true sense of the word. My wife drank very little as opposed to what people think. She left a lot of drinks around the house but she sipped more than she drank."

Mickey was asked why the bathroom door was locked when Judy was in the room, dead. He explained: "Judy always locked the bathroom door.

She told me this habit went back to her MGM days when she was a little girl of twelve standing in a slip with men walking all around her and she felt self-conscious."

Judy's doctor was asked if Judy's drinking habits were those of an alcoholic. The answer was an emphatic no.

On Friday, June 27, everything went along as scheduled. Mickey Rooney arrived early at the chapel but had to leave quickly—he was too overcome to remain for the services.

James Mason flew in from Switzerland to deliver the eulogy, which read:

> The thing about Judy Garland was that she was so alive. You close your eyes and you see a small vivid woman sometimes fat, sometimes thin, but vivid. Vivacity, vitality . . . that's what our Judy had, and still has as far as I'm concerned. I did not see much of her during the last ten years. Maybe I saw her sometimes when she was low or sick or not at the top of her form but it did not in the least impair the unbreakable image which remained constant—unchanged even up to and including today.
>
> Beyond the walls of this church there are millions of people in the United States, who know Judy Garland and love her; and there are millions more in other countries; and each individual cherishes his own special image. Each such image is registered firmly in a living brain; each one is alive in fact. And those images will remain alive until in turn each life is switched off and its memory fades. When the youngest of those who today love Judy is no longer alive only then will the idea of Judy as we know her, be finally rendered extinct and she will become instead a chapter in the history of show business.
>
> Those who read this chapter will wonder what she was and will ask why contemporaries raved about her and carried on so.
>
> There is a German saying which is worth quoting in this context: "Die machweltfeicht dem mimen keine kranze." Kranze means wreaths or better still, garlands, so it means: "Posterity weaves no garlands for actors."
>
> Once an actor's work is done and the memories of those who saw him or her are extinguished, no effort on the part of posterity can put him together again.
>
> It may seem ironical that some of our newspapers and magazines are prepared to devote more space to this final event than to any of Judy's achievements during her life. But let's not fret too much about that. Let us make the best of the moment and weave garlands while we may. If only for the sake of the future student of show business history who will try to make something of that chapter that survives of Judy, let us make an effort to define this lady's greatness.
>
> Fortunately, there will be many people much better equipped for the job than I. Perhaps even in this church there are those who knew Judy when she was a child performer, one of The Gumm Sisters. Tonight in Hollywood, veterans will reminisce deep into the night

about the teenage Judy in her early days at MGM. There are many here in this church, I am sure, who witnessed her spectacular rebirth as a star at The Palace Theatre in 1951. I was thrilled by the echoes that reverberated in California but I remained a witness by hearsay only. The performances. Of the people who were close to her during those and all her later triumphs and setbacks I am sure that many are here now and could give us a blow by blow account.

I travelled in her orbit only for a while but it was an exciting while and one during which it seemed that the joys in her life outbalanced the miseries. The little girl whom I knew who had a little curl right in the middle of her forehead, when she was good she was not only very, very good, she was the most sympathetic, the funniest, the sharpest and the most stimulating woman I ever knew.

She was a lady who gave so much and richly both to her vast audience whom she entertained and to the friends around her whom she loved that there was no currency in which to repay her. And she needed to be repaid, she needed devotion and love beyond the resources of any of us.

People took from her what they wanted most. Had I ever been in a position to take what I wanted from her it would have been a long program of funny funny movies since I firmly believed that she was the funniest girl in the world. But she was so touching that she was invariably in demand to do the purely emotional thing. It was this very touching quality that made her such a great comedian. In these great funny films that I dreamed of she would have developed a line of whacky comedy which would have been the more effective being played without a trace of emotion in the framework of a harrowing plot.

She had pursued this line very effectively, if briefly, during the early stages of her movie career. But the lines had been discontinued, and the hopes for its revival which I long cherished must now at last be abandoned.

I think that I have a hint for the Judy Garland student yet unborn. Her special talent was this: she could sing so that it would break your heart. What is a tough audience? A tough audience is a group of high income bracket cynics at a Hollywood party. Judy's gift then was to wring tears from men with hearts of rock.

The person who probably of all the world knew Judy best is her older daughter, Liza Minnelli. Since I do not have an ending of my own to this eulogy, I will again quote from Lisa Minelli's moving statement, which she issued after the death of her mother (see page 136):

> I wish you would mention the joy she had for life. That's what she gave me. If she was the tragic figure they said she was, I would be a wreck, wouldn't I?
> It was her love of life that carried her through everything. The middle of the road was never for her. It bored her. She

wanted the pinnacle of excitement. If she was happy she wasn't just happy. She was ecstatic. And when she was sad she was sadder than anyone.

She had lived eight lives in one. And yet I thought she would outlive us all. She was a great talent and for the rest of my life I will be proud to be Judy Garland's daughter.

In addition to Mason, others present at the funeral were Lauren Bacall, Jack Benny, Sammy Davis, Jr., Katharine Hepburn, Burt Lancaster, Dean Martin, Lana Turner, Patricia Kennedy Lawford, Spyros Skouras, Kay Thompson, Pamela Mason, Earl Wilson, Adolph Green, Betty Comden, Otto Preminger, Harold Arlen, Mayor and Mrs. John Lindsay, Ray Bolger, and Mr. and Mrs. Alan King.

The Reverend Peter Delaney, who had blessed Judy and Mickey following their marriage in London some three months earlier, closed the services by reading from I Corinthians, chapter 13, verses 1 through 13, which begins:

If I speak with the tongues of men and angels, but have not love, I am become sounding brass or a clanging cymbal. And if I have the gift of prophecy, and know all mystery and all knowledge, and if I have all faith, so as to move mountains but have not love . . .

and concludes:

Now abideth faith, hope, love, these three; and the greatest of these is love . . .

And so read this passage, which always had a special meaning for Judy. Outside the funeral home 2,000 fans were waiting to see Judy make her last journey—to Ferncliff Cemetery in Hartsdale, New York, just five minutes from where she had lived in Scarsdale in 1961. The casket made the journey covered with a bed of yellow roses, a gift from her children.

And so, as Judy Garland lay in a white metal casket, in a white marble vault, Richard Barstow, her former director, wrote: "The stars have lost their glitter."

One couldn't help but think of Judy's appearance on a New York television show the preceding Christmas, when she sang a song especially written for her. The last words were:

When life is through,
When all my days are done,
By every star above,
It's you I love,
The only one.

And let them say,
This much is true,
It was all for you,
All for you.*

And so it was.

Judy on Records

DECCA SINGLES—78's

848   "Swing Mr. Charlie"
         "Stompin' at the Savoy"
         The Bob Crosby Orchestra—*recorded June 12, 1936*

1332   "Everybody Sing"
         "When Two Love Each Other"—The Henry King Orchestra—*no vocal*
         The Georgie Stoll Orchestra—*recorded August 30, 1937*

1432   "All God's Chillun Got Rhythm"
         "Everybody Sing"
         The Georgie Stoll Orchestra—*recorded August 30, 1937*

1463   "(Dear Mr. Gable) You Made Me Love You"
         "You Can't Have Everything"
         The Harry Sosnick Orchestra—recorded September 24, 1937

1796   "Cry, Baby, Cry"
         "Sleep, My Baby, Sleep"
         The Harry Sosnick Orchestra—recorded April 24, 1938

2017   "It Never Rains But What It Pours"
         "Ten Pins in the Sky"
         The Harry Sosnick Orchestra—recorded August 21, 1938

2672   "Over the Rainbow"
         "The Jitterbug"
         The Victor Young Orchestra—recorded September 28, 1939

2881   "Embraceable You"
           "Swanee"
           The Victor Young Orchestra—recorded October 16, 1939

3165   "Friendship" (with Johnny Mercer)
           "Wearing of the Green"
           The Bobby Sherwood Orchestra—recorded April 10 & April 15, 1940

3174   "Buds Won't Bud"
           "I'm Nobody's Baby"
           The Bobby Sherwood Orchestra—recorded June 10, 1940

3231   "The End of the Rainbow"
           "The End of the Rainbow"—The Woody Herman Orchestra—no vocal
           The Bobby Sherwood Orchestra—recorded June 10, 1940

3593   "Our Love Affair"
           "I'm Always Chasing Rainbows"
           The David Rose Orchestra—recorded December 18, 1940

3604   "It's a Great Day for the Irish"
           "A Pretty Girl"
           The David Rose Orchestra—recorded December 18, 1940

4050   "The Birthday of a King"
           "Star of the East"
           The David Rose Orchestra

4072   "How About You?"
           "F. D. R. Jones"
           The David Rose Orchestra—recorded October 24, 1941

4081   "Blues in the Night"
           "The End of the Rainbow"
           The David Rose Orchestra—recorded October 24, 1941
           The Bobby Sherwood Orchestra—recorded June 10, 1940

15045   "In Between"
           "Sweet Sixteen"
           The Victor Young Orchestra

18320   "Poor You"
           "Last Call for Love"
           The David Rose Orchestra

18480   "For Me and My Gal" (with Gene Kelly)
           "When You Wore a Tulip" (with Gene Kelly)
           The David Rose Orchestra—recorded July 26, 1942

18524   "I Never Knew"
           "On the Sunny Side of the Street"
           The David Rose Orchestra

18540   "That Old Black Magic"
           "Poor Little Rich Girl"
           The David Rose Orchestra—March 3, 1942

18543   "Zing! Went the Strings of My Heart"
           "Fascinatin' Rhythm"
           The Victor Young Orchestra—recorded July 29, 1939

18484   "No Love, No Nothin' "
           "A Journey to a Star"
           The Georgie Stoll Orchestra—recorded December 22, 1943

18660   "This Heart of Mine"
           "Love"
           The Victor Young Orchestra—recorded January 26, 1945

23303   "Embraceable You"
           "Could You Use Me?" (with Mickey Rooney)
           The Georgie Stoll Orchestra—recorded November, 1943

23309   "But Not For Me"
           "Treat Me Rough"—Mickey Rooney
           The Georgie Stoll Orchestra—recorded November, 1943

23310   "Bidin' My Time"
           " I Got Rhythm"
           The Georgie Stoll Orchestra recorded November 2, 1943

23360   "Meet Me in St. Louis, Louis"
           "Skip to My Lou"
           The Georgie Stoll Orchestra—recorded April 24, 1944

23361   "The Trolley Song"
           "Boys and Girls Like You and Me"
           The Georgie Stoll Orchestra—recorded April, 1944

23362   "Have Yourself a Merry Little Christmas"
           "The Boy Next Door"
           The Georgie Stoll Orchestra—recorded April 20, 1944

23410   "Yah-Ta-Ta, Yah-Ta-Ta" (with Bing Crosby)
           "You've Got Me Where You Want Me" (with Bing Crosby)
           The Joseph Lilley Orchestra

23436   "If I Had You" (with the Merry Macs)

"On the Atchison, Topeka and the Sante Fe" (with the Merry Macs)
The Lyn Murray Orchestra—recorded May 14 and July 7, 1945

23438   "On the Atchison, Topeka and the Sante Fe"
"In the Valley When the Evening Sun Comes Down"
The Lennie Hayton Orchestra—recorded September 2, 1945

23459   "Wait and See"—Kenny Baker
"Round and Round"
The Lennie Hayton Orchestra—recorded September 2, 1945

23460   "It's a Great Big World" (with Betty Russell and Virginia O'Brien)
"The Wild, Wild West"—Virginia O'Brien
The Lennie Hayton Orchestra—recorded September 2, 1945

23539   "Smilin' Through"
"You'll Never Walk Alone"
The Lyn Murray Orchestra and chorus—recorded July 10, 1945

23658   "Birthday of a King"
"Star of the East"
The David Rose Orchestra

23687   "For You, For Me, Forevermore" (with Dick Haymes)
"Aren't You Kinda Glad We Did" (with Dick Haymes)
The Gordon Jenkins Orchestra

23688   "Changing My Tune"
"Love"
The Gordon Jenkins Orchestra—recorded September 11, 1946
The Victor Young Orchestra—recorded January 26, 1945

23746   "There Is No Breeze"
"Don't Tell Me That Story"
The Gordon Jenkins Orchestra

23804   "Connecticut" (with Bing Crosby)
"Mine" (with Bing Crosby)
The Joseph Lilley Orchestra

23962   "Over the Rainbow"
"The Jitterbug"
The Victor Young Orchestra—recorded September 28, 1939

24469   "I Wish I Were in Love Again"
"Nothing But You"
With the Goodwin and Griffen Twin Pianos

25043   "It's a Great Day for the Irish"

"A Pretty Girl"
The David Rose Orchestra—recorded December 18, 1940

25115 "For Me and My Gal" (with Gene Kelly)
"When You Wore a Tulip" (with Gene Kelly)
The David Rose Orchestra—recorded July 26, 1942

25393 "(Dear Mr. Gable) You Made Me Love You"
"Sleep, My Baby, Sleep"
The Harry Sosnick Orchestra—recorded September 24, 1937 & April 24, 1938

25493 "(Dear Mr. Gable) You Made Me Love You"
"Over the Rainbow"
The Harry Sosnick Orchestra—recorded September 24, 1937
The Victor Young Orchestra—recorded September 28, 1939

25494 "The Trolley Song"
"Meet Me in St. Louis, Louis"
The Georgie Stoll Orchestra—recorded April 24, 1944

28210 "Mine" (with Bing Crosby)
"You've Got Me Where You Want Me" (with Bing Crosby)
The Joseph Lilley Orchestra

29233 "In Between"
"Sweet Sixteen"
The Victor Young Orchestra

DECCA SINGLES—45's

9-23539 "Smilin' Through"
"You'll Never Walk Alone"
The Lyn Murray Orchestra—recorded July 10, 1945

9-23658 "The Birthday of a King"
"Star of the East"
The David Rose Orchestra

9-23961 "Over the Rainbow"
"The Jitterbug"
The Victor Young Orchestra—recorded September 28, 1939

9-25043 "It's a Great Day for the Irish"
"A Pretty Girl"
The David Rose Orchestra—recorded December 18, 1940

9–25115   "For Me and My Gal" (with Gene Kelly)
"When You Wore a Tulip" (with Gene Kelly)
The David Rose Orchestra—recorded July 26, 1942

9–25493   "(Dear Mr. Gable) You Made Me Love You"
"Over the Rainbow"
The Harry Sosnick Orchestra—recorded September 24, 1937
The Victor Young Orchestra—recorded September 28, 1939

9–25494   "The Trolley Song"
"Meet Me in St. Louis, Louis"
The Georgie Stoll Orchestra—recorded April 24, 1944

9–28210   "Mine" (with Bing Crosby)
"You've Got Me Where You Want Me" (with Bing Crosby)
The Joseph Lilley Orchestra

9–29295   "Have Yourself a Merry Little Christmas"
"You'll Never Walk Alone"
The Georgie Stoll Orchestra—recorded April 24, 1944
The Lyn Murray Orchestra—recorded July 10, 1945

9–29296   "The Boy Next Door"
"Smilin' Through"
The Georgie Stoll Orchestra—recorded April 24, 1944
The Lyn Murray Orchestra—recorded July 10, 1945

9–40219   "In Between"
"Sweet Sixteen"
The Victor Young Orchestra

MGM SINGLES—78's

30002   "Look for the Silver Lining"
"Life Upon the Wicked Stage"—Virginia O'Brien
The Lennie Hayton Orchestra—recorded 1946
(From the MGM film, *Till the Clouds Roll By*)

30003   "Who?"
"Can't Help Lovin' Dat Man"—Lena Horne
The Lennie Hayton Orchestra—recorded 1946
(From the MGM film, *Till the Clouds Roll By*)

30097   "Be a Clown" (with Gene Kelly)
"Pirate Ballet"—Orchestra only

The Lennie Hayton Orchestra—recorded 1948
(From the MGM film, *The Pirate*)

30098   "Love of My Life"
"You Can Do No Wrong"
The Lennie Hayton Orchestra—recorded 1948
(From the MGM film, *The Pirate*)

30099   "Mack the Black"
"Nina"—Gene Kelly
The Lennie Hayton Orchestra—recorded 1948
(From the MGM film, *The Pirate*)

30172   "Johnny One Note"
"I Wish I Were in Love Again" (with Mickey Rooney)
The Lennie Hayton Orchestra—recorded 1948
(From the MGM film, *Words and Music*)

30185   "Easter Parade" (with Fred Astaire)
"A Fella With an Umbrella" (with Peter Lawford)
Johnny Green and the MGM Orchestra—recorded 1948
(From the MGM film, *Easter Parade*)

30186   "A Couple of Swells" (with Fred Astaire)
"I Love a Piano," "Snooky Ookums," "When the Midnight Choo Choo
Leaves For Alabam" (with Fred Astaire)
Johnny Green and the MGM Orchestra—recorded 1948
(From the MGM film, *Easter Parade*)

30187   "Better Luck Next Time"
"It Only Happens When I Dance With You"—Fred Astaire
Johnny Green and the MGM Orchestra—recorded, 1948
(From the MGM film, *Easter Parade*)

30431   "Who?"
"Look For the Silver Lining"
The Lennie Hayton Orchestra—recorded 1946
(From the MGM film, *Till the Clouds Roll By*)

50025   "Put Your Arms Around Me, Honey"
"Meet Me Tonight in Dreamland"
The Georgie Stoll Orchestra—recorded 1949
(From the MGM film, *In the Good Old Summertime*)

50026   "Play That Barbershop Chord"
"I Don't Care"
The Georgie Stoll Orchestra—recorded 1949
(From the MGM film, *In the Good Old Summertime*)

30212 "Merry Christmas"
The Georgie Stoll Orchestra—recorded 1949
(From the MGM film, *In the Good Old Summertime*)
"Look for the Silver Lining"
The Lennie Hayton Orchestra—recorded 1946
(From the MGM film, *Till the Clouds Roll By*)

30251 "Happy Harvest"
"If You Feel Like Singing, Sing"
Johnny Green and the MGM Orchestra—recorded 1950
(From the MGM film, *Summer Stock*)

30254 "Friendly Star"
"Get Happy"
Johnny Green and the MGM Orchestra—recorded 1950
(From the MGM film, *Summer Stock*)

MGM SINGLES—45's

MGM KGC–166 "Over the Rainbow"
The MGM Orchestra conducted by Victor Young—recorded 1939
(From the MGM film, *The Wizard of Oz*)
"(Dear Mr. Gable) You Made Me Love You"
The Georgie Stoll Orchestra—recorded 1937
(From the MGM film, *Broadway Melody of 1938*)

(X–45) 30212 "Merry Christmas"
The Georgie Stoll Orchestra—recorded 1939
(From the MGM film, *In the Good Old Summertime*)
"Look for the Silver Lining"
The Lennie Hayton Orchestra—recorded 1946
(From the MGM film, *Till the Clouds Roll By*)

(X–45) 30254 "Get Happy"
"Friendly Star"
Johnny Green and the MGM Orchestra—recorded 1950
(From the MGM film, *Summer Stock*)

COLUMBIA SINGLES—78's

40010 "Send My Baby Back to Me"
"Without a Memory"
The Ray Heindorf Orchestra—recorded 1954

40023   "Go Home, Joe"
         "Heartbroken"
         The Ray Heindorf Orchestra—recorded 1954

40270   "The Man That Got Away"
         "Here's What I'm Here For"
         The Ray Heindorf Orchestra—recorded 1954
         (From the Warner Brothers film, *A Star Is Born*)

WARNER BROTHERS SINGLES—45's

5310   "Little Drops of Rain"
         "Paris Is a Lonely Town"
         The Mort Lindsey Orchestra—recorded 1962
         (From the Warner Brothers film, *Gay Purr-ee*)

CAPITOL SINGLES—45's

4624   "Zing! Went the Strings of My Heart"
         "Rockabye Your Baby"
         The Mort Lindsey Orchestra—recorded 1961

4656   "Comes Once in a Lifetime"
         "Sweet Danger"
         The Mort Lindsey Orchestra—recorded 1962

4938   "Hello Bluebird"
         "I Could Go on Singing"
         The Mort Lindsey Orchestra—recorded 1962
         (From the United Artists film, *I Could Go on Singing*)

5497   "Hello Dolly" (with Liza Minnelli)
         "He's Got the Whole World in His Hands" (with Liza Minnelli)
         The Harry Robinson Orchestra—recorded 1964

6128   "Maybe I'll Come Back"
         The Nelson Riddle Orchestra—recorded 1956
         "Over the Rainbow"
         The Jack Cathcart Orchestra—recorded 1955

6125   "San Francisco"
         "Chicago"
         The Mort Lindsey Orchestra—recorded 1961

6126   "The Man That Got Away"
The Mort Lindsey Orchestra—recorded 1961
"April Showers"
The Nelson Riddle Orchestra—recorded 1956

6129   "Swanee"
"That's Entertainment"
The Mort Lindsey Orchestra—recorded 1961

6127   "Come Rain or Come Shine"
"Rockabye Your Baby"
The Mort Lindsey Orchestra—recorded 1961

BRUNSWICK SINGLES (BRITISH DIVISION OF DECCA)—78's

02656   "Ten Pins in the Sky"
"It Never Rains But What It Pours"
The Harry Sosnick Orchestra—recorded August 21, 1938

02953   "Oceans Apart"
"Figaro"

02969   "Zing! Went the Strings of My Heart"
"I'm Just Wild About Harry"
The Victor Young Orchestra—recorded July 29, 1939

V-DISC SINGLES (FOR TROOPS OVERSEAS DURING WORLD WAR II)—78's

335A   "Over the Rainbow"
"I May Be Wrong But I Think You're Wonderful"
The Tommy Dorsey Orchestra—recorded 1943

EMI SINGLES (BRITISH DIVISION OF CAPITOL)—45's

45–CL–14791   "It's Lovely to Be Back Again in London"
"By Myself"
Recorded 1957

DECCA ALBUMS—78's

A–74   *The Wizard of Oz* (with Victor Young and his Orchestra, the Ken Darby Singers, and Cliff Edwards) Four-record set.

       2672—"Over the Rainbow"
               "The Jitterbug"

A–76   *The Judy Garland Souvenir Album*

       1463—"(Dear Mr. Gable) You Made Me Love You"
               "You Can't Have Everything"

       2873—"Figaro"
               "Oceans Apart"

       15045—"In Between"
               "Sweet Sixteen"

A–97   *George Gershwin Songs, Volume Two* (with Connie Boswell, Tony Martin, Francis Langford, the Foursome, and Victor Young and his Orchestra)

       2881—"Swanee"
               "Embraceable You"

A–347   *Christmas Candle* (with Tony Martin and the King's Men)

       4050—"Birthday of a King"
               "Star of the East"

A–349   *The Judy Garland Second Souvenir Album*

       18480—"For Me and My Gal" (with Gene Kelly)
               "When You Wore a Tulip" (with Gene Kelly)

       18540—"That Old Black Magic"
               "Poor Little Rich Girl"

       18543—"Zing! Went the Strings of My Heart"
               "Fascinatin' Rhythm"

       18524—"On the Sunny Side of the Street"
               "I Never Knew"

A–362   *Girl Crazy* (with Mickey Rooney and the Georgie Stoll Orchestra)

       23308—"Embraceable You"
               "Could You Use Me?" (with Mickey Rooney)

23309—"But Not for Me"
    "Treat Me Rough"—Mickey Rooney

23310—"Bidin' My Time"
    "I Got Rhythm"

A–380   *Meet Me in St. Louis* (with the Georgie Stoll Orchestra)

23360—"Meet Me in St. Louis, Louis"
    "Skip to My Lou"

23361—"The Trolley Song"
    "Boys and Girls Like You and Me"

23362—"Have Yourself a Merry Little Christmas"
    "The Boy Next Door"

A–388   *The Harvey Girls* (with Kenny Baker, Virginia O'Brien, Betty Russell, and the Lennie Hayton Orchestra)

23458—"On the Atchison, Topeka and the Sante Fe"
    "In the Valley"

23459—"Round and Round"
    "Wait and See"—Kenny Baker

23460—"It's a Great Big World" (with Virginia O'Brien and Betty Russell)
    "The Wild, Wild West"—Virginia O'Brien

A–631   *Bing Crosby Sings* (with Judy Garland, Mary Martin, and Johnny Mercer)

23410—"Yah-Ta-Ta, Yah-Ta-Ta" (with Bing Crosby)
    "You Got Me Where You Want Me" (with Bing Crosby)

23804—"Mine" (with Bing Crosby)
    "Connecticut" (with Bing Crosby)

A–488   *Christmastime* (with various Decca artists)

23658—"Birthday of a King"
    "Star of the East"

A–671   *The Judy Garland Third Souvenir Album*

18524—"On the Sunny Side of the Street"
    "I Never Knew"

18540—"That Old Black Magic"
"Poor Little Rich Girl"

18543—"Zing! Went the Strings of My Heart"
"Fascinatin' Rhythm"

18660—"This Heart of Mine"
"Love"

A–588   *The Wizard of Oz* (with Victor Young and his Orchestra, the Ken Darby Singers, and Cliff Edwards)

23961—"Over the Rainbow"
"The Jitterbug"

A–682   *Judy Garland Sings* (with Dick Haymes, Gene Kelly, the Merry Macs, and the Gordon Jenkins Orchestra)

23436—"If I Had You" (with the Merry Macs)
"On the Atchison, Topeka and the Sante Fe" (with the Merry Macs)

23687—"Aren't You Kinda Glad We Did?" (with Dick Haymes)
"For You, For Me, Forevermore" (with Dick Haymes)

23746—"Don't Tell Me That Story" (with the Gordon Jenkins Orchestra)
"There Is No Breeze" (with the Gordon Jenkins Orchestra)

25115—"For Me and My Gal" (with Gene Kelly)
"When You Wore a Tulip" (with Gene Kelly)

A–899   *Judy at the Palace*

25115—"For Me and My Gal" (with Gene Kelly)
"When You Wore a Tulip" (with Gene Kelly)

25493—"(Dear Mr. Gable) You Made Me Love You"
"Over the Rainbow"

25494—"The Trolley Song"
"Meet Me in St. Louis, Louis"

40219—"In Between"
"Sweet Sixteen"

9–73   *Christmastime* (with various Decca artists)

"Star of the East," "Birthday of a King"

9–287   *Judy at the Palace*

"For Me and My Gal" (with Gene Kelly), "When You Wore a Tulip" (with Gene Kelly), "(Dear Mr. Gable) You Made Me Love You," "Over the Rainbow," "The Trolley Song," "Meet Me in St. Louis, Louis," "In Between," "Sweet Sixteen"

9–325   *The Wizard of Oz* (with Victor Young and his Orchestra, the Ken Darby Singers, and Cliff Edwards)

"Over the Rainbow," "The Jitterbug"

ED–620   *Judy at the Palace*

"For Me and My Gal" (with Gene Kelly), "When You Wore a Tulip" (with Gene Kelly), "(Dear Mr. Gable) You Made Me Love You," "Over the Rainbow," "The Trolley Song," "Meet Me in St. Louis, Louis," "In Between," and "Sweet Sixteen"

ED–661   *The Wizard of Oz* (with Victor Young and his Orchestra, the Ken Darby Singers, and Cliff Edwards)

"Over the Rainbow," "The Jitterbug"

ED–1700   *A Musical Autobiography of Bing*

"Yah-Ta-Ta, Yah-Ta-Ta" (with Bing Crosby)

ED–2020   *Girl Crazy*

"Bidin'My Time," "I Got Rhythm," "Embraceable You," "But Not for Me"

ED–2050   *Judy Garland, Volume Two*

"Smilin' Through," "You'll Never Walk Alone," "The Boy Next Door," "I'm Always Chasing Rainbows"

DX–151   *Bing*

"Yah-Ta-Ta, Yah-Ta-Ta" (with Bing Crosby)

DECCA ALBUMS—33 1/3's

DL-4000 *Original Hit Performances—The Late 30's* (with various Decca artists)

     "(Dear Mr. Gable) You Made Me Love You"

DL-4001 *Original Hit Performances—Into the 40's* (with various Decca artists)

     "Over the Rainbow," "For Me and My Gal" (with Gene Kelly)

DL-4007 *Original Hit Performances—The 40's* (with various Decca artists)

     "The Trolley Song"

     Released in Great Britain as Brunswick LAT-8369

DL-4199 *The Magic of Judy Garland*

     "I Never Knew," "Zing! Went the Strings of My Heart," "On the Sunny Side of the Street," "F. D. R. Jones," "But Not for Me," "I'm Always Chasing Rainbows," "Our Love Affair," "That Old Black Magic," "A Pretty Girl," "On the Atchison, Topeka and the Sante Fe," "Embraceable You," "I'm Nobody's Baby"

     Released in Great Britain as Ace of Hearts AH-128

DL-4205 *Open House* (with various Decca artists)

     "Meet Me in St. Louis, Louis"

DL-4206 *House Party* (with various Decca artists)

     "Wearing of the Green"

DL-5152 *The Wizard of Oz* (with Victor Young and his Orchestra, the Ken Darby Singers, and Cliff Edwards) (10")

     "Over the Rainbow," "The Jitterbug"

DL-5412 *Girl Crazy* (with Mickey Rooney) (10")

     "Embraceable You," "Could You Use Me?" (with Mickey Rooney), "Bidin My Time," "I Got Rhythm," "But Not for Me"

DL-6020 *Judy at the Palace* (10")

     "For Me and My Gal" (with Gene Kelly), "When You Wore a Tulip" (with Gene Kelly), "(Dear Mr. Gable) You Made Me Love You," "Over the Rainbow," "The Trolley Song," "Meet Me in St. Louis, Louis," "In Between," and "Sweet Sixteen"

Released in Great Britain as Brunswick LAT-8725

DL–8075   *A Musical Autobiography of Bing*

"Yah-Ta-Ta, Yah-Ta-Ta" (with Bing Crosby)

Released in Great Britain as Brunswick LAT-8054

DL–8190   *Judy Garland—Greatest Performances*

"The Trolley Song," "Meet Me in St. Louis, Louis," "Poor Little Rich Girl," "Sweet Sixteen," "When You Wore a Tulip" (with Gene Kelly), "You'll Never Walk Alone," "(Dear Mr. Gable) You Made Me Love You," "Over the Rainbow," "How About You?", "In Between," "Love," "For Me and My Gal" (with Gene Kelly)

Released in Great Britain (minus "Love" and "Poor Little Rich Girl") as Ace of Hearts AH-11

DL–8387   *The Wizard of Oz* (with Victor Young and his Orchestra, the Ken Darby Singers, and Cliff Edwards) / *Pinnochio*

"Over the Rainbow," "The Jitterbug"

Released in Great Britain as Ace of Hearts AH-121

DL–8498   *Selections from The Harvey Girls and Meet Me in St. Louis* (with Virginia O'Brien, Kenny Baker, and Betty Russell)

"Meet Me in St. Louis, Louis," "The Trolley Song," "The Boy Next Door," "Have Yourself a Merry Little Christmas," "Boys and Girls Like You and Me," "Skip to My Lou," "On the Atchison, Topeka and the Sante Fe," "In the Valley," "Round and Round," "It's a Great Big World" (with Virginia O'Brien and Betty Russell)

DL–9056   *Around the Christmas Tree* (with various Decca artists)

"Have Yourself a Merry Little Christmas"

Released in Great Britain as Ace of Hearts AH-125

DXB–172/   *The Best of Judy Garland*
DXSB–7172

"(Dear Mr. Gable) You Made Me Love You," "Over the Rainbow," "F. D. R. Jones," "In Between," "Sweet Sixteen," "For Me and My Gal" (with Gene Kelly), "Love," "The Trolley Song," "Meet Me in St. Louis," "Poor Little Rich Girl," "When You Wore a Tulip" (with Gene Kelly), "You'll Nver Walk Alone," "I Never Knew," "On the Sunny Side of the Street," "The Boy Next Door," "But Not for Me," "I'm Always Chasing Rainbows," "Our Love Affair," "A Pretty Girl," "That Old Black Magic," "On the Atchison, Topeka and the Sante Fe," "Have Yourself a Merry Little Christmas," "Zing! Went the Strings of My Heart," "I'm Nobody's Baby"

Also released as MCA 24003

DL–78387   *The Wizard of Oz* (With Victor Young and his Orchestra, the Ken Darby Singers, and Cliff Edwards) / *Pinnochio*

"Over the Rainbow," "The Jitterbug"

DL–75150   *Judy Garland's Greatest Hits*

"(Dear Mr. Gable) You Made Me Love You," "Over the Rainbow," "I'm Nobody's Baby," "I'm Always Chasing Rainbows," "A Pretty Girl," "For Me and My Gal" (with Gene Kelly), "When You Wore a Tulip" (with Gene Kelly), "Meet Me in St. Louis, Louis," "The Boy Next Door," "The Trolley Song," "Have Yourself a Merry Little Christmas," "On the Atchison, Topeka and the Sante Fe"

DEA 7–5   *Judy Garland—Collector's Items (1936–1945)*

"Stompin at the Savoy," "Swing Mr. Charlie," "Everybody Sing," "All God's Chillun Got Rhythm," "You Can't Have Everything," "Sleep, My Baby, Sleep," "Blues in the Night," "No Love, No Nothin," "A Journey to a Star," "This Heart of Mine," "If I Had You," "Smilin' Through," "Cry, Baby, Cry," "Ten Pins in the Sky," "It Never Rains But What It Pours," "Oceans Apart," "The End of the Rainbow," "Buds Won't Bud," "Swanee," "Embraceable You," "I Got Rhythm," "Wearing of the Green," "It's a Great Day for the Irish," "How About You?"

Released in Great Britain on Coral as *Collectors Items, Volume One* and *Collectors Items, Volume Two*—CP53 and CP54.

MGM ALBUMS—78's

M–1   *Till the Clouds Roll By*

30002—"Look for the Silver Lining"
          "Life Upon the Wicked Stage" (Virginia O'Brien)

30003—"Who?"
"Can't Help Lovin' That Man" (Lena Horne)

M-21   *The Pirate*

30097—"Be a Clown" (with Gene Kelly)
"Pirate Ballet" (Orchestra)

30098—"Love of My Life"
"You Can Do No Wrong"

30099—"Mack the Black"
"Nina" (Gene Kelly)

M-37   *Words and Music*

30172—"Johnny One Note"
"I Wish I Were in Love Again"

M-40   *Easter Parade*

30185—"Easter Parade" (with Fred Astaire)
"A Fella With an Umbrella" (with Peter Lawford)

30186—"A Couple Of Swells" (with Fred Astaire)
"I Love a Piano," "Snooky Ookums," "When the Midnight
Choo Choo Leaves for Alabam" (with Fred Astaire)

30187—"Better Luck Next Time"
"It Only Happens When I Dance With You" (Fred
Astaire)

L-11   *In the Good Old Summertime*

50025—"Put Your Arms Around Me, Honey"
"Meet Me Tonight in Dreamland"

50026—"Play That Barbershop Chord"
"I Don't Care"

M-54   *Summer Stock*

30251—"Happy Harvest"
"If You Feel Like Singing, Sing"

30254—"Friendly Star"
"Get Happy"

M–169   *Merry Christmas* (with various MGM artists)

        "Merry Christmas"

MGM ALBUMS—45's

X–1   *Till the Clouds Roll By*

        "Who?", "Look For The Silver Lining"

X–21   *The Pirate*

        "Be a Clown" (with Gene Kelly), "Love of My Life," "You Can Do No Wrong," "Mack the Black"

X–37   *Words and Music*

        "Johnny One Note," "I Wish I Were in Love Again" (with Mickey Rooney)

X–40   *Easter Parade*

        "A Couple of Swells" (with Fred Astaire), "A Fella With an Umbrella" (with Peter Lawford), "Easter Parade" (with Fred Astaire), "Medley: I Love a Piano, Snooky Ookums, When the Midnight Choo Choo Leaves for Alabam" (with Fred Astaire), "Better Luck Next Time"

X–42   *The MGM Silver Anniversary Album* (with various MGM artists)

X–56   *Summer Stock*

        "Happy Harvest," "If You Feel Like Singing, Sing," "Friendly Star," "Get Happy"

X–240   *The MGM Thirtieth Anniversary Album* (with various MGM artists)

        "Easter Parade" (with Fred Astaire)

X–268   *Judy Garland*

        "Who?", "Look for the Silver Lining," "Play That Barbershop Chord," "Last Night When We Were Young," "Put Your Arms Around Me Honey," "Love of My Life," "Get Happy," "Johnny One Note"

X–1038   *Get Happy*

"Who?", "Look for the Silver Lining," "Love of My Life," "Get Happy"

X–1116   *Look for the Silver Lining*

"Put Your Arms Around Me, Honey," "Look for the Silver Lining," "Play That Barbershop Chord," "Last Night When We Were Young"

X–3464ST   *The Wizard of Oz*

"Over the Rainbow," "If I Only Had a Brain" (with Ray Bolger, Buddy Ebsen, and Bert Lahr), "Ding, Dong the Witch Is Dead" (with the Munchkins), and "We're Off to See the Wizard" (with Ray Bolger, Buddy Ebsen, and Bert Lahr)

MGM ALBUMS—33 1/3's

E–501   Till the Clouds Roll By (10")

"Who?", "Look for the Silver Lining"

E–21   *The Pirate* (10")

"Be a Clown" (with Gene Kelly), "Love of My Life," "You Can Do No Wrong," "Mack the Black"

E–42   *The MGM Silver Anniversary Album* (with various MGM artists)(10")

E–505   *Words and Music* (10")

"Johnny One Note," "I Wish I Were in Love Again" (with Mickey Rooney)

E–502   *Easter Parade* (10")

"Easter Parade" (with Fred Astaire), "A Fella With an Umbrella" (with Peter Lawford), "A Couple of Swells" (with Fred Astaire), "Medley: I Love a Piano, Snooky Ookums, When the Midnight Choo Choo Leaves for Alabam" (with Fred Astaire), "Better Luck Next Time"

Released in Great Britain as D-140.

E–519   *Summer Stock* (10")

"Happy Harvest," "If You Feel Like Singing, Sing," "Get Happy,"
"Friendly Star"

E–82   *Judy Garland Sings* (10")

"Get Happy," "Love of My Life," "Johnny One Note," "Look for the
Silver Lining," "Play That Barbershop Chord," "Last Night When We
Were Young," "Put Your Arms Around Me, Honey"

M–169   *Merry Christmas* (10") (with various MGM artists)

"Merry Christmas"

E 3231   *Till the Clouds Roll By / Gentlemen Prefer Blondes*

"Who?", "Look for the Silver Lining"

E–3234   *The Pirate / Summer Stock*

"Be a Clown" (with Gene Kelly), "Love of My Life," "You Can Do No
Wrong," "Mack the Black," "If You Feel Like Singing, Sing," "Get
Happy," "Happy Harvest," "Friendly Star"

In Great Britain, *The Pirate* was released on C-763 backed by *Les Girls*
instead of *Summer Stock.*

E–3233   *Words and Music / Two Weeks in Love*

"I Wish I Were in Love Again" (with Mickey Rooney)

In Great Britain, *Words and Music* was released on C-853 backed by
Seven Brides for Seven Brothers instead of *Two Weeks in Love.*

E–3227   *Easter Parade / Annie Get Your Gun*

"Easter Parade" (with Fred Astaire), "A Fella With an Umbrella" (with
Peter Lawford), "A Couple of Swells" (with Fred Astaire), "Medley: I
Love a Piano, Snooky Ookums, and When the Midnight Choo Choo
Leaves for Alabam" (with Fred Astaire)

E–3232   *In the Good Old Summertime / An American in Paris*

"I Don't Care," "Put Your Arms Around Me Honey," "Play That
Barbershop Chord," "I Don't Care"

E–3118   *The MGM 30th Anniversary Album* (with various MGM artists)

"Easter Parade" (with Fred Astaire)

E–3149   *Judy Garland*

"Last Night When We Were Young," "Play That Barbershop Chord," "Put Your Arms Around Me Honey," "I Don't Care," "Meet Me Tonight in Dreamland," "Get Happy," "Johnny One Note," "Better Luck Next Time," "If You Feel Like Singing, Sing," "Who?", "Look for the Silver Lining," "Love of My Life"

E–3464ST   *The Wizard of Oz*

"Over the Rainbow," "If I Only Had a Brain" (with Ray Bolger, Buddy Ebsen, and Bert Lahr), "Ding, Dong the Witch Is Dead" (with the Munchkins), and "We're Off to See the Wizard" (with Ray Bolger, Buddy Ebsen, and Bert Lahr)

Released in Great Britain as C-757

E–3989P   *The Judy Garland Story—The Star Years*

"Last Night When We Were Young," "Play That Barbershop Chord," "Put Your Arms Around Me Honey," "I Don't Care," "Meet Me Tonight in Dreamland," "Get Happy," "Johnny One Note," "Better Luck Next Time," "If You Feel Like Singing, Sing," "Who?", "Look for the Silver Lining," "Love of My Life"

Released in Great Britain as C-886

E–4005P   *The Judy Garland Story—VOLUME TWO—The Hollywood Years*

"Over the Rainbow," "(Dear Mr. Gable) You Made Me Love You," "Bei Mir Bist Du Schoen," "I'm Nobody's Baby," "I Cried for You," "Singing in the Rain," "Danny Boy," "The Trolley Song," "But Not for Me," "Johnny One Note," "The Boy Next Door," "You Can't Get a Man With a Gun"

Released in Great Britain as C-887

E–4017   *Magnificent Moments from MGM Movies* (with various MGM artists)

"Over the Rainbow," "Johnny One Note"

E/SE–4171   *The Very Best of Motion Picture Musicals* (with various MGM artists)

"Over the Rainbow," "Johnny One Note"

E–3770   Till the Clouds Roll By / Singing in the Rain

250

"Who?", "Look for the Silver Lining"

E–3771   *Words and Music / Good News*

"Johnny One Note," "I Wish I Were in Love Again" (with Mickey Rooney)

E/SE–4204   *The Very Best of Judy Garland*

"Over the Rainbow," "(Dear Mr. Gable) You Made Me Love You," "The Trolley Song," "Johnny One Note," "Look for the Silver Lining," "The Boy Next Door," "I Cried for You," "Get Happy," "If You Feel Like Singing, Sing," "I Don't Care," "Singing in the Rain," "But Not for Me"

E/SE–4241   *The Very Best of Jerome Kern* (with various MGM artists)

"Look for the Silver Lining"

E/SE–4238   *The Very Best of Rodgers and Hart* (with various MGM artists)

"Johnny One Note"

E/SE–4240   *The Very Best of Irving Berlin* (with various MGM artists)

"Better Luck Next Time," "You Can't Get a Man With a Gun"

E–3996   *The Wizard of Oz*

"Over the Rainbow," "If I Only Had a Brain" (with Ray Bolger, Buddy Ebsen, and Bert Lahr), "Ding Dong the Witch Is Dead" (with the Munchkins), "We're Off to See the Wizard" (with Ray Bolger, Buddy Ebsen, and Bert Lahr).

L–70118   *Girls and More Girls* (with various MGM artists)

"Love of My Life"

M/MS–505   *Judy Garland* (Metro Division)

"Danny Boy," "Meet Me Tonight in Dreamland," "Friendly Star," "I'm Nobody's Baby," "I Cried for You," "The Boy Next Door," "Singing in the Rain," "The Trolley Song," "Put Your Arms Around Me Honey," "Play That Barbershop Chord"

M/MS–581   *Judy Garland in Song* (Metro Division)

"Over the Rainbow," "Get Happy," "If You Feel Like Singing, Sing," "But Not for Me," "You Can't Get a Man With a Gun," "Last

251

Night When We Were Young," "(Dear Mr. Gable) You Made Me Love You," "Bei Mir Bist Du Schoen," "Better Luck Next Time," "I Don't Care"

M/MS–578   *Till the Clouds Roll By* (Metro Division)

"Who?", "Look for the Silver Lining"

M/MS–580   *Words and Music* (Metro Division)

"Johnny One Note," "I Wish I Were in Love Again" (with Mickey Rooney)

GAS–113   *Judy Garland—The Golden Archive Series*

"Over the Rainbow," "The Trolley Song," "(Dear Mr. Gable) You Made Me Love You," "Singing in the Rain," "Look for the Silver Lining," "Put Your Arms Around Me Honey," "I Cried for You," "You Can't Get a Man With a Gun," "The Boy Next Door," "I'm Nobody's Baby"

SUPL–2   *Judy Garland, The Golden Years at MGM*

"(Dear Mr. Gable) You Made Me Love You," "Bei Mir Bist Du Schoen," "Over the Rainbow," "I'm Nobody's Baby," "I Cried for You," "Who?", "Look for the Silver Lining," "You Can't Get a Man With a Gun," "Love of My Life," "Johnny One Note," "Danny Boy," "Singing in the Rain," "But Not for Me," "The Trolley Song," "The Boy Next Door," "Better Luck Next Time," "I Don't Care," "Last Night When We Were Young," "If You Feel Like Singing, Sing," "Friendly Star," "Get Happy"

PX–102   *Forever Judy*

"Over the Rainbow," "The Trolley Song," "(Dear Mr. Gable) You Made Me Love You," "Singing in the Rain," "Look for the Silver Lining," "Put Your Arms Around Me Honey," "I Cried for You," "You Can't Get a Man With a Gun," "The Boy Next Door," "I'm Nobody's Baby"

PX–104   *The Wizard of Oz*

"Over the Rainbow," "If I Only Had a Brain" (with Ray Bolger, Buddy Ebsen, and Bert Lahr), "Ding Dong the Witch Is Dead" (with the Munchkins), "We're Off to See the Wizard" (with Ray Bolger, Buddy Ebsen, and Bert Lahr)

2SES–40–ST   *Easter Parade/Singing in the Rain*

"Easter Parade" (with Fred Astaire), "A Fella With An Umbrella" (with Peter Lawford), "A Couple Of Swells" (with Fred Astaire), "Better Luck Next Time," "Medley: I Love A Piano, Snooky Ookums, When The Midnight Choo Choo Leaves For Alabam" (with Fred Astaire)

2SES–43–ST   *The Pirate/Hit the Deck/Pagan Love Song*

"Mack The Black," "You Can Do No Wrong," "Love Of My Life," "Be A Clown" (with Gene Kelly)

2SES–45–ST   *Till the Clouds Roll By/Three Little Words*

"Who?", "Look For The Silver Lining"

COLUMBIA ALBUMS—78's

BM–1201   *A Star Is Born* (With Ray Heindorf and his Orchestra)

8005—"Gotta Have Me Go With You"
"Lose That Long Face"

8006—"The Man That Got Away"
"Someone at Last"—Part II

8007—"Born in a Trunk"—Part I
"Someone At Last"—Part I

8008—"Born in a Trunk"—Part II
"It's a New World"

8009—"Born in a Trunk"—Part III
"Here's What I'm Here For"

COLUMBIA ALBUMS—45's

BA–1201   *A Star Is Born* (with Ray Heindorf and his Orchestra)

"Gotta Have Me Go With You," "The Man That Got Away," "Born in a Trunk," "Someone At Last," "Here's What I'm Here For," "It's a New World," "Lose That Long Face"

253

B–2598   *Judy Garland*

"Born in a Trunk"

COLUMBIA ALBUMS—33 1/3's

CL–6299   *A Star Is Born—House Party* (10")

"Gotta Have Me Go With You," "Lose That Long Face," "Some-one At Last," "The Man That Got Away," "It's a New World," "Here's What I'm Here For"

BL–1201   *A Star Is Born* (with Ray Heindorf and his Orchestra)

"Gotta Have Me Go With You," "Lose That Long Face," "Some-one At Last," "Born in a Trunk," "It's a New World," "The Man That Got Away," "Here's What I'm Here For," "Lose That Long Face"

Released in Great Britain as follows: Phillips BBL-7007, CBS Realm RM/RMS 52063, and Hallmark SHM-654.

CL–1101/   *A Star Is Born* (with Ray Heindorf and his Orchestra)
CS–8740

"Gotta Have Me Go With You," "The Man That Got Away," "Born in a Trunk," "Here's What I'm Here For," "It's a New World," "Someone At Last," "Lose That Long Face"

HS–11366   *A Star Is Born* (with Ray Heindorf and his Orchestra) (Harmony Division)

"Gotta Have Me Go With You," "The Man That Got Away," "Born in a Trunk," "Here's What I'm Here For," "It's a New World," "Someone At Last," "Lose That Long Face"

WARNER BROTHERS ALBUM—33 1/3

B/BS–1479   *Gay Purr-ee* (with Robert Goulet, Red Buttons, Paul Frees, and Mort Lindsey and his Orchestra)

"Gay Purr-ee Overture," "Little Drops of Rain," "Take My Hand

Paree," "Paris Is a Lonely Town," "Roses Red, Violets Blue," "The Mewsette Finale" (with Robert Goulet and chorus)

Released in Great Britain as W/WS-8021.

COLPIX ALBUM—33 1/3

CP/CPS–507   *Pepe*

"The Far Away Part of Town"

Released in Great Britain as Pye International NPL-28015

UNITED ARTISTS ALBUM—33 1/3

UXS–54
UXL–4   *Three Billion Millionaires* (A special album recorded by some of the greatest names in show business. The profits were given to the United Nations.)

"One More Lamb" (with children's chorus)

CAPITOL ALBUMS—45's

EDM–676   *Miss Show Business* (with the Jack Cathcart Orchestra)

"While We're Young," "You Made Me Love You," "For Me and My Gal," "The Boy Next Door," "The Trolley Song," "A Pretty Girl," "Rockabye Your Baby," "Happiness Is Just a Thing Called Joe," "Judy at the Palace Medley," "Carolina in the Morning," "Danny Boy," "After You've Gone," "Over the Rainbow"

EAP–734   *Judy* (sold in three separate record jackets as EAP-734-1, EAP-734-2, EAP-734-3) (with the Nelson Riddle Orchestra)

"Last Night When We Were Young," "Dirty Hands, Dirty Face," "Lucky Day," "Just Imagine," "Life Is Just a Bowl Of Cherries," "April Showers," "Anyplace I Hang My Hat Is Home," "Come Rain or Come Shine," "I Feel a Song Comin On," "I Will Come Back," "Memories of You"

EAP-835   *Alone* (sold in three separate record jackets as EAP-835-1, EAP-835-2, EAP-835-3) (with the Gordon Jenkins Orchestra)

"Me and My Shadow," "Among My Souvenirs," "I Get the Blues When It Rains," "Just a Memory," "I Gotta Right to Sing the Blues," "Mean to Me," "Happy New Year," "By Myself," "Little Girl Blue," "How About Me," "Blue Prelude"

EAP–1636   *Judy in Love* (sold in three separate record jackets as EAP-1636-1, EAP-1636-2, EAP-1636-3) (with the Nelson Riddle Orchestra)

"I Can't Give You Anything But Love," "More Than You Know," "This Is It," "I Concentrate on You," "Zing! Went the Strings of My Heart," "Day In, Day Out," "Do I Love You," "I Am Loved," "I Hadn't Anyone Till You," "I'm Confessin'," "Do It Again"

EAP–1569   *Judy at Carnegie Hall* (with Mort Lindsey and his Orchestra)

"When You're Smiling," "Almost Like Being in Love / This Can't Be Love," "Do It Again," "You Go to My Head," "Alone Together," "Who Cares?", "How Long Has This Been Goin On?", "Just You, Just Me," "Puttin On the Ritz," "The Man That Got Away," "San Francisco," "I Can't Give You Anything But Love," "That's Entertainment," "Come Rain or Come Shine," "If Love Were All," "A Foggy Day," "Zing! Went the Strings of My Heart," "Stormy Weather," "You Made Me Love You / For Me and My Gal / The Trolley Song," "Rockabye Your Baby," "Over the Rainbow," "Swanee," "After You've Gone," "Chicago"

CAPITOL ALBUMS—33 1/3's

W/DW–676   *Miss Show Business* (with the Jack Cathcart Orchestra)

"While We're Young," "You Made Me Love You / The Boy Next Door / For Me and My Gal / The Trolley Song," "A Pretty Girl," "Rockabye Your Baby," "Happiness Is Just a Thing Called Joe," "Judy at the Palace Medley," "Carolina in the Morning," "Danny Boy," "After You've Gone," "Over the Rainbow"

Released in Great Britain as LCT-6103

T/DT–734   *Judy* (with the Nelson Riddle Orchestra)

"Last Night When We Were Young," "Dirty Hands, Dirty Face," "Lucky Day," "Just Imagine," "Life Is Just a Bowl of Cherries," "April Showers," "Anyplace I Hang My Hat Is Home," "Come

Rain or Come Shine," "I Feel a Song Comin On," "I Will Come Back," "Memories of You"

Released in Great Britain as LCT-6121

T/DT–835   *Alone* (with the Gordon Jenkins Orchestra)

"Me and My Shadow," "Among My Souvenirs," "I Got a Right to Sing the Blues," "I Get the Blues When It Rains," "Just a Memory," "Mean to Me," "Happy New Year," "By Myself," "Little Girl Blue," "How About Me," "Blue Prelude"

Released in Great Britain as LCT-6136. Also released by the World Record Club as TP-154.

T/ST–1036   *Judy in Love* (with the Nelson Riddle Orchestra)

"I Can't Give You Anything But Love," "More Than You Know," "This Is It," "I Concentrate on You," "Zing! Went the Strings of My Heart," "Day In, Day Out," "Do I Love You," "I Am Loved," "I Hadn't Anyone Till You," "I'm Confessin," "Do It Again"

T/ST–1118   *Garland at the Grove* (with the Freddie Martin Orchestra)

"When You're Smiling," "Zing! Went the Strings of My Heart," "Purple People Eater," "You Made Me Love You / For Me and My Gal / The Trolley Song," "When the Sun Comes Out," "Rockabye Your Baby," "Over the Rainbow," "After You've Gone," "A Pretty Girl," "Swanee"

SN–1   *What's New - Volume One* (with other Capitol artists)

"That's All There Is, There Isn't Anymore"

TAO–1188   *The Letter* (with John Ireland, the Ralph Brewster Singers, and the Gordon Jenkins Orchestra)

"Beautiful Trouble," "Love in the Village," "The Worst Kind of Man," "That's All There Is, There Isn't Anymore," "Love in Central Park," "The Red Balloon," "The Fight," "At the Stroke of Midnight," "Come Back"

Released in Great Britain as T/ST-1188.

T/ST–1467   *Judy! That's Entertainment* (with the Jack Marshall Orchestra)

"That's Entertainment," "Who Cares?", "I've Confessed to the Breeze," "If I Love Again," "Yes," "Puttin' on the Ritz," "Old

Devil Moon," "Down With Love," "How Long Has This Been Going On?", "It Never Was You," "Just You, Just Me," "Alone Together"

WBO/
SWBO–1569

Judy at Carnegie Hall (with the Mort Lindsey Orcestra)

"Overture," "When You're Smiling," "Almost Like Being In Love / This Can't Be Love," "Do It Again," "You Go to My Head," "Alone Together," "Who Cares?", "How Long Has This Been Going On?", "Just You, Just Me," "Puttin' on the Ritz," "San Francisco," "The Man That Got Away," "I Can't Give You Anything But Love," "That's Entertainment," "Come Rain or Come Shine," "If Love Were All," "A Foggy Day," "You're Nearer," "Zing! Went the Strings of My Heart," "Stormy Weather," "You Made Me Love You / For Me and My Gal / The Trolley Song," "Rockabye Your Baby," "Over the Rainbow," "Swanee," "After You've Gone," "Chicago"

Released in Great Britain as W/SW-11569 and 21569.

T/ST–1941

Our Love Letter (with John Ireland, the Ralph Brewster Singers, and the Gordon Jenkins Orchestra)

"Beautiful Trouble," "Love in the Village," "The Worst Kind of Man," "That's All There Is, There Isn't Any More," "Love in Central Park," "The Red Balloon," "The Fight," "At the Stroke of Midnight," "Come Back"

W/WS–1710

The Garland Touch (with the Mort Lindsey Orchestra)

"Lucky Day," "I Happen to Like New York," "Comes Once in a Lifetime," "Judy at the Palace Medley," "Happiness Is Just a Thing Called Joe," "Sweet Danger," "You'll Never Walk Alone," "Do I Love You?", "More Than You Know," "It's a Great Day for the Irish"

Released in Great Britain by the World Record Club as T/ST-675, *You'll Never Walk Alone.*

T/ST–1999

The Hits of Judy Garland

"You Made Me Love You / For Me and My Gal / The Trolley Song," "Over the Rainbow," "Swanee," "Come Rain or Come Shine," "The Man That Got Away," "Chicago," "I Can't Give You Anything But Love," "Zing! Went the Strings of My Heart," "April Showers," "Rockabye Your Baby," "When You're Smiling"

258

| W/WS–1861 | *I Could Go on Singing* (Original soundtrack recording with Mort Lindsey and his Orchestra) |

"I Could Go on Singing," "Hello Bluebird," "I Am the Monarch Of the Sea," "It Never Was You," "By Myself," "I Could Go on Singing" (reprise)

| W/DW–2062 | *Just for Openers* (with the Mort Lindsey Orchestra) |

"It's a Good Day," "That's All," "Some People," "More," "Island in the West Indies," "As Long As He Needs Me," "Get Me to the Church on Time," "Fly Me to the Moon," "I Wish You Love," "Jamboree Jones," "Battle Hymn of the Republic," "I Will Come Back"

WBO/
| SWBO–2295 | *Judy Garland and Liza Minnelli, Live at the Palladium* (with Harry Robinson and the Palladium Orchestra) |

"The Man That Got Away," "Hello Dolly" (with Liza), "Together" (with Liza), "Medley: Bob White, We Could Make Such Beautiful Music Together" (with Liza), "Love Medley" (with Liza), "Smile," "What Now My Love," "Make Someone Happy," "His Is the Only Music That Makes Me Dance," "He's Got the Whole World in His Hands / When the Saints Go Marching In" (with Liza), "Never, Never Will I Marry," "Swanee" (with Liza), "Chicago," (with Liza), "Over the Rainbow," "San Francisco" (with Liza)

Released in Great Britain as W/SW 2205. Also released in Great Britain by the World Record Club as ST/764/5.

| STCL–2988 | *The Deluxe Judy Garland Set* |

"Over the Rainbow," "Rockabye Your Baby," "April Showers," "Last Night When We Were Young," "That's Entertainment," "If I Love Again," "Puttin' on the Ritz," "Old Devil Moon," "Down With Love," "How Long Has This Been Going On?", "It Never Was You," "Just You, Just Me," "Alone Together," "Maybe I'll Come Back," "Zing! Went the Strings of My Heart," "I Can't Give You Anything But Love," "It Never Was You," "More Than You Know," "I Am Loved," "I Hadn't Anyone Till You," "I Concentrate on You," "I'm Confessin'," "Do I Love You?", "Do It Again," "Come Rain or Come Shine," "Day In, Day Out," "Just Imagine," "Swanee," "The Man That Got Away," "Chicago"

PC–3053   *I Feel A Song Comin On* (Pickwick Division)

"I Feel a Song Comin On," "Among My Souvenirs," "Do I Love You?", "It's a Great Day for the Irish," "Happiness Is Just a Thing Called Joe," "Little Girl Blue," "By Myself," "I Concentrate on You," "Life Is Just a Bowl of Cherries," "Anyplace I Hang My Hat Is Home"

Also released by Sears-Roebuck as *By Myself* Sp-430.

PC–3078   *Judy Garland Over the Rainbow* (Pickwick Division)

"Over the Rainbow," "Come Rain or come Shine," "Just You, Just Me," "A Pretty Girl," "When You're Smiling," "Old Devil Moon," "I Can't Give You Anything But Love," "Down With Love," "It Never Was You," "That's Entertainment"

PTP–2010   *Judy Garland: Her Greatest Hits* (Pickwick Division)

"Over the Rainbow," "Come Rain or Come Shine," "Just You, Just Me," "A Pretty Girl," "When You're Smiling," "Old Devil Moon," "I Can't Give You Anything But Love," "Down With Love," "It Never Was You," "That's Entertainment," "I Feel a Song Coming On," "Among My Souvenirs," "Do I Love You," "It's a Great Day for the Irish," "Happiness Is Just a Thing Called Joe," "Little Girl Blue," "I Concentrate on You," "Life Is Just a Bowl of Cherries," "Anyplace I Hang My Hat Is Home"

94407   *Judy in London* (with Norrie Paramour and his Orchestra)

"Lucky Day," "You Made Me Love You / For Me and My Gal / - The Trolley Song," "Happiness Is Just a Thing Called Joe," "Rock-abye Your Baby," "Stormy Weather," "The Man That Got Away," "San Francisco," "I Can't Give You Anything But Love," "Chicago," "Do It Again," "Over the Rainbow," "After You've Gone," "I Happen to Like New York," "Why Was I Born?", "You Go to My Head," "Judy at the Palace Medley," "It's a Great Day for the Irish," "Come Rain or Come Shine," "Swanee," "You'll Never Walk Alone"

SL–6524   *Showstoppers* (with other Capitol artists)

"I Concentrate on You," "Zing! Went the Strings of My Heart"

SLER06528   *That's Entertainment* (with other Capitol artists)

"Zing! Went the Strings of My Heart," "Last Night When We Were Young," "I Concentrate on You," "Little Girl Blue," "Over the Rainbow"

ST–11191   *Judy Garland—Liza Minnelli: Live at the London Palladium*

> "Together" (with Liza), "The Man That Got Away," "Love Medley" (with Liza), "What Now My Love," "Hello Dolly" (with Liza), "Swanee" (with Liza), "Over The Rainbow," "When The Saints Go Marching In/He's Got The Whole World In His Hands" (with Liza)

ABC PARAMOUNT ALBUM—33 1/3

ABC/
ABCS–620   *Judy Garland: At Home at the Palace* (with the Bobby Cole Orchestra, and Lorna and Joe Luft)

> "I Feel a Song Comin' On," "Almost Like Being in Love / This Can't Be Love," "You Made Me Love You / For Me and My Gal / - The Trolley Song," "What Now My Love," "Bob White" (with Lorna), "Jamboree Jones" (with Lorna), "Together" (with Lorna and Joe), "Old Man River," "That's Entertainment," "I Loved Him," "Rockabye Your Baby"

> Released in Great Britain by Stateside Records as SL/SSL-10220

LONGINES SYMPHONETTE SOCIETY ALBUMS—33 1/3's

SY5217,
218,219,
220,221,   *The Immortal Judy Garland*

> "Story Weather," "The Man That Got Away," "Chicago," "Rockabye Your Baby," "Over the Rainbow," "Last Night When We Were Young," "I Feel a Song Comin On," "Who Cares?", "Life Is Just a Bowl of Cherries," "By Myself," "The Battle Hymn of the Republic," "I Can't Give You Anything But Love," "Comes Once in a Lifetime," "A Pretty Girl," "You're Nearer," "Lucky Day," "I'm Confessin'," "April Showers," "I Hadn't Anyone Till You," "Come Rain or Come Shine," "Zing! Went the Strings of My Heart," "A Foggy Day," "Swanee," "I Am Loved," "Me and My Shadow," "After You've Gone," "What Now My Love," "Smile," "Little Girl Blue," "I Gotta Right to Sing the Blues," "Get Me to the Church on Time," "Fly Me to the Moon," "It's a Great Day for the Irish," "Sam Francisco," "Some People," "Puttin on the Rite," "Do It Again," "Island in the West Indies," "Anyplace I Hang My Hat Is Home," "You'll Never Walk Alone," "I Concentrate on

261

You," "Do I Love You?", "Just You, Just Me," "The Music That Makes Me Dance," "It Never Was You," "That's Entertainment," "Old Devil Moon," "Down With Love," "More Than You Know," "When You're Smiling"

SY5222   *I Could Go on Singing Forever*

"I Could Go on Singing," "You Made Me Love You / For Me and My Gal / The Boy Next Door / The Trolley Song," "Happiness Is Just a Thing Called Joe," "This Is It," "Among My Souvenirs," "Just Imagine," "Make Someone Happy"

TUCKER ALBUM—33 1/3

TLP–201   *Judy: All Alone*

"I'm Always Chasing Rainbows," "I'm Nobody's Baby," "The Man That Got Away," "Battle Hymn of the Republic," "Poor Butterfly," "All Alone," "When the Sun Comes Out," "Stormy Weather," "Suppertime," "I Gotta Right to Sing the Blues," "Why Can't I," "By Myself"

JUNO ALBUM—33 1/3

S–1000   *Judy. London. 1969.*

"I Belong to London," "Get Happy," "The Man That Got Away," "I'd Like to Hate Myself in the Morning," "Just in Time," "You Made Me Love You," "For Me and My Gal," "The Trolley Song," "For Once in My Life," "San Francisco," "Over the Rainbow"

Released in Great Britain by Sunset Records as 50196

RADIANT ALBUMS—33 1/3's

711–0101   *Judy* (with the Mort Lindsey Orchestra)

"Come Rain or Come Shine," "Smile," "I Can't Give You Anything But Love," "Hey Look Me Over," "By Myself," "San Francisco," "Fly Me to the Moon," "Do It Again," "After You've Gone," "All Alone," "It's Gonna Be a Great Day"

262

711–0102   *Judy in Hollywood* (with the Mort Lindsey Orchestra)

"Love of My Life," "A Couple of Swells," "That's Entertainment," "The Boy Next Door," "How About Me?", "If I Had a Talking Picture of You," "Toot, Toot, Tootsie," "You Made Me Love You," "For Me and My Gal," "The Trolley Song," "As Long As He Needs Me," "Dirty Hands, Dirty Face," "A Pretty Girl Milking Her Cow," "Puttin' on the Ritz"

711–0103   *Judy—The Legend*

"Do I Love You?", "What'll I Do?", "Oh Lord, I'm On My Way," "Judy At The Palace Medley," "Don't Ever Leave Me," "I'm Nobody's Baby," "That's Entertainment," "More," "Chicago," "Almost Like Being In Love/This Can't Be Love," "Here's That Rainy Day," "Through The Years"

711–0104   *Judy's Portrait in Song* (with the Mort Lindsey Orchestra)

"From This Moment On," "San Francisco," "Sweet Danger," "When Your Lover Has Gone," "Some People," "Oh, Shenandoah," "A Couple of Swells," "Almost Like Being in Love," "This Can't Be Love," "Anyplace I Hang My Hat Is Home," "Never, Never Will I Marry," "I'm Old Fashioned," "Old Devil Moon"

711–0105   *The Unforgettable Judy Garland* (with the Mort Lindsey Orchestra)

"Lucky Day," "Lost in the Stars," "I'll Show Them All," "Paris Is a Lonely Town," "Through the Years," "Island in the West Indies," "A Long, Long Trail," "Give My Regards to Broadway," "This Could Be the Start of Something Big," "I Love You," "Last Night When We Were Young," "Just in Time," "Seventy-six Trombones," "The Battle Hymn of the Republic"

RADIOLA ALBUM—33 1/3

Music 3 & 4   *Hollywood on the Air*

Excerpts from *Babes in Arms* ("Good Morning" with Mickey Rooney), *Pigskin Parade* ("It's Love I'm After," "The Texas Tornado," "Balboa"), *For Me and My Gal* ("For Me and My Gal" with Gene Kelly, "World War I Medley" with Gene Kelly), and *Little Nellie Kelly* ("Singing in the Rain")

STARTONE ALBUMS—33 1/3's

ST–201   *Judy Garland (1935–1959)*

"Broadway Rhythm," "Smiles," "Over the Rainbow," "Nobody," "America," "I May Be Wrong But I Think You're Wonderful," "I Don't Care," "Pretty Baby" (with Al Jolson), "For Me and My Gal" (with Bing Crosby), "Who?" (with Bing Crosby), "Embraceable You" (with Bing Crosby), "Alexander's Ragtime Band," "Wish You Were Here," "A Pretty Girl," "Carolina in the Morning," "You Belong to Me," "Rockabye Your Baby"

ST–208   *The Judy Garland Musical Scrapbook (1935–1949)*

"Zing Went The Strings Of My Heart," "The Texas Tornado," "It's Love I'm After," "The Balboa," "I Never Knew," "That Old Black Magic," "This Is The Army, Mr. Jones," "Gotta Get Out And Vote," "There's A Tavern In The Town" (Autolite commercial with Dick Haymes), "Somebody Love Me," "Can't Help Lovin' That Man," "Love," "Liza," "Wait Till The Sun Shines Nellie" (with Bing Crosby), "I've Got You Under My Skin," "Tearbucket Jim" (with Bing Crosby, William Frawley, and Leo McCarey), "Ma He's Making Eyes At Me" (with Bing Crosby), "Why Was I Born?"

JUDY'S BRITISH RELEASES

(This is the same material available in the United States but packaged differently. The following list does not include British releases mentioned elsewhere in this discography.)

BRUNSWICK ALBUMS—33 1/3's

A.H. 48   *Miss Show Biz*

"Friendship" (with Johnny Mercer), "It's a Great Big World" (with Virginia O'Brien and Betty Russell), "On the Atcheson, Topeka and the Sante Fe," "If I Had You," "Love," "Changin My Tune," "Bidin My Time," "Fascinatin Rhythm," "Poor Little Rich Girl," "Nothing But You"

A.H. 69   *Hollywood Sings, Volume Three* (with various Decca artsits)

"Could You Use Me?" (with Mickey Rooney), "Aren't You Kinda Glad We Did?" (with Dick Haymes)

MGM Albums—33 1/3's

D–134   *Born to Sing* (10")

"A Couple of Swells" (with Fred Astaire), "I Love A Piano / Snooky Ookums / When the Midnight Choo Choo Leaves For Alabam" (with Fred Astaire), "Put Your Arms Around Me, Honey," "Johnny One Note," "Get Happy," "A Fella With an Umbrella" (with Peter Lawford), "I Don't Care," "I Wish I Were in Love Again" (with Mickey Rooney), "Love of My Life," "Easter Parade" (with Fred Astaire)

D–139   *Words and Music / Three Little Words* (10")

"I Wish I Were in Love Again" (with Mickey Rooney)

2353033   Words and Music / Three Little Words

"I Wish I Were in Love Again" (with Mickey Rooney), "Johnny One Note"

2353038   *If You Feel Like Singing, Sing (Summer Stock) / Good News*

"Get Happy," "If You Feel Like Singing, Sing," "Happy Harvest," "Friendly Star"

2353044   *The Wizard of Oz*

"Over the Rainbow," "If I Only Had a Brain" (with Ray Bolger, Buddy Ebsen, and Bert Lahr), "Ding, Dong the Witch Is Dead" (with the Munchkins), "We're Off to See the Wizard" (with Ray Bolger, Buddy Ebsen, and Bert Lahr)

2353067   *Till the Clouds Roll By / Gentlemen Prefer Blondes*

"Who?", "Look for the Silver Lining"

23530   *The Pirate / Easter Parade*

"Be a Clown" (with Gene Kelly), "Mack the Black," "You Can Do No Wrong," "Love of My Life," "Easter Parade" (with Fred Astaire), "A

Fella With an Umbrella" (with Peter Lawford), "A Couple of Swells" (with Fred Astaire), "Better Luck Next Time," "I Love a Piano / Snooky Ookums / When the Midnight Choo Choo Leaves for Alabam" (with Fred Astaire)

2683005   *Judy Garland—The Hollywood Years*

"Last Night When We Were Young," "Play That Barbershop Chord," "Look for the Silver Lining," "Who?", "Put Your Arms Around Me, Honey," "Love of My Life," "Get Happy," "Friendly Star," "Better Luck Next Time," "If You Feel Like Singing, Sing," "I Don't Care," "Meet Me Tonight in Dreamland," "You Made Me Love You," "Bei Mir Bist Du Schoen," "I'm Nobody's Baby," "I Cried for You," "Singing in the Rain," "Danny Boy," "The Trolley Song," "But Not for Me," "Johnny One Note," "The Boy Next Door," "You Can't Get a Man With a Gun," "Over the Rainbow"

MUSIC FOR PLEASURE ALBUMS—33 1/3's

MFP–1003   *Judy Garland—The Star Years*

Selections from MGM LP's *Judy Garland—The Star Years* and *Judy Garland—The Hollywood Years*

MFP–1237   *Over the Rainbow With Judy Garland*

Selections from MGM LP's *Judy Garland—The Star Years* and *Judy Garland—The Hollywood Years*

Capitol Albums—45's

EAP–20051   *A Garland for Judy*

"Over the Rainbow," "Rockabye Your Baby," "You Made Me Love You / For Me and My Gal / The Trolley Song / The Boy Next Door"

CL–14791   *Maggie May*

"Maggie, Maggie May," "There's Only One Union," "It's Yourself," "The Land of Promises"

WORLD RECORD CLUB ALBUM—33 1/3

TP–461   *Miss Show Business*

"While We're Young," "A Pretty Girl," "Carolina in the Morning," "Life Is Just a Bowl of Cherries," "Anyplace I Hang My Hat Is Home," "This Is IT," "I Am Loved," "I Hadn't Anyone Till You," "I Concentrate on You," "I'm Confessin'," "Day In, Day Out"

Judy on Film

THE OLD LADY IN THE SHOE (Warner Brothers) 1929

With The Meglin Kiddies

EVERY SUNDAY AFTERNOON (MGM) 1936

Directed by Felix Fiest.
Cast included: Deanna Durbin and Sid Silvers.
Judy's Songs: "America," "Opera vs. Jazz" (with Durbin), "Waltz in Springtime" (with Durbin).

PIGSKIN PARADE (Twentieth Century–Fox) 1936

Directed by David Butler. Associate Producer: Bogart Rogers. Screenplay by Harry Tugend, Jack Wellan, and Mark Kelly. Musical direction by David Buttolph. Music and lyrics by Lew Pollock, Sidney M. Mitchell, and the Yacht Club Boys. Costumes by Gwen Wakeling. Photographed by Arthur Miller. Running time: 95 minutes.
Cast included: Stuart Erwin, Patsy Kelly, Jack Haley, Johnny Downs, Betty Grable, Arline Judge, Dixie Dunbar, Anthony (Tony Martin).
Judy's Songs: "It's Love I'm After," "The Texas Tornado," "The Balboa" (with principals and chorus). Recorded but not used: "Hold That Bulldog."

BROADWAY MELODY OF 1938 (MGM) 1937

Directed by Roy Del Ruth. Produced by Jack Cummings. Screenplay by Jack McGowan. Original story by Jack McGowan, Sid Silvers. Music and lyrics by Nacio Herb Brown and Arthur Freed. Dance direction by Dave Gould. Musical direction by Georgie Stoll. Arrangement by Roger Edens. Costumes by Adrian. Photographed by William Daniels. Running time: 110 minutes.

Cast included: Robert Taylor, Eleanor Powell, George Murphy, Binnie Barnes, Sophie Tucker, Buddy Ebsen, Charles Gorin, Raymond Walburn, Robert Benchley.

Judy's Songs: "(Dear Mr. Gable) You Made Me Love You," "Everybody Sing," "Yours and Mine" (with Powell, Taylor, et al.), "Finale" (with Ebsen, Murphy, Gorin, Tucker, and chorus).

THOROUGHBREDS DON'T CRY (MGM) 1937

Directed by Alfred E. Green. Produced by Harry Rapf. Screenplay by Lawrence Hazard. Original story by Eleanore Griffin and J. Walter Rubin. Music and lyrics by Nacio Herb Brown and Arthur Freed. Musical direction by William Axt. Costumes by Dolly. Photographed by Leonard Smith. Running time: 80 minutes.

Cast included: Mickey Rooney, Sophie Tucker, C. Aubrey Smith, Ronald Sinclair, Forrester Harvey, Helen Troy, Charles Brown, Frankie Darro, Henry Kolker.

Judy's Songs: "Gotta Pair of New Shoes." Recorded but not used: "Sun Showers."

EVERYBODY SING (MGM) February, 1938

Directed by Edwin L. Marin. Produced by Harry Rapf. Screenplay by Florence Ryerson and Edgar Allan Woolf from their original story. Additional dialogue by James Gruen. Musical direction by Dr. William Axt. Arrangement by Roger Edens. Music and lyrics by Gus Kahn, Bronislau Kaper, Walter Jurmann, Harry Ruby, and Bert Kalmer. Costumes by Dolly Tree. Photographed by Joseph Ruttenberg. Running time: 80 minutes.

Cast included: Allan Jones, Fannie Brice, Reginald Owen, Billie Burke, Reginald Gardner, Lynne Carver, Helen Troy, Monty Woolley.

Judy's songs: "Sweet Chariot," "Down on Melody Farm," "Swing, Mr. Mendelssohn," "Why? Because" (with Fannie Brice), "Bus Sequence" (with Jones, Carver, and Gardner).

LISTEN, DARLING (MGM) October, 1938

Directed by Edwin L. Marin. Produced by Jack Cummings. Screenplay by Elaine Ryan and Anne Morrison Chapin. Original story by Katherine Brush. Musical direction by Georgie Stoll. Arrangements by Roger Edens. Songs by Al Hoffman, Al Lewis, Murray Mancher, Joseph McCarthy, and Milton Ager. Costumes by Dolly Tree. Photographed by Charles Lawton, Jr. Running time: 70 minutes.

Cast included: Freddie Bartholomew, Mary Astor, Walter Pidgeon, Alan Hale, Charlie Grapewin, Scotty Beckett, Gene Lockhart, Barnett Parker, Byron Foulger.

Judy's Songs: "Ten Pins in the Sky," "Zing! Went the Strings of My

Heart," "On the Bumpy Road to Love" (with Bartholemew, Astor, Pidgeon, and Beckett).

LOVE FINDS ANDY HARDY (MGM) July, 1938

Directed by George B. Seitz. Produced by Lou Ostrow. Screenplay by William Ludwig. Based upon characters created by Aurania Rouverol and stories by Vivien R. Breatherton. Songs by Mack Gordon, Harry Revel, and Roger Edens. Vocal arrangements by Roger Edens. Musical score by David Snell. Costumes by Jeanne. Photographed by Lester White. Running time: 90 minutes

Cast included: Lewis Stone, Mickey Rooney, Cecilia Parker, Ann Rutherford, Lana Turner, Fay Holden, Don Castle, Gene Reynolds, Marie Blake, George Breakstone.

Judy's Songs: "Meet the Beat of My Heart," "In Between." Recorded but not used: "It Never Rains But What It Pours" and "Bei Mir Bist Du Schoen."

THE WIZARD OF OZ (MGM) August, 1939

Directed by Victor Fleming. Produced by Mervyn LeRoy. "Over the Rainbow" sequence directed by King Vidor. Screenplay by Noel Langley and Florence Ryerson. Original story by L. Frank Baum. Character makeup by Jack Dawn. Music and lyrics by Harold Arlen and Yip Harburg. Musical numbers directed by Bobby Connolly. Costumes by Adrian. Photographed by Harold Rossen. Running time: 100 minutes.

Cast included: Frank Morgan, Ray Bolger, Bert Lahr, Jack Haley, Billie Burke, Margaret Hamilton, Clara Blandick, Charley Grapewin, Pat Walshe.

Judy's Songs: "Over the Rainbow," "Follow the Yellow Brick Road" (with Bolger, Lahr, and Buddy Ebson,)* "We're Off to See the Wizard" (with Bolger, Lahr, and Ebsen), "Munchkinland" (with Billie Burke). Recorded but not used: "The Jitterbug" (with Bolger, Lahr, and Ebsen)*

BABES IN ARMS (MGM) December, 1939

Directed by Busby Berkeley. Produced by Arthur Freed. Screenplay by Jack McGowan and Kay Van Riper. Original book by Richard Rodgers and Lorenz Hart, based on their Broadway production. Music and lyrics by Rodgers and Hart. Musical direction by Georgie Stoll. Costumes by Dolly Tree. Photographed by Ray June. Running time: 98 minutes.

Cast included: Mickey Rooney, Charles Winninger, June Preisser, Grace Hayes, Betty Jaynes, Douglas McPhail, Margaret Hamilton, Guy Kibbee, Rand Brooks, Ann Shoemaker, Henry Hull.

Judy's Songs: "I Cried for You," "Good Morning" (with Rooney),

*Buddy Ebsen supplied the singing voice for Jack Haley.

271

"Where or When," "God's Country" (with Rooney, Jaynes, and MacPhail), "Opera vs. Jazz" (with Jaynes).

ANDY HARDY MEETS DEBUTANTE (MGM) July, 1940

Directed by George B. Seitz. Produced by J. J. Cohn, Screenplay by Annalee Whitmore and Thomas Seller. Based upon characters created by Aurania Rouverol. Songs by Nacio Herb Brown, Arthur Freed, Benny Davis, Milton Ager, and Lester Santley. Musical score by David Snell. Musical arrangements by Roger Edens. Vocal and orchestrations by Arnaud, Salinger, Van Eps, and Haglin. Photographed by Sidney Wanger. Costumes by Dolly Tree. Running time: 87 minutes.

Cast included: Lewis Stone, Mickey Rooney, Cecilia Parker, Fay Holden, Ann Rutherford, Diana Lewis, George Breakstone, Sara Haden, George Lessey, Harry Tyler.

Judy's Songs: "I'm Nobody's Baby," "Alone." Recorded but not used: "Buds Won't Bud," "All I Do Is Dream of You."

STRIKE UP THE BAND (MGM) September, 1940

Directed by Busby Berkeley. Produced by Arthur Freed. Screenplay by John Monks, Jr. and Fred Finklehoffe. Music and lyrics by Roger Edens. Additional songs by George and Ira Gershwin, Arthur Freed and Roger Edens, Leo Arnaud and Conrad Salinger. Musical direction by Georgie Stoll. Musical presentation by Merrill Pye. Photographed by Ray June. Running time: 120 minutes.

Cast included: Mickey Rooney, June Preisser, William Tracy, Larry Nunn, Margaret Early, Ann Shoemaker, Frances Pielot, Virginia Brissac.

Judy's Songs: "Nobody," "Drummer Boy" (with Six Hits and a Miss), "Do the La Conga" (with Rooney, Six Hits and a Miss, and chorus), "Nell of New Rochelle" (with Rooney, Early, Nunn, and Tracy), "Our Love Affair" (with Rooney), "The Finale" (with Rooney, Six Hits and a Miss, and chorus).

LITTLE NELLIE KELLY (MGM) November, 1940

Directed by Norman Taurog. Produced by Arthur Freed. Screenplay by Jack McGowan. Based on the musical comedy written and produced by George M. Cohan. Other song: "Singing in the Rain" by Nacio Herb Brown and Arthur Freed. Musical adaptation by Georgie Stoll. Costumes by Dolly Tree. Photographed by Ray June. Running time: 100 minutes.

Cast included: George Murphy, Charles Winninger, Douglas McPhail, Arthur Shields, James Burke, Robert Homans, Thomas P. Dillon, Rita Page, Henry Blair, Frederic Worlock.

Judy's Songs: "A Pretty Girl Milking Her Cow," "Singing in the Rain," "It's a Great Day for the Irish" (with Douglas McPhail and chorus), "Nellie Kelly, I Love You" (with Murphy, Winninger, and chorus). Recorded but not used: "Danny Boy."

272

THE ZIEGFIELD GIRL (MGM) April, 1941

Directed by Robert Z. Leonard. Produced by Pandro S. Berman. Screenplay by Marguerite and Sonya Levien. Written by William Anthony McGuire. Musical numbers by Busby Berkeley. Songs by Nacio Herb Brown, Gus Kahn, Roger Edens, Harry Carroll, Joseph McCarthy, Edward Gallagher, and Al Shean. Vocal arrangements and orchestrations by Leo Arnaud, George Bassman, and Conrad Salinger. Musical direction by Georgie Stoll. Gowns and costumes by Adrian. Photographed by Ray June. Running time: 134 minutes.

Cast included: Hedy Lamarr, Lana Turner, James Stewart, Tony Martin, Ian Hunter, Jackie Cooper, Charles Winninger, Edward Everett Horton, Philip Dorn, Dan Dailey, Jr., Paul Kelly, Al Shean, Fay Holden, Eve Arden.

Judy's Songs   "Minnie from Trinidad" (with Tony Martin and chorus), "Ziegfeld Girl" (with chorus), "Laugh? I Thought I'd Split My Sides" (with Charles Winninger), "I'm Always Chasing Rainbows," "The Finale" (with Martin, Six Hits and a Miss).

WE MUST HAVE MUSIC (MGM) 1941

Short subject explaining the purpose of the studio's music department. It used scenes from Judy's portions of *Ziegfeld Girl.*

LIFE BEGINS FOR ANDY HARDY (MGM) August, 1941

Directed by George B. Seitz. Produced by J. J. Cohn. Screenplay by Agnes Christine Johnson. Based upon characters created by Aurania Rouverol. Musical direction by Georgie Stoll. Costumes by Kalloch. Photographed by Lester White. Running time: 100 minutes.

Cast included: Mickey Rooney, Lewis Stone, Fay Holden, Ann Rutherford, Sara Haden, Patricia Dane, Ray McDonald, George Breakstone, Pierre Watkin.

Judy's Songs: Judy recorded four songs for use in this film but all of them were deleted: "Easy to Love," "Abide With Me," "The Rosary," "America."

BABES ON BROADWAY (MGM) December, 1941

Directed by Busby Berkeley. Produced by Arthur Freed. Screenplay by Fred Finklehoffe and Elaine Ryan. Original story by Fred Finklehoffe. Songs by Yip Harburg, Burton Lane, Ralph Freed, Roger Edens, and Harold J. Rome. Musical adaptation by Roger Edens. Musical direction by Georgie Stoll. Costumes by Kalloch. Photographed by Lester White. Vocal arrangements by Leo Arnaud, Conrad Salinger, and George Bassman. Running time: 118 minutes.

Cast included: Mickey Rooney, Fay Bainter, Virginia Weidler, Ray McDonald, Richard Quine, Donald Meek, James Gleason,

Emma Dunn, Frederick Burton, Alexander Woolcott, Donna Reed, Cliff Clark.

Judy's Songs: "Mary's a Grand Old Name," "Rings on My Fingers," "How About You?" (with Rooney), "Chin Up. Cheerio, Carry On," "Bombshell from Brazil" (with Rooney, Quine, McDonald, Weidler), "Hoe Down" (with Rooney, Six Hits and a Miss, and Five Music Maids), "Minstrel Show" (with Rooney and chorus).

FOR ME AND MY GAL (MGM) October, 1942

Directed by Busby Berkeley. Produced by Arthur Freed. Screenplay by Richard Sherman, Fred Finklehoffe, and Sid Silvers. Written by Howard Emmett Rogers. Song "For Me and My Gal" by George W. Meyer, Edgar Leslie, and E. Ray Goetz. Musical adaptation by Roger Edens. Dance direction by Bobby Connolly. Vocal and orchestration by Conrad Salinger, George Mussman, and Leo Arnaud. Costumes by Kalloch. Photographed by William Daniels. Running time: 104 minutes.

Cast included: George Murphy, Gene Kelly, Marta Eggerth, Ben Blue, Richard Quine, Keenan Wynn, Horace (Stephen) McNally, Lucille Norman.

Judy's Songs: "After You've Gone," "How Ya Gonna Keep 'Em Down on the Farm," "Ballin' the Jack" (with Kelly), "Where Do We Go from Here Boys?" (with the King's Men and chorus), "For Me and My Gal" (with Kelly), "Oh, You Beautiful Doll" (with Murphy and Norman), "World War I Medley."

PRESENTING LILY MARS (MGM) May, 1943

Directed by Norman Taurog. Produced by Joseph Pasternak. Screenplay by Richard Connell and Gladys Lehman. Based on the novel by Booth Tarkington. Songs by Walter Jurmann, Paul Francis Webster, Yip Harburg, Burton Lane, Roger Edens. Musical direction by Georgie Stoll. Dance direction by Ernest Matray. Photographed by Joseph Ruttenberg. Gowns by Shoup. Running time: 102 minutes.

Cast included: Van Heflin, Fay Bainter, Richard Carlson, Spring Byington, Marta Eggerth, Connie Gilchrist, Leonid Kinskey, Ray McDonald, Charles Walters. Also: Bob Crosby and his Orchestra, Tommy Dorsey and his Orchestra.

Judy's Songs: "When I Look at You," "Tom, Tom the Piper's Son," "Every Little Movement" (with Gilchrist), "The Finale"—including "Three O'Clock in the Morning" and "Broadway Rhythm" (with chorus). Recorded but not used: "Caro Mono," "Paging Mr. Greenback."

GIRL CRAZY (MGM) November, 1943

Directed by Norman Taurog. Produced by Arthur Freed. Screenplay by Fred Finklehoffe. Original story by Gus Bolton and Jack McGowan. Music and lyrics by George and Ira Gershwin. Musical adaption by Roger Edens. Musical direction by Georgie Stoll. Costumes by Irene. Photographed by William Daniels and Robert Flank. Running time: 99 minutes.

Cast included: Mickey Rooney, Gil Stratton, Robert E. Strickland, Rags Ragland, June Allyson, Nancy Walker, Guy Kibbee, Frances Rafferty, Howard Freeman, Henry O'Neill.

Judy's Songs: "But Not for Me," "Boy What Love Has Done for Me," "I Got Rhythm," "Embraceable You," "Bidin' My Time."

THOUSANDS CHEER (MGM) October, 1943

Directed by George Sidney. Produced by Joseph Pasternak. Screenplay by Paul Jerricho and Richard Collins, based on their story "Private Miss Jones." Music and lyrics by Ferde Grofe and Harold Adamson; Lew Brown, Ralph Freed, Burton Lane, Walter Jurmann, and Paul Francis Webster; Earl Brent and Yip Harburg; Dmitri Shostakovich, Harold Rome and Yip Harburg. Musical direction by Herbert Stothart. Photographed by George Folsey. Costume supervision by Irene. Running time: 125 minutes.

Cast included: Kathryn Grayson, Gene Kelly, Mary Astor, Jose Iturbi, John Boles, Dick Simmons, Ben Blue, Frank Jenks, Frank Sully, Frances Rafferty, Odette Myrtel, Will Kaufman, Mickey Rooney, Red Skelton, Eleanor Powell, Ann Sothern, Lucille Ball, Virginia O'Brien, June Allyson, Gloria DeHaven, John Conte, Sara Haden, Frank Morgan, Kay Kyser and his Orchestra, Bob Crosby and his Orchestra.

Judy's Song: "The Joint Is Really Jumpin' Down at Carnegie Hall."

MEET ME IN ST. LOUIS (MGM) December, 1944

Directed by Vincente Minnelli. Produced by Arthur Freed. Screenplay by Irving Beecher and Fred Finklehoffe. Based on the book by Sally Benson. Musical adaption by Roger Edens. Musical direction by Georgie Stoll. Songs by Arthur Freed, Nacio Herb Brown, Kerry Mills, Andrew B. Sterling, Hugh Martin, Ralph Blane, Richard Rodgers and Oscar Hammerstein II. Dance direction by Charles Walters. Photographed by George Folsey. Costumes supervised by Irene and designed by Shariff. Running time: 112 minutes.

Cast included: Margaret O'Brien, Mary Astor, Lucille Bremer, Tom Drake, Marjorie Main, Leon Ames, Harry Davenport, June Lockhart, Henry Daniels, Jr., Joan Carroll, Hugh Marlowe, Chill Wills.

Judy's Songs: "The Boy Next Door," "Have Yourself a Merry Little Christmas," "The Trolley Song" (with chorus), "Skip to My Lou" (with Drake, Bremer, and chorus), "Over the Bannister" (with Drake), "Under the Bamboo Tree" (with O'Brien), "Meet Me in St. Louis" (with Bremer, Davenport, Carroll, and chorus). Recorded but not used: "Boys and Girls Like You and Me."

275

THE CLOCK (MGM) April, 1945

(Released in England as *Under the Clock.*) Directed by Vincente Minnelli. Produced by Arthur Freed. Screenplay by Robert Nathan and Joseph Schrank. Based on a story by Paul Gallico and Pauline Gallico. Musical score by George Bassman. Photographed by George Folsey. Costumes by Irene and Marion Herwood Keyes. Running time: 90 minutes.

Cast included: Robert Walker, James Gleason, Keenan Wynn, Marshall Thompson, Lucille Gleason, Ruth Brady, Moyna Macgill.

THE HARVEY GIRLS (MGM) January, 1946

Directed by George Sidney. Produced by Arthur Freed. Associate Producer: Roger Edens. Screenplay by Edmond Beloin and Nathaniel Curtis. Original story by Samuel Hopkins Adams, Eleanore Griffin, and William Rankin. Music and lyrics by Johnny Mercer and Harry Warren. Musical direction by Lennie Hayton. Special effects created by Warren Newcombe. Costumes by Irene. Photographed by George Folsey. Running time: 101 minutes.

Cast included: John Hodiak, Ray Bolger, Preston Foster, Virginia O'Brien, Angela Lansbury, Marjorie Main, Chill Wills, Kenny Baker, Selena Royale, Cyd Charisse, Ruth Brady.

Judy's Songs: "On the Atchison, Topeka and the Sante Fe," "In the Valley When the Evening Sun Comes Down," "Swing Your Partner" (with chorus), "It's a Great Big World" (with Charisse and O'Brien).

THE ZIEGFELD FOLLIES (MGM) March, 1946

Directed by Vincent Minnelli. Produced by Arthur Freed. Songs by Harry Warren, Arthur Freed, George and Ira Gershwin, Ralph Blane, Hugh Martin, Kay Thompson, and Roger Edens. Musical direction by Lennie Hayton. Vocal arrangements by Kay Thompson. Costume supervision by Irene. Costumes designed by Helen Rose. Running time: 115 minutes.

Cast included: Fred Astaire, Lucille Ball, Fannie Brice, Kathryn Grayson, Lena Horne, Gene Kelly, James Melton, Victor Moore, Red Skelton, Esther Williams, William Powell, Edward Arnold, Marion Bell, Bunin's Puppets, Cyd Charisse, Hume Cronyn, William Frawley, Robert Lewis, Virginia O'Brien, Keenan Wynn.

Judy's Songs: "The Interview"—a musical-comedy sketch. Recorded but not used: "Liza."

TILL THE CLOUDS ROLL BY (MGM) December, 1946

Directed by Richard Whorf. Produced by Arthur Freed. Screenplay by Myles Connolly and Jean Halloway. Story by Guy Bolton. Adapted by George Wells. Based on the life and music of Jerome Kern. Musical direction by Lennie Hayton. Orchestrations by Conrad Salinger. Musical numbers staged and directed by Robert Alton. Judy Garland's numbers directed by Vincente Minnelli. Photographed by Harry Stradling. Costumes by Helen Rose and supervised by Irene. Running time: 137 minutes.

Cast included: Robert Walker, Lucille Bremer, Van Heflin, Paul Langdon, Dorothy Patrick, Mary Nash, Van Johnson, Dinah Shore, Harry Hayden, Paul Maxey, John Wells, June Allyson, Angela Lansbury, Ray McDonald, Cyd Charisse, Gower Champion, the Wilde Twins, Tony Martin, Kathryn Grayson, Virginia O'Brien, Lena Horne, Caleb Peterson, Johnny Johnston, Frank Sinatra.

Judy's Songs: "Who?", "Look for the Silver Lining."

THE PIRATE (MGM) June, 1948

Directed by Vincente Minnelli. Produced by Arthur Freed. Screenplay by Albert Hackett and Frances Goodrich. Based on a play by S. N. Behrman. Dance direction by Robert Alton and Gene Kelly. Songs by Cole Porter. Musical direction by Lennie Hayton. Instrumental arrangements by Conrad Salinger. Photographed by Harry Stradling. Costumes by Irene, Tom Keogh, and Karinska. Running time: 101 minutes.

Cast included: Gene Kelly, Walter Slezak, Gladys Cooper, Reginald Owen, George Zucco, Nickolas Brothers, Lola (Albright) Deem, Lester Allen, Ellen Ross, Mary Jo Ellis, Jean Dean.

Judy's Songs: "Love of My Life," "Mack the Black," "You Can Do No Wrong," "Be a Clown" (with Kelly). Recorded but not used: "Voodoo."

EASTER PARADE (MGM) July, 1948

Directed by Charles Walters. Produced by Arthur Freed. Screenplay by Sidney Sheldon, Francis Goodrich, and Albert Hackett. Original story by Hackett and Goodrich. Music and lyrics by Irving Berlin. Musical direction by Johnny Green. Orchestrations by Conrad Salinger, Van Cleave, and Leo Arnaud. Vocal arrangements by Robert Tucker. Women's costumes by Irene. Photographed by Harry Stradling. Running time: 112 minutes.

Cast included: Fred Astaire, Peter Lawford, Ann Miller, Clinton Sunderberg, Jules Munshin, Jeni Lagon, Jimmy Bates, Richard Beavers, Dick Simmons.

Judy's Songs: "A Fella With an Umbrella" (with Peter Lawford), "It Only Happens When I Dance With You," "Better Luck Next Time," "A Couple of Swells" (with Astaire), "I Want to Go Back to Michigan," "Medley: I Love a Piano, When the Midnight Choo Choo Leaves for Alabam, and Snooky Ookums" (with Astaire). Recorded but not used: "Mr. Monotony."

WORDS AND MUSIC (MGM) December, 1948

Directed by Norman Taurog. Produced by Arthur Freed. Screenplay by Fred Finklehoffe. Story by Guy Bolton and Jean Holloway. Adaption by Ben Feiner, Jr. Musical numbers directed by Robert Alton. Music and lyrics by Richard Rodgers and Lorenz Hart. Photographed by Charles Rosher and Harry Stradling. Women's costumes by Helen Rose. Running time: 100 minutes.

Cast included: Mickey Rooney, Perry Como, Ann Sothern, Tom Drake, Betty Garrett, Janet Leigh, Marshall Thompson, Jeanette Nolan, Richard Quine, Clinton Sunderberg, Harry Antrim, Ilka Gruning, June Allyson, Lena Horne, Gene Kelly, Vera-Ellen, Cyd Charisse, Mel Torme, the Blackburn Twins, Allyn McLerie.

Judy's Songs: "I Wish I Were in Love Again" (with Rooney), "Johnny One Note."

IN THE GOOD OLD SUMMERTIME (MGM) July, 1949

Directed by Robert Z. Leonard. Produced by Joseph Pasternak. Screenplay by Albert Hackett, Frances Goodrich, and Ivan Tors. Based on a scenario by Samson Raphaelson and a play by Miklos Laszlo. Musical sequences directed by Robert Alton. Musical direction by Georgie Stoll. Photographed by Harry Stradling. Women's costumes by Helen Rose. Running time: 102 minutes.

Cast included: Van Johnson, S. Z. (Cuddles) Sakall, Spring Byington, Marcia Van Dyke, Clinton Sunderberg, Lillian Bronson, Ralph Sanford, Buster Keaton.

Judy's Songs: "Merry Christmas," "Meet Me Tonight in Dreamland," "I Don't Care," "In the Good Old Summertime" (with chorus), "Put Your Arms Around Me," "Play That Barbershop Chord." Recorded but not used: "Last Night When We Were Young."

SUMMER STOCK (MGM) August, 1950

Directed by Charles Walters. Produced by Joseph Pasternak. Screenplay by George Wells and Sy Gomberg. Story by Sy Gomberg. Music and lyrics by Harry Warren and Mack Gordon. Dances staged by Nick Castle. Musical direction by Johnny Green and Saul Chaplin. Orchestrations by Conrad Salinger and Skip Martin. Photographed by Robert Planck. Costumes by Walter Plunkett. Running time: 108 minutes.

Cast included: Gene Kelly, Phil Silvers, Marjorie Main, Gloria DeHaven, Eddie Bracken, Ray Collins, Nita Bieber, Carleton Carpenter, Hans Conreid.

Judy's Songs: "Friendly Star," "If You Feel Like Singing, Sing," "Happy Harvest," "You Wonderful You" (with Kelly), "All for You" (with Kelly), "Get Happy."

A STAR IS BORN (Warner Brothers) September, 1954

Directed by George Cukor. Produced by Sidney Luft. Screenplay by Moss Hart based on a screenplay by Dorothy Parker, Alan Campbell, and Robert Carson. Original story by William A. Wellman and Robert Carson. Musical direction by Ray Heindorf. New songs by Harold Arlen and Ira Gershwin. "Born in a Trunk" by Leonard Gershe. Dances created and staged by Richard Barstow. Costumes for "Born in a Trunk" by Irene Shariff. Other costumes by Jean Louis. Vocal arrangements by Jack Cathcart. Orchestrations by Skip Martin. Photographed by Sam Leavitt. Running time: 182 minutes.

Cast included: James Mason, Charles Bickford, Tommy Noonan, Lucy Marlowe, Amanda Blake, Irving Bacon, Hazel Shermet, James Brown, Lotus Robb.

Judy's Songs: "The Man That Got Away," "Gotta Have Me Go With You," "Here's What I'm Here For," "It's a New World," "Someone at Last," "Lose That Long Face," "Born in a Trunk."

JUDGMENT AT NUREMBERG (United Artists) December, 1961

Directed by Stanley Kramer. Produced by Stanley Kramer. Associate producer: Philip Langner. Screenplay by Abby Mann adapted from his teleplay. Photographed by Ernest Laszlo. Music by Ernest Gould. Wardrobe by Joe King. (Filmed in Hollywood and Germany). Running time: 178 minutes.

Cast included: Spencer Tracy, Burt Lancaster, Richard Widmark, Marlene Dietrich, Maximilian Schell, Montgomery Clift, William Shatner, Edward Binns, Kenneth Mackenna, Werner Klemperer, Alan Baxter, Torben Meyer.

PEPE (Columbia) 1960

Directed by George Sidney.

Judy did not appear in this all-star film but was heard singing one song, "The Far Away Part of Town."

GAY PURR—EE (Warner Brothers) 1962

Cast included: Hermione Gingold, Robert Goulet, Red Buttons.
Judy's songs: "Take My Hand, Paree," "Paris Is a Lonely Town," "Roses Red, Violets Blue," "Little Drops of Rain," "Mewsette Finale" (with Goulet).

A CHILD IS WAITING (United Artists) January, 1963

Directed by John Cassavetes. Produced by Stanley Kramer. Screenplay by Abby Mann based on his teleplay. Music by Ernest Gould. Running time: 104 minutes.

279

Cast included: Burt Lancaster, Gena Rowlands, Bruce Ritchey, Steven Hill.

I Could Go on Singing (United Artists) March, 1963

Directed by Ronald Neame. Produced by Stuart Miller and Lawrence Turman. Screenplay by Mayo Simon. Story by Robert Dozier. Songs by Harold Arlen and Yip Harburg. Musical supervision by Saul Chaplin. Music by Mort Lindsey. Photographed by Arthur Ibbetson. Costumes by Edith Head. Running time: 99 minutes.

Cast included: Dirk Bogarde, Jack Klugman, Gregory Phillips, Aline MacMahon, Pauline Jameson, Jeremy Burnham.

Judy's Songs: "I Could Go on Singing," "Hello Bluebird," "It Never Was You," "By Myself," "I Am the Monarch of the Sea" (with chorus).

Judy on Television

"THE FORD STAR JUBILEE." *September 24, 1955.* CBS.

Guests: David Wayne, the Goofers, Mitsuko. Starring Judy Garland.

Judy's songs included: "You Made Me Love You," "Swanee," "The Palace Medley," "Delovely" (with Wayne and Mitsuko), "While We're Young," "But Not for Me," "For Me and My Gal" (with Wayne), "The Boy Next Door," "The Trolley Song," "Rockabye Your Baby," "A Couple of Swells" (with Wayne), "Over the Rainbow."

"THE GENERAL ELECTRIC THEATRE." *April 8, 1956.* CBS.

Guests: Starring Judy Garland with an introduction by Ronald Reagan.

Judy's songs included: "I Will Come Back," "Last Night When We Were Young," "I Feel a Song Comin On," "Life Is Just a Bowl of Cherries," "Dirty Hands, Dirty Face," "April Showers."

"THE JUDY GARLAND SHOW." *February 25, 1962.* CBS.

Guests: Frank Sinatra, Dean Martin. With Mort Lindsey and his orchestra.

Judy's songs included: "Just in Time," "You Do Something to Me" (with Martin and Sinatra), "The Man That Got Away," "When You're Smiling," "I Can't Give You Anything But Love," "Medley: Let There Be Love, You're Nobody Till Somebody Loves You" (with Martin and Sinatra), "You Made Me Love You," "The Trolley Song," "Rockabye Your Baby," "Swanee," "San Francisco."

"THE JACK PAAR SHOW." *December, 1962.* NBC.

Guests: Judy Garland, Robert Goulet.

Judy's songs included: "Little Drops of Rain," "Paris Is a Lonely Town," "Mewsette" (with Goulet).

"JUDY AND HER GUESTS." *March 19, 1963.* CBS.

Guests: Robert Goulet, Phil Silvers. With Mort Lindsey and his orchestra.

Judy's songs included: "Hello Bluebird," "I Happen to Like New York," "Here I'll Stay" (with Goulet), "Manhattan Sketch" (with Silvers), "Through the Years," "Love Is a Lovely Thing" (with Goulet), "Get Happy," "Almost Like Being in Love / This Can't Be Love," "By Myself," "I Could Go on Singing."

"SUNDAY NIGHT AT THE PALLADIUM" (British Television). *March, 1963.*

Portions of this program were later telecast on "The Ed Sullivan Show."

Judy's songs included: "Almost Like Being in Love / This Can't Be Love," "Smile," "Comes Once in a Lifetime," "I Could Go on Singing."

"THE ED SULLIVAN SHOW." *March, 1963.* CBS.

(see above)

"THE JUDY GARLAND SHOW." *September 29, 1963.* CBS.

Guests: Donald O'Connor, Jerry Van Dyke.

Judy's songs included: "Call Me Irresponsible," "Keep Your Sunny Side Up" (with O'Connor and Van Dyke), "Medley: Inka Dinka Do, If You Knew Susie, Mammy, Indian Love Song, Rose Marie, Sweetheart, Stout-Hearted Men, Italian Street Song, Ah Sweet Mystery of Life" (with O'Connor), "Fly Me to the Moon," "Be My Guest" (with O'Connor), "Medley: Wicky Wacky Woo, Yacka Hoola Hicke Doola, Dancin at the Motion Picture Ball, The Old Soft Shoe" (with O'Connor), "I Will Come Back," "Chicago."

"THE JUDY GARLAND SHOW." *October 6, 1963.* CBS.

Guests: Barbra Streisand, the Smothers Brothers, Jerry Van Dyke.

Judy's songs included: "Comes Once in a Lifetime," "Be My Guest" (with Streisand, the Smothers Brothers, and Van Dyke), "Just in Time," "Happy Days Are Here Again / Get Happy" (with Streisand), "There's No Business Like Show Business" (with Streisand and Ethel Merman—a surprise guest), "Happy Harvest" (with Streisand), "Medley: Hooray for Love, After You've Gone, By Myself, 'S Wonderful, How About You, Lover Come Back to Me, You and the Night and the Music, It All Depends on You" (with Streisand), "Medley: You Made Me Love You and The Trolley Song," "I Will Come Back."

"THE JUDY GARLAND SHOW." *October 13, 1963.* CBS.

Guests: Lena Horne, Terry-Thomas.

Judy's songs included: "Day In, Day Out" (with Horne), "A Foggy Day," "Medley: Honeysuckle Rose, Meet Me in St. Louis, Deed I Do, Zing! Went the Strings of My Heart, It's Alright With Me, The Trolley Song, and Love" (with Horne), "Mad Dogs and Englishmen" (with Horne and Thomas), "The Man That Got Away," "I Will Come Back."

"THE JUDY GARLAND SHOW." *October 20, 1963.* CBS.

Guests: George Maharis, Jack Carter, the Dillards, Leo Durocher, Jerry Van Dyke.

Judy's songs included: "Alexander's Ragtime Band," "Be My Guest" (with Maharis and Carter), "I Wish You Love," "Side By Side" (with Maharis), "Take Me Out to the Ball Game" (with Durocher), "Y'All Come," "Somebody Touched Me," "Way in the Middle of the Air," "Swanee," "I Will Come Back."

"THE JUDY GARLAND SHOW." *October 27, 1963.* CBS.

Guests: Steve Lawrence, June Allyson, Jerry Van Dyke.

Judy's songs included: "Life Is Just a Bowl of Cherries," "Happiness Is Just a Thing Called Joe," "Be My Guest" (with Lawrence), "Have You Been Through This Before" (with Lawrence), "The Doodlin Song" (with Allyson), "Medley: Buckle Down Winsocki, Honey, Cleopatterer, Thou Swell, Till the Clouds Roll By, Look for the Silver Lining" (with Lawrence and Allyson), "San Francisco," "I Will Come Back."

"THE JUDY GARLAND SHOW." *November 3, 1963.* CBS.

Guests: Zina Bethune, Vic Damone, George Jessel.

Judy's songs included: "From This Moment On," "Be My Guest" (with Damone and Bethune), "Moon River," "Getting to Know You" (with Bethune), "Porgy and Bess Medley: Where's My Bess, Summertime, It Ain't Necessarily So, I Got Plenty of Nothin, Dere's a Boat That's Leavin Soon for New York, Bess You Is My Woman Now" (with Damone), "My Bill," "Medley: Auld Lang Syne, Deck the Halls, Easter Parade, Brother Can You Spare a Dime, I'm a Yankee Doodle Dandy, You're a Grand Old Flag, Happy Birthday to You, Thank Heavens for Little Girls, Me and My Shadow, M-O-T-H-E-R" (with Damone and Bethune), "Smile," "Rockabye Your Baby," "I Will Come Back."

"THE JUDY GARLAND SHOW." *November 10, 1963.* CBS.

Guests: Count Basie, Mel Torme, Judy Henske, Jerry Van Dyke.

Judy's songs included: "The Sweetest Sounds / Strike Up the Band" (with Basie), "Memories of You" (with Basie), "I've Got My Love to Keep Me Warm," "April in Paris" (with Torme), "A Cottage for Sale," "Hey Look Me Over," "I Will Come Back."

"THE JUDY GARLAND SHOW." *November 17, 1963.* CBS.

Guests: Liza Minnelli, Soupy Sales, the Brothers Castro, Jerry Van Dyke.

Judy's songs included: "Liza," "Come Rain or Come Shine," "Together" (with Minnelli), "We Could Make Such Beautiful Music Together / The Best Is Yet to Come / Bye Bye Baby / Bob White" (with Minnelli), "As Long As He Needs Me," "Let Me Entertain You" (with Minnelli), "Two Lost Souls" (with Minnelli), "I Will Come Back" (with Minnelli).

"THE JUDY GARLAND SHOW." *December 1, 1963.* CBS.

Guests: Jack Carter, Peggy Lee, Carl Reiner.

Judy's songs included: "It's a Good Day," "Never, Never Will I Marry," "I Love Bein Here With You" (with Lee), "Broadway Medley: My Defenses Are Down, They Say It's Wonderful, This Nearly Was Mine, I'm Gonna Wash That Man Right Out of My Hair, I've Grown Accustomed to Her Face, Too Close for Comfort, Mr. Wonderful" (with Carter), "Medley: I Like Men, You Make Me Feel So Young, I Had a Man, Fever, It's So Nice to Have a Man Around the House, Charlie My Boy, Oh Johnny, Big Bad Bill, Won't You Come Home Bill Bailey" (with Lee), "How About Me," "When You're Smiling," "I Will Come Back".

"THE JUDY GARLAND SHOW." *December 8, 1963.* CBS.

Guests: Mickey Rooney, Jerry Van Dyke.

Judy's songs included: "I Feel a Song Comin On," "When the Sun Comes Out," "You're So Right for Me" (with Rooney), "Medley: Where or When, But Not For Me, Fascinatin Rhythm, God's Country, Could You Use Me, Our Love Affair" (with Rooney), "Too Late Now," "Who Cares," "Old Man River," "I Will Come Back."

"THE JUDY GARLAND SHOW." *December 15, 1963.* CBS.

Guests: Tony Bennett, Dick Shawn, Jerry Van Dyke.

Judy's songs included: "Yes Indeed" (with Bennett and Shawn), "Medley: Night Train, Lullaby of Broadway, Carolina in the Morning, Kansas City Here I Come, When the Midnight Choo Choo Leaves for Alabam, I Left My Heart in San Francisco" (with Bennett), "That's All," "One for My Baby," "My Buddy" (with Shawn), "Stormy Weather," "I Will Come Back."

"THE JUDY GARLAND SHOW." *December 22, 1963.* CBS.

Guests: Lorna Luft, Joseph Luft, Liza Minnelli, Tracy Everitt, Jack Jones, Mel Torme.

Judy's songs included: "Have Yourself a Merry Little Christmas," "Consider Yourself" (with Lorna, Liza, and Joe), "Little Drops of Rain," "Jingle Bells" (with Jones), "Sleigh Ride" (with Jones and Liza), "Winter Wonderland," "The Christmas Song" (with Torme), "What Child Is This," "Deck the Halls" (with everyone), "Over the Rainbow."

"THE JUDY GARLAND SHOW." *December 29, 1963.* CBS.

Guests: Bobby Darin, Bob Newhart.

Judy's songs included: "Hello Bluebird," "If Love Were All," "Zing! Went the Strings of My Heart," "More," "Medley: Sentimental Journey, Going Home Train, Blues in the Night, Goin' Home, Chattanooga Choo Choo, On the Atchison, Topeka and the Sante Fe, Some of These Days, Bye Bye Blackbird, Toot Toot Tootsie, Beyond the Blue Horizon, I Know That You Know, I've Been Working on the Railroad, Lonesome Road" (with Darin), "Do It Again," "Get Me to the Church on Time," "I Will Come Back."

"THE JUDY GARLAND SHOW." *January 5, 1964.* CBS.

Guests: Steve Allen, Jayne Meadows, Mel Torme.

Judy's songs included: "This Could Be the Start of Something Big," "Be My Guest" (with Allen and Torme), "Here's That Rainy Day," "Medley: I Love You Today, When I'm in Love, I'll Show Them All" (with Allen), "The Party's Over" (with Torme), "Medley: Ain't Misbehavin, Makin Whoopee, The Glory of Love, Way Back Home, You Took Advantage of Me, Mean To Me, The Girl Friend, Tiptoe Through the Tulips, Nice Work If You Can Get It, The Gypsy in My Soul, Let's Fall in Love, My Heart Stood Still" (with Allen and Torme), "Island in the West Indies," "Through the Years," "I Will Come Back."

"THE JUDY GARLAND SHOW." *January 12, 1964.* CBS.

Guests: Ethel Merman, Shelley Berman, Peter Gennaro.

Judy's songs included: "Everybody's Doin It" (with everyone), "Let's Do It" (with everyone), "Shenandoah," "Medley: Friendship, Let's Be Buddies, You're the Top, You're Just in Love, It's Delovely, Together" (with Merman), "A Pretty Girl Milking Her Cow," "Puttin on the Ritz," "The Battle Hymn of the Republic."

"THE JUDY GARLAND SHOW." *January 19, 1964.* CBS.

Guests: Vic Damone, Louis Nye, Chita Rivera.

Judy's songs included: "They Can't Take That Away From Me," "I Believe in You" (with Rivera), "By Myself," "West Side Story Medley: Maria, Somewhere, Something's Coming, Tonight" (with Damone), "Better Luck Next Time, "Almost Like Being in Love / This Can't Be Love," "I Will Come Back."

"THE JUDY GARLAND SHOW." *January 26, 1964.* CBS.

Guests: Martha Raye, Peter Lawford, Rich Little, Ken Murray.

Judy's songs included: "Seventy-six Trombones," "I'm Old Fashioned," "Glenn Miller Medley: I've Heard That Song Before, Moonlight Cocktails, Pennsylvania 6-5000, Elmer's Tune, At Last, St Louis Blues" (with Raye), "The Boy Next Door" (Rock version), "All Alone," "Oh Lord! I'm on My Way."

"THE JUDY GARLAND SHOW." *February 2, 1964.* CBS.

Guests: The Kirby Stone Four, Ken Murray, Louis Jourdan.

Judy's songs included: "San Francisco," "Whisperin" (with Kirby Stone Four), "Paris Is a Lonely Town," "Smoke Gets in Your Eyes," "Children's Medley: I'm Popeye the Sailor Man, Huckleberry Hound, Give a Little Whistle, Little Lulu, When You Wish Upon a Star, Who's Afraid of the Big Bad Wolf, Zip-A-Dee Doo-

Da, Some of These Days" (with Jourdan), "What'll I Do," "The Battle Hymn of the Republic."

"THE JUDY GARLAND SHOW." *February 9, 1964.* CBS.

Judy in Concert with Mort Lindsey and his Orchestra.

Judy's songs included: "Swing Low-Sweet Chariot," "He's Got the Whole World in His Hands," "World War I Medley: When Johnny Comes Marchin' Home, There's a Long Long Trail, Keep the Home Fires Burning, Give My Regards to Broadway, Boy of Mine, My Buddy, Oh How I Hate to Get Up in the Morning, Over There," "That's Entertainment," "Make Someone Happy," "Liza," "Happiness Is Just a Thing Called Joe," "Lorna," "Rockabye Your Baby," "A Couple of Swells," "America the Beautiful."

"THE JUDY GARLAND SHOW." *February 16, 1964.* CBS.

Guests: Mel Torme, Diahann Carroll.

Judy's songs included: "Hey Look Me Over," "Smile," "I Can't Give You Anything But Love," "After You've Gone," "Alone Together," "Come Rain or Come Shine," "A Stranger in Town," "The Trolley Song" (with Torme), "Arlen-Rodgers Medley: It's Only a Paper Moon, He Dances on the Ceiling, That Old Black Magic, The Gentleman Is a Dope, Ill Wind, It Might As Well Be Spring, Hit the Road to Dreamland, The Surrey With the Fringe on Top, Let's Take the Long Way Home" (with Carroll), "Don't Ever Leave Me," "A Great Day."

"THE JUDY GARLAND SHOW." *February 23, 1964.* CBS.

Guests: Jack Jones, Ken Murray.

Judy's songs included: "Swanee," "Almost Like Being In Love / This Can't Be Love," "Just in Time," "A Foggy Day," "If Love Were All," "Just You, Just Me," "Last Night When We Were Young," "Palace Medley: Shine On Harvest Moon, Some of These Days, My Man, I Don't Care," "Operetta Medley: San Francisco, Rosalie, I'll See You Again, Lover Come Back to Me, The Donkey Serenade" (with Jones), "When The Sun Comes Out."

"THE JUDY GARLAND SHOW." *March 1, 1964.* CBS.

Guests: Ray Bolger, Jane Powell, Jerry Van Dyke.

Judy's songs included: "I've Got a Lot of Living to Do," "Be My Guest" (with Powell, Bolger, and Van Dyke), "Hello Bluebird," "If Love Were All," "Zing! Went the Strings of My Heart," "On the Sunny Side of the Street," "If I Only Had a Brain" (with Bolger), "We're Off to See the Wizard" (with Bolger), "The Jitterbug" (with Bolger and Powell), "When Your Lover Has Gone," "Some People," "I Will Come Back."

"THE JUDY GARLAND SHOW." *March 8, 1964.* CBS.

Judy in Concert with Mort Lindsey and his Orchestra.

Judy's songs included: "Just Once in a Lifetime," "I Feel a Song Comin On," "Toot Toot Tootsie," "If I Had a Talking Picture of You," "Dirty Hands, Dirty Face," "Love of My Life," "The Boy Next Door," "On the Atchison, Topeka and the Sante Fe," "Alexander's Ragtime Band," "You're Nearer," "Steppin Out With My Baby," "I'm Always Chasing Rainbows," "I'm Nobody's Baby," "The Man That Got Away," "Be a Clown," "Just Once in a Lifetime."

"THE JUDY GARLAND SHOW." *March 15, 1964.* CBS.

Guest: Vic Damone.

Judy's songs included: "Lucky Day," "Sweet Danger," "Do I Love You?", "I Love You," "When Your Love Has Gone," "Down With Love," "Old Devil Moon," "Never, Never Will I Marry," "Anyplace I Hang My Hat Is Home," "Chicago," "Kismet Medley: The Night of My Nights, He's in Love, This Is My Beloved" (with Damone), "Lost in the Stars."

"THE JUDY GARLAND SHOW." *March 22, 1964.* CBS.

Guest: Robert Cole Trio.

Judy's songs included: "Sail Away," "Comes Once in a Lifetime," "I Am Loved," "Life Is Just a Bowl of Cherries," "Why Can't I," "I've Gotta Right to Sing the Blues," "Joey, Joey, Joey," "Love," "Get Happy," "As Long As He Needs Me," "Poor Butterfly" (with Cole), "Old Man River."

"THE JUDY GARLAND SHOW." *March 29, 1964.* CBS.

Judy in Concert with Mort Lindsey and his Orchestra.

Judy's songs included: "After You've Gone," "The Nearness of You," "Time After Time," "That Old Feeling," "Carolina in the Morning," "When You're Smiling," "Almost Like Being in Love / This Can't Be Love," "By Myself," "The Last Dance," "Suppertime," "Just in Time," "A Foggy Day," "If Love Were All," "Just You Just Me," "When the Sun Comes Out."

"THE JACK PAAR SHOW." December, 1964. NBC.

Judy's songs included: "Never, Never Will I Marry," "What Now My Love."

"JUDY AND LIZA LIVE, AT THE LONDON PALLADIUM." *December, 1964.* (British television).

Judy's songs included: "Just Once in a Lifetime," "Hello Liza, Hello Mama" (with Minnelli), "Together" (with Minnelli), "The Man That Got Away," "Medley: Hooray for Love, After You've Gone, By Myself, 'S Wonderful, How About You, Lover Come Back to Me, You and the Night and the Music, It All Depends on You" (with Minnelli), "The Music That Makes Me Dance," "Get Happy / Happy Days Are Here Again" (with Minnelli), "He's Got the Whole World in His Hand" (with Minnelli), "San Francisco," "Over the Rainbow," "Chicago" (with Minnelli).

"ON BROADWAY TONIGHT." *February, 1965.* NBC.

Guests: With the Allen Brothers. Host: Rudy Vallee.

Judy's songs included: "When You're Smiling," "Almost Like Being In Love / This Can't Be Love," "I Wish You Love" (with the Allen Brothers), "The Music That Makes Me Dance," "Rockabye Your Baby."

"THE ACADEMY AWARDS." *April, 1965.* ABC.

Guests: Judy was introduced by Gene Kelly.

Judy's song: A special tribute to Cole Porter. It consisted of a long medley of his better-known works, including "Night and Day," "Don't Fence Me In," "I Get a Kick Out of You," "You're the Top," "Lets Do It," "I Love You."

"KUP'S SHOW." *May, 1965.* Syndicated.

Judy was interviewed by Irv Kupcinet during her visit to Chicago. Others on the panel were Jean-Pierre Aumont, Marisa Pavan, Irna Phillips, and Jan Pierce.

"THE GYPSY ROSE LEE SHOW." *September, 1965.* Syndicated.

Judy was interviewed by Gypsy during her stay in San Francisco while she was appearing at the Circle Star Theatre.

"THE ANDY WILLIAMS SHOW." *September, 1965.* NBC.

Guests: Judy, Charlie Weaver, David McCallum.

Judy's songs included: "On a Wonderful Day Like Today" (with Williams), "Get Happy," "The Man That Got Away," "Medley: Why Don't We Do This More Often, On the Atchison, Topeka and the Sante Fe, Over the Rainbow, Rockabye Your Baby, You Made Me Love You, The Trolley Song" (portions of this medley were sung with Williams).

"THE ED SULLIVAN SHOW." *October, 1965.* CBS.

Judy's songs included: "Come Rain or Come Shine," "By Myself," "Rockabye Your Baby."

"THE HOLLYWOOD PALACE." *November, 1965.* ABC.

Guests: Judy as hostess. Vic Damone, Chita Rivera.

Judy's songs included: "Just Once in a Lifetime," "Medley: Maria, Something's Coming, Somewhere, Tonight" (with Damone), "A Couple of Swells," "I Loved Him," "The Palace Medley: Some of These Days, I Don't Care, My Man, Shine On Harvest Moon."

"THE PERRY COMO SHOW." *February, 1966.* NBC.

Guests: Judy, Bill Cosby.

Judy's songs included: "If You Feel Like Singing, Sing" (with Como), "It's a Grand Night for Singing" (with Como), "What Now My Love," "Just in Time," "In My Baby's Lovin Arms" (with Como), "Medley: Rockabye Your Baby, Over the Rainbow, The Man That Got Away," "Bye Bye Blues" (with Como), "For Me and My Gal" (with Como), "Side by Side" (with Como and Cosby).

"THE SAMMY DAVIS SHOW." *March, 1966.* NBC.

Judy's songs included: "When You're Smiling," "The Man That Got Away," "Give My Regards to Broadway," "Medley: A Couple of Swells, The Lady Is a Tramp, How About You, Bidin My Time, For Me and My Gal, Meet Me in St. Louis, Ding Dong the Witch Is Dead, A New World, Johnny One Note, I Got Rhythm, Get Happy, On the Atchison Topeka and the Sante Fe, Could You Use Me, I Wish I Were in Love Again, Treat Me Rough, If I Only Had a Brain, A Couple of Swells" (with Davis).

"THE SAMMY DAVIS SHOW." *March, 1966.* NBC.

Judy's songs included: "Almost Like Being in Love / This Can't Be Love," "Medley: Let Us Entertain You, Alexander's Ragtime Band, April Showers, Look for the Silver Lining, Keep Your Sunny Side Up, Life Upon the Wicked Stage, Rockabye Your Baby, Smile, Terpsicory, Song and Dance Men, Grand Old Flag, Toot Toot Tootsie, Carolina in the Morning, California Here I Come, Swanee, Born in a Trunk" (with Davis).

"THE HOLLYWOOD PALACE." *May 1, 1966.* ABC.

Guests: Judy as hostess. Johnny Rivers, Van Johnson.

Judy's songs included: "What the World Needs Now Is Love," "Mr. and Mrs. Clown" (with Johnson), "Comes Once in a Lifetime," "By Myself."

"WHAT'S MY LINE?" *March, 1967.* CBS.

Judy appeared as the mystery guest. The panel included Tony Randall, Bennett Cerf, and Arlene Francis. Judy's identity was guessed by Bennett Cerf, who exclaimed: "That voice could only belong to one woman, Judy Garland."

"THE TODAY SHOW." *March, 1967.* NBC.

Judy was in New York for Liza Minnelli's wedding and to announce her participation in *Valley of the Dolls.* Barbara Walters interviewed her, Lorna, and Joe.

"THE JACK PAAR SHOW." *May 14, 1967.* NBC.

Guests: Judy, Bob Newhart.

Judy and Jack Paar told numerous anecdotes about her days in Hollywood.

"THE HERB LYONS SHOW." *September, 1967.* Syndicated.

Judy, in Chicago for concerts, was interviewed by Herb Lyons.

"Kup's Show." *September, 1967.* Syndicated.

Judy was interviewed by Irv Kupcinet during her stay in Chicago.

"The Johnny Carson Show." *June 20, 1968.* NBC.

Judy was interviewed prior to her opening at the Garden State Arts Center.

"The Mike Douglas Show." *July, 1968.* Syndicated.

Guests: Judy, Peter Lawford, Jerry Vale.

Judy's songs included: "For Once in My Life," "How Insensitive," "Over the Rainbow," "Blue Skies" (with Lawford).

"The Dick Cavett Show." *December, 1968.* ABC.

Guests: Judy, Ida Kaminska, Lee Marvin.

Judy's song: "God Bless Johnny."

The Johnny Carson Show. *December, 1968.* NBC.

Judy's songs included: "It's All for You," "Till After the Holidays."

"The Merv Griffin Show." *December, 1968.* CBS.

Judy's songs included: "I'd Like to Hate Myself in the Morning," "The Trolley Song," "Have Yourself a Merry Little Christmas."

"The Merv Griffin Show." *December, 1968.* CBS.

Guests: Rex Reed, Margaret Hamilton, Van Johnson.

Judy's songs included: "Just in Time," "If You Were the Only Boy in the World" (with Arthur Treacher).

"Sunday Night at the Palladium." British television. *February, 1969.*

Judy's songs included: "For Once in My Life," "Get Happy," "I Belong to London."

INDEX

293